# STEINBERG

### *The Breakup of a*

# FAMILY EMPIRE

# STEINBERG

## *The Breakup of a*

# FAMILY EMPIRE

## ANN GIBBON & PETER HADEKEL

MACMILLAN OF CANADA
A Division of Canada Publishing Corporation
Toronto, Ontario, Canada

**Canadian Cataloguing in Publication Data**

Gibbon, Ann, 1960-
   Steinberg : the breakup of a family empire

Includes bibliographical references.
ISBN 0-7715-9102-0

1. Steinberg, Samuel, 1905-1978.   2. Steinberg Inc. –
History.   3. Supermarkets – Quebec (Province) –
History.   4. Businessmen – Canada – Biography.
I. Hadekel, Peter, 1951-      .  II. Title.

HF5469.23.C34S57 1990      381'.456413'0092      C90-094849-3


1 2 3 4 5 FP 94 93 92 91 90

Cover design by Kirk Stephens/Styles Design Inc.

Macmillan of Canada
A Division of Canada Publishing Corporation
Toronto, Ontario, Canada

Printed in Canada

*In loving memory of my brother Scott*
— A.G.

and

*To Anne, Kathleen and Christine*
— P.H.

# ACKNOWLEDGEMENTS

The authors would like to thank the following people for their generous help in putting the book together: our agent, Peter Livingston, for believing in the original idea; the Montreal *Gazette* for giving each of us a leave of absence; Agnes McFarlane, head of the *Gazette*'s library and Barry Gray, the *Gazette*'s photo editor, for help compiling photographs; *Gazette* photographer, John Mahoney; all at Macmillan of Canada and especially our publisher, Denise Schon and our editor, Sheldon Fischer for his expert guidance on the manuscript; Jacques Labrèche for historical and computer consulting as well as moral support; Doug Long, Steinberg Inc.'s former director of communications for compiling a wealth of company archival material; Julian Armstrong for her marketing help and general interest in the project; Linda McKnight for her initial interest in the book; McGill University professor, Henry Mintzberg, for providing us with his invaluable corporate study of Steinberg Inc.; all the people who kindly granted us interviews; each of our families for enduring with us through the preparation of the book; and finally, Steinberg family members and executives for trusting in the project.

# CONTENTS

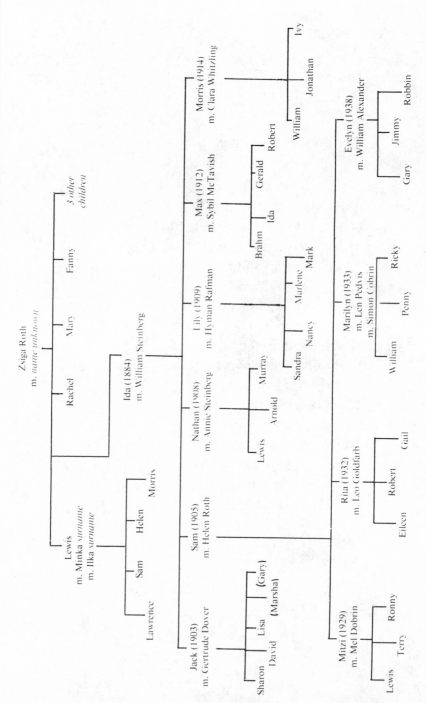

Legend: m. = married; (date) = birth date; (name) = died as child; italic = name unknown.

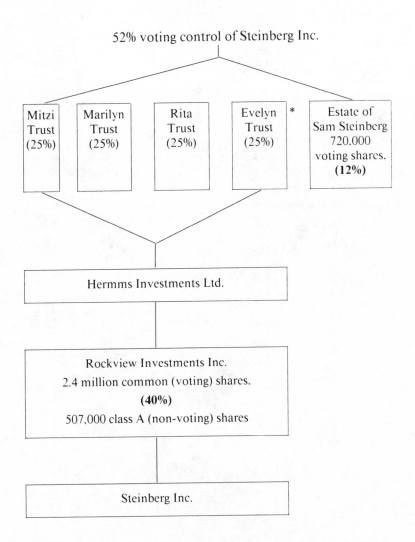

52% voting control of Steinberg Inc.

| Mitzi Trust (25%) | Marilyn Trust (25%) | Rita Trust (25%) | Evelyn Trust (25%) | * | Estate of Sam Steinberg 720,000 voting shares. (12%) |

Hermms Investments Ltd.

Rockview Investments Inc.
2.4 million common (voting) shares.
(40%)
507,000 class A (non-voting) shares

Steinberg Inc.

* Trustees for all the trusts: Mitzi Dobrin, Melvyn Dobrin, Marilyn Cobrin, Simon Cobrin, Evelyn Alexander, William Alexander, Morris Steinberg, as of Nov. 1977.

*I'd like to come back in twenty years to see what's happened to my business.*

—Sam Steinberg, 1969

# Introduction

The idea for this book first emerged in the winter of 1988, when the Steinberg sisters were engaged in a public fight for control of the Montreal-based supermarket and real estate empire they had inherited from their father, Sam Steinberg.

The story had all the elements of a prime-time soap opera: a family dynasty racked by jealousy and back-stabbing; a fight over money and power, and all of it happening in front of a voyeuristic public. As journalists reporting on the lawsuit and the dramatic events it triggered, we realized we were touching only the tip of the iceberg. This family feud was a complicated story, rooted in events and decisions made years before.

We knew we could not reflect the complexity of the story in newspaper articles and columns alone. We wanted to write a book tracing the history of both the family and the company so we could piece together how a once picture-perfect family came to be stricken by such rancor; how a once-thriving company came close to economic disaster and how those two currents came together to provoke the sale of Steinberg Inc.

We also wished to chronicle the story of a company that had been a leader in the Canadian supermarket industry for seven decades and a rich part of Quebec's social heritage. It was a captivating tale: an impoverished immigrant family, led by the charismatic but humble Sam Steinberg, managed to spin a single tiny produce store into what became one of Canada's most important business empires.

Yet we approached the story with some trepidation. Delving into the conflicting emotions, loyalties, and rivalries of a dynasty like the Steinbergs seemed a daunting task. First, there was the obvious hurdle of getting the family to talk to us. This is not an "authorized" book, and when we began the project we had no assurance that any member of the family or any executive in the company would cooperate.

It was a delicate matter to ask the Steinbergs to speak openly about their private lives and their relationships with other family members. Much damage had already been done to the family by the lawsuit Mitzi Steinberg Dobrin filed against her sisters. The family had spent the better part of 1988 under a media microscope and the torn relationships were far from repaired. Moreover the company had become the subject of takeover rumors. Both the family and Steinberg executives had to be careful about what they said in public.

Through the years, the family had always preferred to stay in the background. Sam Steinberg, a shy man who shunned the limelight despite his immense success, had resisted previous attempts by others to tell his personal life story. In the early 1960s, he had reluctantly agreed to allow a book to be written about the company and the family, commissioning two writers from Montreal, H. Gordon Green and Alice Parizeau, for the job. But though he gave the authors access to company files, he and other family members were unwilling to open up much. Finally Sam killed the project and no book was released.

History repeated itself in the 1980s, when Sam's daughter Mitzi asked a well-known Montreal journalist, Gerald Clark, a former editor-in-chief of *The Montreal Star*, to write a book about her late father. But the author's 1986 account, *For Good Measure: The Sam Steinberg Story*, was no more pleasing to the Steinberg family, even if it was kind to Sam's memory. It was published as a limited private edition, carefully circulated by Mitzi Dobrin.

At first, with little confidence that the family would ever confide in us, we began to research the book discreetly. We feared that if word got around about our intentions, everyone would clam up. In late summer of 1988, in the course of our work as business journalists at the Montreal *Gazette*, we were able to obtain an interview with Irving Ludmer, then chief executive officer of Steinberg Inc. It was a freewheeling session that provided us with a revealing glimpse into Steinberg's affairs. During that meeting we told Ludmer of our intention to write a book. The news stopped him dead in his tracks for a moment but after the initial surprise, he was supportive and provided us with close to ten hours of tape-recorded interviews.

The next challenge was to win over the family. We began a sequence of correspondence and phone conversations with each of Sam's children, and consistently ran into dead ends.

For over a year there was only silence from Mitzi Dobrin, who had initiated the lawsuit, and her husband. Then in the fall of 1988, we received a telephone call from Simon Cobrin, the husband of Marilyn Steinberg. He had read our letter and he wanted to talk. He was clearly bitter about the way the Dobrins had handled the dispute. We met for lunch at Gibby's Restaurant in Old Montreal, where he spent several hours giving his views of the dispute between his wife and Mitzi. We had found another ally.

One factor that did work in our favor was the sheer size of the Steinberg family. There were countless cousins and uncles, nephews and nieces, many of whom had worked for Steinberg and knew the family history. We continued our research, speaking with dozens of people: current and former executives, suppliers, family friends, and many members of the family, including Sam's sister Lily and brother Morris.

A crucial break for us was convincing Sam's nephew Arnold Steinberg to cooperate. Arnold was a company "lifer", a senior vice-president at Steinberg and a repository of corporate and family history going back decades. He was wonderfully candid and helpful and devoted many hours of his time to the project.

Next we had to decide what kind of book to write. We didn't want a gossipy account of the lifestyles of the rich and famous. We felt that the Steinberg dispute went straight to the heart of a problem deeply rooted in Canadian business: how to pass a family-owned company down to the next generation without causing a civil war among the heirs.

As other Canadian families who have been embroiled in feuds can attest — the Billeses of Canadian Tire, the Ballards of Maple Leaf Gardens, or the Birks of the jewelry empire of the same name — the family business is a unique and complicated creature, one in

which corporate decisions are based as much on emotion and
family ties as on sound business sense. And as the Steinberg case
amply demonstrated, that can lead to trouble. We soon learned
that Steinberg was almost a textbook example of the many ills that
can befall a family-owned company despite well-intentioned
efforts to avoid them.

The mistakes made here have been repeated in hundreds of
smaller businesses across North America. Many families are agonizing today over how to pass along the business to their children.
They may be frustrated that no child shows an aptitude for the job.
Perhaps they are paralyzed by the fear of appearing to favor one
child over another. Or maybe they just don't know how to pass
along the inheritance without opening up old animosities and
sibling rivalries.

The family business has become a tinderbox of emotion in
Canada and nobody knows how to defuse it. The emotions that
bind a family together can easily blow it apart when money and
corporate power are at stake. A self-help group called the Canadian
Association of Family Enterprise has been set up to help owners of
companies deal with these issues. By listening to the successes and
failures of others, members can learn lessons they can apply to their
own family businesses. There are no hard-and-fast rules, no instant
solutions. Each family situation is different, and each demands a
commitment to communication, honesty, and trust from those
involved. The job of preparing for succession doesn't start when the
founder of the business dies; it has to start years before.

We had completed a year of interviews, without a word from the
sisters themselves, when the company was sold to a group of
Quebec investors, including Michel Gaucher and the province's
powerful pension fund, the Caisse de dépôt et placement. It was the
ultimate solution to the family conflict. Not only did it provide a
dramatic conclusion to the story, but it also gave us renewed hope
that, with the family empire gone, Sam's daughters might finally
agree to talk with us.

The first to do so was Mitzi, who met with us in September 1989.
We saw no heroes or villains, we told her; there was no single
interpretation of events. Each participant in the drama had his or
her own truth to tell and our job was to reconcile those differing
accounts.

She met us in the office of her family's holding company in the affluent Montreal suburb of Westmount, where her son Ronny also works. Inside the office, which is kept locked, the walls are covered with paintings by the celebrated Montreal artist John Little. In the foyer are giant photographic portraits of each of her parents by the Hungarian photographer Laszlo. The pictures radiate warmth: Helen, dressed in satin and pearls, with pink roses at her side; a distinguished-looking Sam on the wall next to her.

Mitzi, wearing a beige woolen jacket, dark skirt, and her signature beige-tinted designer sunglasses, began to tell her story. After a year of opinion and speculation about her motives from other people, we were relieved to hear her side of things. Soon we were able to convince her sisters, Marilyn and Evelyn, to meet with us, although their mother Helen declined.

While the Steinberg story interested us as the story of a family, it is an important business story as well. We wanted to trace the compelling drama of the takeover battle, which left investors and family members hanging in suspense for a good part of 1989. The story required a look at the two principal combatants for Steinberg, an Ontario group called Oxdon Investments Inc. and the Quebec group that finally captured the prize.

Oxdon's principal players declined to speak to us; however, from interviews with their business associates we were able to reconstruct their role in the affair.

As for the Quebec group, they were quite willing to discuss their stunning coup: nothing less than the acquisition of one of Canada's biggest retailing companies.

This, then, is the story of the rise and the fall of a family empire. As a business venture, it may well rise again. As an enterprise run and bound by family ties, it is forever gone.

# 1

# *The Changing of the Guard*

On the morning of August 23, 1989, the employees on the twenty-fourth floor of the Alexis Nihon Plaza in Montreal watched in quiet amazement as a battalion of lawyers, consultants, and accountants marched into the executive offices of Steinberg Inc. The army of occupation was led by Steinberg's new owner, Michel Gaucher, who had just purchased the family-owned company, ending a seventy-two-year dynasty in the Canadian grocery business.

An aggressive dealmaker, Gaucher symbolized the new breed of businessman in Quebec. He was a world apart from the Steinbergs, the Hungarian Jews who had emigrated to Montreal and started their grocery business in 1917. Gaucher knew nothing about groceries. His corporate holdings had been built around development projects in the Third World and his principal investment was in a company called Socanav Inc., which operated a fleet of thirteen oil tankers. Yet it was Gaucher who had convinced the three surviving daughters of the founder, Sam Steinberg, to sell their controlling interest in one of Canada's largest retailers.

His audacious $1.3-billion takeover was financed almost completely by a Quebec government agency — the Caisse de dépôt et placement. In return, the Caisse, a powerful pension investment fund controlling $37-billion of public money, had obtained the right to purchase Steinberg's valuable shopping centers and real estate from Gaucher, leaving him with the retailing side of the business.

On this Wednesday morning, Gaucher was savoring his victory. Just the day before, the Quebec Superior Court had defeated a legal challenge to the takeover from a rival bidder, Toronto-based Oxdon Investments Inc. Oxdon had waged a nineteen-month battle to acquire Steinberg but had finally conceded defeat. Gaucher and the Caisse were left with the prize: Canada's twenty-first largest company with 1988 sales of $4.5-billion, 37,000 employees in Canada and the U.S. and diversified assets in supermarkets, department stores, restaurants, sugar refineries, and real estate.

The new owner's first act of business on this day was a settling of accounts. Gaucher strode into the office of executive vice-president Arnold Steinberg and fired him on the spot, thus severing the last link between the company and the family that had built it into a grocery giant.

Arnold was the nephew of the late Sam Steinberg and had spent thirty-five years in the business. A quiet, analytical man with a degree from the Harvard Business School, Arnold was the company's chief financial officer. He was well-connected in Establishment circles and had become an extremely wealthy man through astute investing. He was a passionate art collector and maintained an apartment in Manhattan, where he and his wife would often go on art-buying jaunts.

Arnold Steinberg, together with his two brothers Lewis and Murray, had owned 17 percent of the company's voting stock before the takeover by Gaucher. He hadn't wanted to sell the business; in fact he had wanted to buy control of it. Arnold and Steinberg chief executive, Irving Ludmer, had spent months desperately trying to put together their own bid to purchase the company, but they had not been able to raise the money.

Arnold's cousins, the three surviving daughters of Sam Steinberg, with their mother Helen, controlled 52 percent of the voting stock and had decided to accept a $75-a-share offer from the Gaucher group. Throughout the lengthy takeover battle that followed, Arnold and his brothers had refused to commit their shares, tendering them only when there was no alternative left. Their holdout had threatened to scuttle the whole deal, because Gaucher had made his offer conditional upon being able to buy at least 90 percent of the shares. Now Gaucher was making Arnold pay for his intransigence.

The new owner of Steinberg was still enraged by Arnold's conduct and their meeting was acrimonious. He accused Arnold of reneging on a deal by which Arnold would have tendered his shares in return for keeping his job as chief financial officer of Steinberg. Gaucher was so furious that he ordered Arnold to leave by the end of the week.

Gaucher then accepted the resignations of two more top executives, Irving Ludmer and Bill Cleman, and appointed himself chairman and chief executive officer. Within days the twelve directors on the Steinberg board were asked to resign and were replaced with Gaucher's own nominees. To be president and chief operating officer he chose Jean-Roch Vachon, a close friend, who was already head of the food division at Steinberg.

The sale of the company felt almost like a death in the family to Arnold Steinberg. Even though he and his brothers wound up collecting more than $76-million from the sale of their shares, Arnold felt a lingering sadness, a sense of shock, that money couldn't erase. The company had been a way of life for him almost since the day he was born. Even after he was sacked, Arnold would find it difficult to shop anywhere else. He still visited the stores to see what was going on. For him, that would never change.

The sale was doubly disappointing to Arnold because Steinberg Inc. had emerged from a troubled decade in the 1980s with the promise of much greater profitability. Through the first half of 1989, profits had been substantially higher under the leadership of Irving Ludmer as chief executive. Arnold had wanted to hold on to the business out of family pride and especially out of a conviction that Steinberg would make even more money in the 1990s. But the sisters' lack of patience with Ludmer's turnaround strategy was a major factor behind the sale. While the family came out of the sale "a winner", Arnold believed it could have come out a bigger winner if it had waited another ten years.

For the Steinberg heiresses, the three daughters who had inherited control of the company from their father Sam, the winnings were substantial. Mitzi, Marilyn, Evelyn, their mother Helen, and the twelve grandchildren of Helen and Sam together collected more than $260-million for their stock. They gained a sort of peace, too, for the sale marked the merciful conclusion of almost four years of tension, bitterness, and squabbling that had thrust the family into the public eye and placed the company's survival in jeopardy. Their feud included a lawsuit by the eldest daughter, Mitzi Dobrin, against her sisters Marilyn Cobrin and Evelyn Alexander and the breakdown of relations between Helen and Marilyn. The dispute had shattered a family that had once been extremely close, had made thousands of employees uneasy, and had led inexorably to the sale of the family empire.

Sam Steinberg would have been inconsolably distressed. "Mr. Sam" had been a legend in the grocery business, a grade-school dropout who became one of the great geniuses of the North American supermarket industry. His intuitive understanding of customer behavior and his skill at adapting and innovating made Steinberg Inc. the unchallenged leader in the Quebec grocery business for decades. His remarkable ability to motivate his employees made him almost universally loved and respected by them.

Yet Sam had been guilty of a major mistake. Like many other successful family patriarchs, he was so obsessed with running his business that he gave no thought to what would happen after he was gone. He never attempted to counsel his daughters on how they should treat their inheritance or manage the company after his death. When he passed away in 1978, Steinberg began a precipitous slide, and lost its leading position in the Quebec grocery market.

Sam had run the company as a "family" business in every sense of the word. His mother Ida had started the first grocery store on Montreal's fabled St. Lawrence Boulevard in 1917 and all six of her children were put to work there. When Sam took over the business as a young man, his four brothers and his wife Helen's three brothers all held important positions. Over the years nepotism flourished as successive generations of Steinbergs took their places in the business.

But with the passage of time, and especially after Sam's death, that emotional attachment waned. One by one, family members fell away from the company. With the exception of Mitzi, a Steinberg vice-president for twelve years, Sam's daughters never got actively involved. He had no sons. His twelve grandchildren, the beneficiaries of the family trusts established to pass on Sam's stock holdings, also remained aloof from the business and by the time the company was sold in 1989, only one of the grandchildren was still employed there.

The Steinberg family had become an absentee landlord, owning an asset that it no longer understood or even cared about very much. The family shareholders had almost no impact on day-to-day operations and decisions. Professional managers ran the company, competently for the most part, but without the visceral attachment that distinguishes the self-made man from the "cool professional". When Arnold Steinberg reflected on the sale of the company, he conceded it was almost inevitable. The same pressures are found in many other family-owned businesses: by the time the second or third generation took control, the family members were no longer involved and they simply wanted the money. They were supposed to be wealthy people but all their holdings were tied up in company stock. It was as if the money was behind a glass door, a family jewel that could be seen but not touched.

Within the Steinberg family, it was Mitzi Dobrin, the one who had been most involved, who had in the end been most determined to sell. It was as if her failure to successfully grasp and manage the empire made her turn to the opposite extreme. Ever since she had left her job at Steinberg in 1985, she had tried to convince her sisters to unload the business. Their resistance prompted her to sue, and it was the lawsuit that grabbed the attention of potential bidders. It was only a matter of time before somebody would offer enough money to satisfy the sisters. In the aftermath of the sale Mitzi felt mainly relief.

If the sisters had regrets, they were felt most acutely by Marilyn, Mitzi's junior by five years. Long after the sale was over, Marilyn still felt grief whenever she went into a Steinberg store. "I really wanted that business," she said after it was sold. Yet she realized that keeping it had become impossible because the family had grown too large and there were too many personal interests to satisfy.

Michel Gaucher skillfully played on the family schisms. In the atmosphere of suspicion that still existed between the sisters, Gaucher and the Caisse de dépôt had insisted on obtaining an exclusive option on the family's shares. With a lockup agreement, none of the sisters could cause trouble later by backing out. And the exclusive option meant Gaucher could not unknowingly be outbid in an auction for the company.

Michel Gaucher looks the very picture of success. Words like "dashing," "articulate," "urbane," and "impeccably bilingual" have been used to describe him. He's married to a striking woman from Ontario, Nancy Orr, who is an accountant by training and the chief financial officer for his holding company. He drives a Porsche; she drives a Jaguar. They have four children and divide their time between a red-brick mansion at the top of Westmount mountain and a rambling country home in Quebec's Eastern Townships. Michel Gaucher cuts such an attractive public figure that he's been seriously wooed by both the federal Conservatives and the Quebec Liberals as an election candidate. Some believe his overriding ambition is to become premier of Quebec one day.

His life story reads like an endless quest for success and recognition. By the age of thirty-two, Gaucher had managed to acquire an engineering degree, a law degree, and a Master's degree in business administration. At thirty-six, he was a millionaire with a profitable business empire in shipping and construction. He seems driven, not only by intellectual curiosity, but also by an overwhelming desire to win, whatever the game.

Born into a prosperous Montreal family, he enjoyed a privileged upbringing in the wealthy Montreal suburb of Outremont. His grandmother, an Anglo-Irishwoman from Toronto, had made money in the jewelry business and his father was a successful insurance executive. Michel was educated at Collège Stanislas, an exclusive private school that turned out many of the best and brightest in French Quebec. At the age of sixteen, he was sent to the Collège Militaire Royal de Saint-Jean for a year of discipline and then enlisted in the Canadian navy for three years.

Returning home, he studied engineering at the Université de Montréal, where he played varsity football and took an active interest in campus politics. In fact, Gaucher got kicked out of school for a month after leading a student strike in 1967. But he wasn't a radical, nor did he share the typical student enthusiasm for Quebec separatism. Gaucher has always marched to his own drumbeat. He says the biggest philosophical influence on his life is Ayn Rand's novel *The Fountainhead*, which celebrates the triumph of individualism over collectivism.

After obtaining his MBA from McGill University, Gaucher joined the Montreal-based multinational Alcan Aluminium Ltd., but he wasn't really sure what he wanted to do in life. He went back to school again, this time earning a law degree at night while working by day. He describes himself as "a pauper" in those days, earning money on weekends by teaching skiing in the Laurentian Mountains. "I had a little beatup '57 Volkswagen. All my friends had Chevys and wives and two kids. I was running around in jeans and still in law school."

Gaucher soon became general manager of Alcan's Mexican subsidiary, moving onto the fast track of one of Canada's leading corporations. But he became disenchanted with life in a big company and left in 1972 to become a consultant. Four years later, he was named president of a small Montreal engineering firm, T. Pringle & Sons.

While working on a project in Africa in the 1970s, Gaucher met a man who would change his life. The man was David Morse, an elderly New York lawyer with impeccable business connnections. He made the young Quebecer his protégé. "David Morse convinced me I could do anything," Gaucher says. Morse had been director-general of the International Labor Organization for two decades and he knew industrialists from all over the world. He introduced Gaucher to executives at International Harvester Co., then the world's leading maker of farming equipment. The meeting soon led to a contract with Gaucher's firm, training Africans to use Harvester's machinery. Before long, Harvester was doing assembly work in Quebec and helping Gaucher set up a new company, Sofati Ltd., to manage development projects and training programs in the Third World.

Sofati made Gaucher a millionaire in short order. The company was profitable from the start because 90 percent of its customers were foreign governments who were able to obtain export financing from Ottawa. The young man proved extremely astute at getting government assistance for his projects. By 1989 he had landed deals worth a total of $1.2-billion in the Third World, including a $109-million contract, financed by Ottawa's Export Development Corporation, to construct six schools in Cameroon and a $250-million deal to build a car-and-truck maintenance facility in Algeria.

But his thirst for success remained unquenched and Gaucher felt the need to establish a business presence at home. "Here I was with 100 percent of my activities overseas, based in Montreal, doing absolutely nothing in this country," he told an interviewer in 1983. His first venture in Quebec, in partnership with a Quebec City businessman named Louis Rochette, was the $43-million purchase of a small fleet of oil tankers that plied the St. Lawrence River and the Great Lakes.

Rochette, a tall, white-haired man with a courtly bearing and a sharp business mind, was president of Davie Shipbuilding at the time. The shipyard was owned by struggling Dome Petroleum Ltd., which later went bust. Dome wanted to sell its fleet of oil tankers and Rochette was an interested buyer. So was Gaucher, although the young man didn't have the money.

The two decided to get together and make a joint bid for the tanker fleet, known then as Branch Lines. They were successful, and the deal marked the beginning of a profitable and unusual business partnership. Rochette is older and more conservative in his approach to business dealings than the often-impetuous Gaucher. "I thought that maybe he needed a partner like me to hold him back at times," says Rochette. "He is sometimes too eager to go after something." The two have become good business part-ners as well as good friends. Rochette entertains the Gaucher family at his Florida home in Key Largo, where they sail together.

It wasn't long before Gaucher and Rochette convinced other major oil companies to sell or lease their fleets of tankers to them, promising they could operate the ships for less than it would cost the oil companies to do so. Gulf Canada, Texaco, Ultramar, and Shell eventually signed long-term contracts with Socanav (the name is a play on the French words for "company" and "ships": société and navires) to move petroleum products through the St. Lawrence Seaway, along the east coast, and in the Arctic. As the business became more successful, Gaucher put his own imprint on it. He named one of the ships after his wife — the Nancy Orr-Gaucher — and another after his father — the Hubert Gaucher.

At the age of 39 Gaucher took another gamble, becoming the first Québécois ship operator in the transatlantic container trade. The decision to get into the ocean shipping business was born out of necessity. Gaucher discovered it was much cheaper to charter his own ships to deliver materials to Africa than it was to deal with existing container lines. Why not extend the ship-chartering service to other destinations?

Gaucher put up $500,000 as an initial investment and Sofati Container Lines was formed in October 1982, with a group of executives who had jumped ship from the rival Cast Container Group. They brought a breath of fresh air to the stuffy Montreal shipping industry. Visitors to Sofati's office were greeted by a little salt-and-pepper dog, a schnauzer named Winnie, whom Gaucher routinely described as the chairman of the board.

This was a tough business and Gaucher found himself in cut-throat competition with Cast and other transatlantic operators. A devastating price war developed. Being a francophone Quebecer didn't hurt, however. Sofati Container Lines was able to win a major shipping contract from the Quebec government's liquor corporation to transport wine from Europe, a contract that helped establish the new shipping firm's credibility.

Eventually the competition proved too much for the rival company, Cast, which was driven to the edge of bankruptcy and was rescued by its principal creditor, the Royal Bank of Canada. It was a Pyrrhic victory for Gaucher. The Royal Bank was determined to salvage its multi-million-dollar investment in Cast and was prepared to stay in for the long haul. Competition between the two companies heated up again; shipping rates dropped; and soon it was Sofati that was pushed to the wall. Sofati suspected that Cast and the Royal Bank were engaged in unfair pricing practices. Gaucher, never one to take a challenge lying down, came very close to taking them to court.

Instead, he took another route out, selling his container line to Cast and leaving the business cleanly. But he had a long memory. When he took over Steinberg in late August 1989, Gaucher discovered the company's principal banker was the Royal Bank. Several weeks later the Bank of Montreal took over the Steinberg account.

Gaucher had aspirations to build a vast industrial conglomerate of the kind put together by his friend, Paul Desmarais, the owner of Power Corporation of Canada. Indeed, *The Financial Post* had once described Gaucher in a flattering profile as "a corporate emperor in the making". Yet for a time after the sale of Sofati Container Lines, he encountered only defeat and disappointment.

Gaucher next tried to buy Canadian Arsenals Ltd., the Crown-owned munitions firm privatized by the federal government, but

his bid fell short. Then he managed to convince the Quebec government to award his firm a $30-million contract to design and build a
new concert hall in downtown Montreal. But when the Parti
Québécois government was defeated in an election, the new Liberal
administration cancelled the project.

Gaucher's oil tanker business, Socanav Inc., was quietly prosper-
ing, becoming one of Canada's busiest marine carriers. He and his
partner, Louis Rochette, took the company public in 1986 with a
$25-million share issue under the Quebec Stock Savings Plan, a
provincial tax shelter. The influx of capital allowed the two partners to pay off the considerable bank debt they were carrying at the
time. Soon after, Socanav acquired a Quebec school-bus company,
Sumabus Inc., in an effort to diversify further.

Up to this point his business had been small-time stuff, and
Gaucher yearned to play in the big time. He assembled a team of
acquisition specialists to study new opportunities and he didn't shy
away from going after big fish. When Texaco Canada Inc. was put
on the auction block by its parent company in the United States,
Gaucher was able to make a fully financed bid worth $650 million
for the refineries and service stations. But once again, he came up
short, and Imperial Oil Ltd. walked away the winner.

Turning his attention to the United States, Gaucher managed to
line up financing for a $1.2-billion offer to buy First Republic Bank
Corp. of Dallas, Texas, in 1988. Even though the troubled bank was
in the process of being bailed out by U.S. regulators, the investment
was attractive to potential buyers because there was so much government money being pumped in. Gaucher spent an entire summer in Washington, D.C., studying how to buy the bank. He was
even prepared to move to Texas to run the operation. Before he had
the chance, a North Carolina bank bought 49 percent of First
Republic for $520-million.

Gaucher was getting hungry and Steinberg soon caught his attention. The Gauchers were friends with then-Governor General
Jeanne Sauvé and her husband Maurice, a corporate "marriage
broker" who matched up buyers and sellers of companies. Maurice
Sauvé was acting on behalf of Mitzi Dobrin, the Steinberg sister
most interested in selling the family business. In March 1989,
Gaucher was advised by Sauvé that the sisters were willing to sell if
the price was right. He wrote immediately to the Steinberg family,

outlining his plans to bid for the company. Later he enlisted the help of the Caisse de dépôt et placement, in an attempt to defeat a rival bid from Toronto's Oxdon Investments.

Gaucher and the Caisse knew that the sisters were under great political pressure to sell Steinberg to a Quebec group. This company had been adopted by Québécois as their very own, becoming part of the province's *patrimoine*. The Steinberg banner was as familiar a landmark in Montreal as the cross on Mount Royal, and hundreds of thousands of French-speaking Quebecers shopped there over the years, making Steinberg an intimate part of their daily lives.

Steinberg had worked its way into the psyche of Quebec because Mr. Sam had grasped a simple truth. If you were going to operate a business in the province, you had to operate in French. Well before other anglophone corporations made the same discovery, Sam Steinberg, with his unaffected charm, was recruiting gifted French-speaking Quebecers at all levels of management, and by 1965 the company had made French its working language. For a time, the in-house joke at Steinberg was that if you wanted a job, it was better to have a French name than a Jewish one.

Steinberg was the third largest employer in Quebec and the biggest purchaser of Quebec produce. It was more than a cultural icon: it was a major economic force in the province. So when the company was put up for sale by the feuding Steinberg sisters, alarm bells began to ring in the corridors of Quebec City. In June 1989, the first bid came from Oxdon Investments Inc., an Ontario group that planned to dismantle the company piece by piece and sell the food stores to Toronto-based Loblaw Cos. Ltd. Premier Robert Bourassa and many other Quebecers felt it was simply unacceptable for Steinberg to be sold to an out-of-province buyer.

A new spirit of economic nationalism had taken hold in Quebec, and the province suddenly felt vulnerable to the wave of mergers and acquisitions sweeping the business world in the late 1980s. Such takeovers were being justified in the name of free trade and global markets, but to many French-speaking Quebecers they threatened to take the levers of economic power out of Quebec's hands. The province had already sustained a couple of major losses: its largest pulp and paper company, Consolidated-Bathurst Inc., had been sold by Montreal financier Paul Desmarais to a U.S.

company, Stone Container Corp. of Chicago; and a large insurance company, Groupe Commerce, was bought by Dutch interests. Now Steinberg was in danger too.

The concern was felt not just by politicians but by some of the most powerful business executives in the province: men like André Bérard, chairman of the National Bank of Canada; Jean Campeau, chairman of the Caisse de dépôt; and Claude Béland, chief executive of the Mouvement Desjardins credit union. They began to speak openly about creating a Quebec defence fund to keep control of major industries within the province. What good were laws protecting the French language and culture or the distinct society of Quebec, they argued, if the major economic decisions were made by outsiders? They proposed to create a pool of financial capital in the province so that institutions could purchase large equity stakes in Quebec companies that were vulnerable to takeover.

Suddenly groceries became a political issue. The bidding war for Steinberg took place before a 1989 provincial election and Premier Robert Bourassa was acutely sensitive to the outcome. He was unhappy that Consolidated-Bathurst had been lost and he wanted to ensure Steinberg would remain a Quebec company. The premier made telephone calls to Gaucher, to the Caisse, and to the Steinberg sisters. The political pressure was building.

When the Caisse made its move, providing almost all the financing for the Steinberg acquisition, critics outside the province were quick to complain. Michel Gaucher and his Socanav partner, Louis Rochette, had put up only $20-million in cash, yet the $1.3-billion takeover offer for Steinberg was made in Socanav's name.

"This was a Caisse-driven undertaking and Gaucher was the puppet and will be forever," a bitter Arnold Steinberg said later. "Gaucher had never been able to raise a penny to do any of these things until the Caisse said it would put up all the dough." Not only had the Caisse agreed to a pre-purchase of Steinberg's enormous Ivanhoe real estate portfolio at a final price of $887-million, it had also assumed $150-million of Ivanhoe debt. It also lent $70-million to Socanav, in the form of debentures.

For its trouble, the Caisse took a 15 percent-equity interest in Socanav. But that stake could rise to 27 percent because the debentures were convertible into shares. The deal looked to critics like nationalization in disguise, an example of the Caisse exceeding its primary mandate to invest Quebecers' pension money in a prudent and profitable fashion. Anonymous voices on Toronto's Bay Street grumbled that the Caisse had become an "insidious" presence in Canadian business, using its enormous power to distort the rules of the marketplace.

This wasn't the first time such accusations had been leveled at the Caisse de dépôt. The fund has been a controversial presence ever since its creation in the mid 1960s to invest deposits in the Quebec Pension Plan and various other public pension and insurance plans. While its main role is to earn a decent rate of return on pensioners' money, the Caisse also has a mandate to develop the economy of Quebec. In doing so, it often behaves in ways that seem blatantly nationalistic, although its chairman at that time, Jean Campeau, disagrees with such criticism. "People say it's nationalistic for us to want to keep a head office in Quebec. My eye. It's selfish," Campeau says. "The bigger we are, the stronger we are. Those people [at Steinberg] are our depositors. They deposit pension premiums and auto insurance premiums. And each time they buy from Quebec farmers, they enrich us."

That kind of enlightened self-interest has made the $37-billion Caisse the biggest stockmarket investor in the country, with a portfolio of more than $13-billion in Canadian stocks. In 1989 the Caisse's principal holdings included $760-million worth of BCE Inc. stock; $420-million worth of Toronto Dominion Bank; $424-million of Canadian Pacific Ltd., and $402-million of Seagram. During the 1980s the Caisse threw its weight around, buying large stakes in resource companies such as Noranda Inc. and Domtar Inc. It even showed serious interest in buying the transportation giant, Canadian Pacific Ltd., prompting the federal government to step in with a bill to keep national transportation companies out of provincial hands. The Caisse controlled large stakes in so many Quebec companies that there was scarcely a deal done in Quebec without its involvement.

The Steinberg transaction was the right deal at the right time for Jean Campeau. The shrewd chairman of the Caisse had successfully diversified the fund's holdings ever since he'd taken it over in 1980. But there was one gap to be filled in the investment plan. The Caisse's real estate portfolio was ten years behind the times, he believed. "It was 2 percent of our assets and a pension fund like us should be at 4 to 6 percent." He believed that a bigger investment in real estate would spread Quebec's pension money around prudently so that it wasn't all tied up in the financial markets.

The Steinberg deal provided just such an opportunity. It was a once-in-a-lifetime chance for the Caisse. In return for helping Michel Gaucher finance the takeover, the Caisse was getting all of the Steinberg real estate held by Ivanhoe Inc., the sixth largest real estate company in Canada. Ivanhoe owned thirty-six prime shopping centers in Quebec and Ontario, evaluated at more than $1.1-billion — by far the most valuable assets in Steinberg. "In a single transaction, we made up ten years, with quality real estate," said Campeau. "Over a period of time, you can't go wrong with that." It was no wonder the normally reserved Campeau celebrated the acquisition by taking all his senior staff out to dinner.

Michel Gaucher was hailed in Quebec as a savior, the man who had snatched Steinberg from the jaws of the Ontario invaders. And he was flushed with optimism at his new purchase. In the dramatic way in which he expresses himself, Gaucher described Steinberg as "a war machine" with the best purchasing power in Quebec. His military strategy was contained in a large red loose-leaf binder that he kept in his office, emblazoned with the letters W.A.R. — Winning at Retail. On the twenty-fourth floor of Steinberg's executive office, Gaucher turned the office of the former chairman, Mel Dobrin, into a "war room" from which the general deployed his troops.

To those who doubted his ability to run a retailing company he replied, "I'm not the type to be laid back. We took a shipping company and we made it the biggest shipping company in Canada, in terms of days. It increased by 400 percent in three years. We're not going to sit idle with this company." Those who know him well say he is as tenacious as a bulldog. "He's very determined, he has a lot of stamina," says Jean Campeau.

But those most familiar with the complex problems that bedeviled Steinberg weren't so sure how much of a triumph this deal really was. While the Caisse laid claim to the prized real estate, Gaucher was left with the struggling retail side of the business and a mountain of debt. He had purchased the Steinberg empire with borrowed money, in the same kind of risky "leveraged buyout" that had forced Canadian financier Robert Campeau's retailing empire into bankruptcy in the United States. The numbers weren't quite as big, but the concept and the risks were exactly the same.

The leveraged buyout was a common phenomenon in the 1980s, whereby an acquisitor borrows most of the money for a takeover and hopes to pay back the debt by selling some of the company's assets and using the company's cash flow. LBOs are risky propositions: if the assets cannot be sold for the expected price, or if interest rates on the mountainous debts rise, the debt load can crush the company.

In this case, Socanav was injecting only $50-million in cash to buy Steinberg and borrowing the rest of the $1.3-billion from the Caisse and a group of other financial institutions. Besides the Caisse's contribution, $330-million in short-term credit was pledged by the Toronto Dominion Bank and the Bank of Montreal and another $50-million by a Quebec government agency. After selling the valuable Ivanhoe real estate to the Caisse, Gaucher was left with the low-profit retail operations: 101 Steinberg supermarkets in Quebec, 68 Miracle Food Marts, and 81 Valdi discount stores in Ontario; 20 department stores in the M Store chain and 24 Arizona-based supermarkets operating under the Smitty's Super Valu name. There was a hodgepodge of other assets in restaurants, sugar refining, and wholesaling that Gaucher planned to sell.

Because he put up so little of his own money to buy the company, however, Gaucher in effect mortgaged the assets in Steinberg. The arithmetic was frightening. Not only did Steinberg assume about $450-million in new debt from the takeover, but there was already $320-million in existing debt on the company's books. When you added it all up, Steinberg was in hock for $770-million, even after the sale of Ivanhoe. The problem was obvious. Now the company was carrying this debt on a much smaller asset base.

Michel Gaucher knew that he couldn't afford to carry that much debt for very long. Moreover, he knew that within three years the rents he would pay at many of Steinberg's prime store locations would double or more. As long as Ivanhoe was part of the Steinberg empire, the rents it charged to the food stores were always kept below market price. In the deal to buy Ivanhoe, the Caisse had insisted that the rents in the food stores move to full market value every five years.

The Caisse de dépôt had been a very tough bargainer, using its tremendous political and economic power to dictate the terms of the takeover deal to Gaucher. Even after they purchased all the shares of Steinberg, Gaucher and the Caisse were still haggling over the final terms of the transaction. "The Caisse is an animal which, if you let it have its own way, will just wipe you out," Gaucher says. "They didn't give a shit about Michel Gaucher or anybody. Contrary to what you may read, the Caisse is only out for itself and the good of the state. . . . They just wanted to get their hands on the real estate."

That was the heart of the problem. Without the real estate, Gaucher was left with the food stores and the department stores — assets of questionable value. Steinberg's supermarkets, while showing a turnaround before the takeover, had slipped to number three in the province. The $11-billion grocery market in Quebec is a tough place to make money because the population isn't growing and there's tough competition from Steinberg's main competitors, Provigo Inc., Métro-Richelieu Inc., and IGA-Boniprix.

Not the least of Gaucher's problems was the combative Steinberg union, local 500 of the United Food and Commercial Workers. Steinberg had a long history of labor trouble and was the highest-cost operator in the Quebec food business. In 1988, under the previous ownership, Steinberg had threatened to sell off its food division unless the union agreed to substantial concessions. The Quebec government wound up mediating the dispute in a marathon bargaining session in Quebec City. It had helped draft a new contract that provided for six years of labor peace and wage cuts totaling $11-million.

But as part of that deal the union claimed Steinberg had agreed to maintain a network of at least fifty corporate-owned stores in the Montreal area. Michel Gaucher just as adamantly maintained he knew nothing of such a commitment. The issue was important because Gaucher had made it clear that he intended to franchise as many of the Montreal stores as possible. Franchising — the common practice among Steinberg's principal competitors in Quebec — was clearly the way of the future in the grocery industry, combining the entrepreneurial initiative of an independent store owner with the resources of a major wholesale buyer.

Of course franchising was anathema to the union. It meant the end of corporate-wide contract negotiations for union members, since each franchise owner would be able to set his own terms with unionized employees. While cashiers made $12 an hour in a corporate store, they earned an average of only $9.75 in a franchise. Two months after Gaucher bought Steinberg, the union initiated legal action that sought to overturn the takeover and prevent Steinberg from selling off any more stores to franchisees. They lost their case in court but they vowed to continue the fight against franchising.

The new ruler of Steinberg would have his hands full. It was in the food stores where the success or failure of his gamble would be determined.

# 2

# A Day in the Life of Store Number Four

6:00 a.m.: Daybreak casts a gentle glow on the Steinberg store at the corner of Sherbrooke Street and Victoria Avenue in the Montreal suburb of Westmount. In a couple of hours this intersection will be enveloped in the madness of morning rush hour. But for now, the only discernible activity outside is the flashing of streetlights and the arrival of delivery vans behind the store. Inside, seven employees are already at work, changing prices and displays, getting the specials ready and putting out the fresh fruit, vegetables, and cuts of meat for the day. The store's bakery has been busy since 5:00 a.m.

It's Monday morning and the store's manager, Graham Fletcher, will soon be waking in his home in Châteauguay, on the south shore of the St. Lawrence River, to prepare for another busy week at Store Number Four. Fletcher and his employees will reenact a daily drama as they struggle to serve the hundreds of grocery shoppers who come to the store each day. The same scenes will be played out with small variations in more than 100 Steinberg-owned supermarkets in Quebec and Ontario.

Keeping the customers satisfied was Sam Steinberg's principal challenge when his mother started the business in 1917 and the same is true today for its new owner, Michel Gaucher. It's the only thing that really counts in the highly competitive grocery business. A supermarket is a low-profit-margin operation that will make money only if the goods on its shelves turn over quickly and the customers keep streaming in the doors. Volume is everything in this business.

To satisfy the clientele, a steady procession of delivery trucks arrives and departs during the early morning hours. Deliveries start here at 5:00 a.m. and the fresh meat and produce shipments have already arrived. Two vans are now discharging the day's order of yogurt and dairy products. Shipments are unloaded early so as not to clog the small parking lot during store hours. The lot can handle only forty cars, and later today there will be customer lineups of up to a dozen cars waiting to get in. The congestion causes such traffic problems on the street that police sometimes ticket the line of waiting cars. That's bad for business and it upsets Graham Fletcher so much that he once went up on the roof to snap pictures of the police at their work so he could give them to city hall.

Store Number Four occupies 19,000 square feet (5,800 square metres) in one of Montreal's choicest retailing districts. It's small compared to the sprawling new super-stores opening up around town, which often combine a supermarket with a drugstore, but the location makes up for it. The neighboring blocks are filled with trendy boutiques catering to the affluent residents of Westmount. The store has five cashiers on the Sherbrooke Street side and six on the Victoria Avenue side. But the store's layout is poor: the stock and refrigeration rooms are downstairs in the basement, for example, requiring the constant use of an elevator. These days, new stores are always built on one level for the convenient handling of goods.

Despite that handicap, Store Number Four is one of the few really profitable outlets in the Steinberg chain. It attracts between 17,000 and 18,000 customers a week, grossing up to $450,000 in a good week and $22-million in a good year. When Michel Gaucher purchased Steinberg, this was one of the first stores he visited, "probably because he couldn't believe how much money we're making," says Graham Fletcher proudly.

7:15 a.m.: Fletcher has driven across the Mercier Bridge, beating the rush-hour traffic by a good half hour and arriving an hour and forty-five minutes before opening time. After pouring himself a coffee, he begins to pace the aisles, making his customary round of checks. Despite the long day ahead of him, he likes to get in early and make sure everything is all right. He nods at his produce manager, who arrived at 4:00 a.m. to stock his counters, well before he's required to do so under the union agreement. "That's what you like to see," Fletcher says. "He doesn't have to be here this early but he wants to get organized for the week." Fletcher has a boyish face topped with red hair. He's bright and easygoing, and has earned the respect of his employees for his straight-shooting manner. "He's a very nice guy, certainly compared to some of the SOBs we've had around here," says the head cashier, Anita Knappe.

As he makes his rounds, greeting employees, Fletcher finds one problem to solve on this Monday morning. There's an absentee in the dairy department and the dairy manager will need help today because he will be busy stocking yogurt. The customers at this store have a particular fondness for yogurt. It's amazing how much of the stuff they buy — more than 100 cases of it last week alone. The store stocks over 100 different brands and flavors, and "we could easily put in another four feet of shelf space for the yogurt," Fletcher says.

Indeed, customers here buy enormous amounts of all kinds of food. On this day alone, the dairy manager expects to sell 320 cartons of 2 percent milk, 180 cartons of 1 percent, 160 of skim, and 90 of whole milk. The bakery section is even busier. On a Saturday, 1,000 loaves of bread will be sold and when English muffins are on special, 900 packages will be snapped up in a day.

7:30 a.m.: Office manager Monique Plouffe — "the singing office girl", as Fletcher calls her — is organizing schedules for the 60 full-time and 60 part-time workers at the store, a job she shares with the head cashier. She's also balancing last week's sales and receipts in her books. Plouffe has thirty years of experience at Steinberg and a plaque on the wall commemorates her first twenty-five. She's a slightly built, dark-haired woman with a lilting voice. Most mornings she starts at eight o'clock, a half hour before she has to report. "It's like a sickness with me," she says. "I have to be here early to get things ready.

"I check if they deposited the right amount of money on Saturday. I balance all my sales from the previous day. Everything has to balance to the penny. If there's an error, it's possible to go back and find it [through the central computer system that controls the cash registers]. Then I check the money in the safe." When the cashiers arrive, Plouffe will open the safe and hand each of them a blue satchel of cash with her name and seal on it.

This initial cash float provides change for the cashier. Every time she accumulates $600 from customers, the cashier turns it over to the office for deposit in the safe upstairs. Accuracy is demanded of cashiers ringing in prices or code numbers and handling change. Mistakes aren't tolerated for long, although each cashier is given a one-cent margin of error on every transaction handled and a $3.25 credit every twelve weeks.

Plouffe glances at one of her charts and finds an example. "Look at this girl. For the whole week, we picked up $16,000 from her cash. She's out by $1.74. That's okay." On average, each cashier punches up 845 customers in one week, giving her an $8.45 margin of error, plus the prorated portion of her $3.25 credit. If she's short or over by more than that amount during a twelve-week period, she goes back to training school. If it happens a second time, she's gone. Each cashier gets 30 to 32 hours of training at school and most recruits don't survive the weeding-out process.

"If I send five, I'm lucky if I get two that pass," says Plouffe. "Some can't multiply 30 by 10 or they can't add. The first time they see customers, they go blank. And when they quit, it's because of the stress. It's too hard on them. They're always moving. At the end of the day, they're dead."

8:00 a.m.: Moving around the store, Fletcher ensures that the new specials for the week are properly displayed. Last week the big loss leader was blade roast at 98 cents a pound. Fletcher sold 125 cases of that. Peaches were on sale for $2.99 a basket and went fast, selling close to 800 cases. Today they're back up to $4.99 a basket. This week's specials are scrawled on blackboards above the aisles: FBI fruit juice for 89 cents a litre, down from the regular $1.39; Viau cookies, $2.99 a pack, down from $3.77; Dr. Ballard's cat food for 79 cents a can, down from $1.25; and Miracle Whip for $1.89 for 1500 ml, down from $2.69.

Decisions on the specials are made by head office. "There's almost a regular pattern to it," Fletcher says. Each major brand gets its turn, and almost every week you can count on a special promotion for a soft drink, a soap, a brand of spaghetti, some kind of beef, almost any staple. "Some people, the only thing they buy is what's on special," he says. "The average family can't afford to buy four rib steaks, so when steak's on sale, people stock up." However, while specials are important, they're supposed to be just a teaser to bring people into the store. "If the only thing you sell is low-margin stuff, it's a nightmare for the store."

Ordering the right quantities of food is no simple task. Fletcher gives a lot of responsibility to his department heads. The fruit, dairy, meat, fish, cheese, and bakery managers do their own forecasting and ordering. "All I try to do is make sure that nothing is empty," he says. "The idea is not to get stuck with too much, because until it's sold it's costing you interest. It can be a nightmare for head office, too. Let's say they need 40,000 cases of Tide. Then they find they're short another 20,000. The stuff has to be shipped in from Toronto.

"We keep records here to guide us. I have a rough idea how much of a special will sell. Like last Monday, we calculated we would need 800 cases of peaches for the week. But you can't do that with all the items. Take an item that sells a case a month. You have to be on the ball and follow it every day." And even then, you never know when a strike or a labor dispute could interrupt the next shipment of goods, he says. The store's bakery — a profitable operation with high markups on everything from muffins to croissants — needs especially careful attention. "You have to be careful you don't bake too much or it goes in the garbage," Fletcher explains. "We like to bake it throughout the day, so it's always fresh and we're never stuck with too much. Besides, when the customers come in, they like the smell of fresh baking."

He relies on his service manager and head cashier to plan staff use and "make sure we can meet the rushes". That can be tricky. "Wait for a morning when four cashiers call in sick," he says. "That'll be the busiest day of the week — it's Murphy's Law. Normally we run with eleven cashiers, but say there's going to be a snowstorm or somebody's sick or it's going to be really busy. It's hard to call in extra people [part-timers]. We'll call them at 6:00 or 7:00 a.m. on a Saturday, but they don't want to answer the phone. Some weeks, with absenteeism, we need upwards of 200 hours of replacement time out of a total schedule of 2,900 hours a week. The company makes only $1.50 on a $100 order, so you don't want to waste it on bad scheduling."

There are times when Fletcher views the employees and customers at his store as some strange hybrid version of an extended family — a family of which he is patriarch. "I've got 120 kids here and 17,000 in-laws," he jokes. And like any father, he occasionally has problems with his offspring, the biggest one being their proclivity to steal time. A 15-minute break often turns into a 25-minute one. For the most part, however, he is happy with his workers' productivity. "This store is only as good as the staff that works here, and fortunately we're blessed with good staff."

He can't complain much about the customers either, although there are always a few oddballs and belligerents. He seems to know them all. "Some customers are so regular, you can set your watch by them. One guy comes in here at two o'clock every day." Others distinguish themselves by their lavish spending habits. "We have orders of up to $300 or $400 sometimes."

There is also loyalty and affection from longtime customers. Fletcher recalls receiving a letter from a blind woman who had been a regular customer for many years before she moved to British Columbia. She used to phone in her order and the staff would fill it and deliver it. "She wrote us to thank us," he says with pride.

Fletcher has spent twenty-four years with Steinberg at a score of different stores. He started working part-time while at high school and never really tried anything else. At twenty-one, he was a full-time assistant grocery manager, at twenty-three a grocery manager, and later a customer-service manager. This was the standard route of advancement for anybody working under Sam Steinberg. No matter how much education you had, you started at the bottom to get a feel for the business and you worked your way up. Over the years, the management ranks of Steinberg were filled with people who started as stock-boys or packers.

"I've been happy at all my jobs. I've had a chance to do everything," Fletcher says. But ask him what he'd really like to be doing and he'll say, "live on a farm". Press him further and he'll concede that a work schedule that gives him Wednesdays and Sundays off is less than ideal for a family man with four little kids at home. On Thursdays he doesn't leave the store until 10:00 at night, after putting in a fifteen-hour day, and on most other nights, he's not home until 7:30, which means "I don't see the kids much at night."

The responsibilities of his job mean he's on call all the time. Just the day before, on a Sunday, he was called in to deal with a leak in the refrigeration system. "When the phone rang at home, my wife tried to tell me, 'Don't answer it'," he laughs. At 12:30 a.m. one New Year's Eve, while the rest of the world was celebrating, he was in the store to help repair a broken sump pump.


8:10 a.m.: Some cashiers have already arrived and are checking the cigarette inventory at the front desk. As Fletcher watches them, he sympathizes with their lot. "The cashiers have a grueling job," he says. "They pass through hundreds of people a day at the checkout counters, punching an average of twenty items per minute. And Saturday is a zoo in here, it's really tough on them." That's the day people line up outside the store at 8:30 a.m. like racehorses awaiting the bugle call. When the doors open, shoppers race through the store, filling their carts within five or ten minutes, trying to beat the Saturday crush. The phenomenon is particularly pronounced on the first warm day of summer, when people want to get out of town fast and head to the cottage or the campground.

Eight cashiers are expected today. The store will be busiest during the noon hour, when some cashiers are taking their lunch break, and during the late rush, when there will be as many as 100 shoppers in the store around the 6:00 p.m. closing time. The place is also busy throughout the day. It's not like some so-called weekend stores in the chain, where almost nobody comes early in the week but the dam breaks on Thursdays, Fridays, and Saturdays. Some say it's easier to operate that kind of store, but there is no such good fortune for Fletcher. He's running a high-volume operation that caters to families with long shopping lists. By comparison, the other Steinberg store serving Westmount, in the Alexis Nihon shopping plaza adjacent to a Métro station, has double the customers but a smaller sales volume. For the most part it handles walk-in traffic, people who come in for a quart of milk or a loaf of bread.

8:30 a.m.: Fletcher takes the elevator downstairs, then walks through the stockroom, where boxes filled with everything from jam to bathroom cleanser are piled high on both sides. In the far corner of the room is the bottle department, where as much as $5,000 worth of empties are stacked. "It takes one guy 40 or 50 hours a week, just sorting out the empties," he complains. "That's all he does. It doesn't give us any money. Then somebody with a bottle drive will come along, like the Boy Scouts, and take away three or four van loads of them."

Striding down the basement corridor, Fletcher turns and steps into the frigid domain of the meat department, where all the cuts are prepared, wrapped, and checked for freshness daily. In the cutting room it's 30°F. (1°C) and in the wrapping room, 45°F. (7°C). His voice betrays the admiration he feels for these employees. "It's cold down here and they won't see much sunlight today."

He stops to talk with two women who are putting chicken into Styrofoam packaging with plastic wrapping. The packages are then placed on a conveyor belt that moves them onto a computerized scale where they are weighed and stamped with a price. The women will spend all day at this task — from 7:00 a.m. to 4:00 p.m. — carefully scraping the frost off each piece before wrapping it. "You can imagine what their hands feel like at the end of the day," says Fletcher. "They're rough and red." The work is even colder and tougher in the cutting room, where the butchers trim their meat orders in below-freezing temperatures with electric saws. "The guys working in the cutting room should be getting danger pay," Fletcher comments.

Of course, health-conscious consumers are buying less red meat these days, substituting chicken, fish, and vegetarian fare, and that means less work for the butchers downstairs. The change is one of many that Fletcher has observed in his years in the business. There's no barometer like a supermarket for keeping track of the changes, not only in consumers' grocery tastes but also in general lifestyles and values. Single-parent families, two-income families, and fast-food restaurants have completely revolutionized the supermarket business.

"When I was growing up there were no fast-food restaurants," he remembers. "My dad would come home with ten bags of groceries.

Nowadays, how many people will come back with ten bags? It would cost you $150. It's easier and cheaper to call out for something or buy a ready-to-serve meal. I was a packer when they came in with the first disposable diapers, twenty years ago. Nobody ever thought they would sell. Look at them now."

As the transition to new products quickens, there remains an immutable rule in stocking a supermarket: every time you bring in something new, you have to take something out. Composition of the shelves has literally changed before Fletcher's eyes. When the frozen-food section began to expand, it took space away from other products. Now, there is a twelve-foot section for frozen pizzas alone. When margarine sales declined in Quebec, because of a provincial government order that margarines must be dyed a different color from butter, Fletcher adjusted by adding another four feet of shelf space for the yogurt. When consumers became more concerned about the health risks of cholesterol and salt, they showed a ready willingness to pay for specialty cheeses, cut and wrapped individually, rather than the mass-produced brands of cheddar. That's why this particular store has its own cheese "boutique" with 135 different varieties.

9:01 a.m.: The doors are unlocked and the first few customers of the day walk in.

9:02 a.m.: A Brinks truck pulls up to collect the weekend receipts and to provide the store with change. "Once Brinks goes upstairs to the safe," says Fletcher, "nobody can go into the office, not even me."

9:07 a.m.: The produce manager walks up to Fletcher holding a half-eaten banana he has rescued from a fruit counter. "We've got a customer who is half-hungry today," he says, brandishing the banana in disbelief. Fletcher sees more than enough examples of bizarre customer behavior in an average day: people singing in the aisles, loiterers, shoplifters, people leaving their personal belongings in the shopping carts.

And there's the inevitable abuse he gets from customers. "When you're taking a deposit from a cashier, and the customer is stuck waiting at the checkout counter, they'll always complain, 'Why me?' Or you'll get a customer with a long list of items to buy and she'll find everything she needs except two or three things, yet she'll complain that 'this store has nothing.' Or just after you've finished sweeping the floors and cleaning the counters, somebody will say, 'This is the dirtiest store I've ever seen.' The problem is that if something falls on the floor, the store is sometimes so crowded that you can't do a proper job of cleaning it up."

One of Fletcher's continuing problems is loiterers. He watches a zombie-like woman walk listlessly through an open service door and into the store. "They like to come in and sit down," he says. Fletcher doesn't make a move to stop her, and a few minutes later she walks out again in the same trance-like state.

At night, he is responsible for checking the store after closing time to make sure there are no derelicts or homeless people hiding in the building. He recalls one time when he was checking in the employee washroom and noticed a pair of large boots in view under a toilet-stall door. He was afraid to open the door. When he finally mustered the nerve to look, he found a drunk snoozing comfortably on the toilet seat. Fletcher hustled him out.

9:31 a.m.: Fletcher is walking down an aisle when he spots a woman trying to conceal a $4 bottle of shampoo under her dress. When she sees him coming, she drops the bottle and runs. Fletcher has encountered her before. "I'm glad I didn't have to reach under her dress for that bottle," he says.

The store occasionally uses plainclothes security staff to deter shoplifting, but often it's Fletcher himself who must play policeman. He looks for telltale signs of mischief. "If I see a guy with long hair and jeans piling rib steaks into a cart, then I know something's up. Those are the guys who like to steal steaks and sell them to the taverns." Once, Fletcher was standing near the meat counter, talking with one of his butchers, when he apprehended a young man calmly stuffing about $300 worth of steaks into an Adidas sports bag.

On another occasion, one of his employees spotted a man who had stuffed a piece of steak inside his pants and then tried to walk out of the store. The employee alerted a cashier. "She said, 'You've got a steak in there, hand it over.' The guy denied it. Then she said, 'Okay, drop your pants.' So the guy dropped his pants with a smile on his face and sure enough the steak was there. She looked at him and said, 'I want that. No, not *that*, the piece of steak.'" By the time Fletcher arrived on the scene, the man was becoming belligerent. "Out of the blue he picked up a chair and was going to swing it at me, but he stopped just short of my face. That brought my head wrapper over." The man pulled a knife and a chase began, with the knife-wielding shoplifter pursued out of the store by the head wrapper and by Fletcher, who was armed with a broom.

10:00 a.m.: The computer in Fletcher's office shows $1,875 in sales in the first hour of business. One hundred and nine customers have passed through the checkout counter, spending an average of $17.21 each. Six lines are open.

10:47 a.m.: Accurate pricing is just as important as accurate stocking, and this morning a checker is walking through the store, verifying the prices on 650 items. He's making sure the price listed on the UPC sticker (those familiar tags with the black lines that are scanned by the cashier's computer) is the same as the price printed on the package. So far he has found 11 mistakes. He can do 300 price checks an hour, using a computerized gun that communicates with a head office computer. "There's always human error in pricing," says Fletcher, "and there's nothing more frustrating for the customer than finding the wrong price on an item. During the week we'll also check the cashiers. We'll take every item of an order and make sure that everything has been punched right, with the right price and attributed to the right department." With the UPC system now in place, cashiers are using computer-scanning on just over 50 percent of the items they punch. Eventually they'll scan 100 percent of them or close to it.

11:15 a.m.: Graham Fletcher pours himself another coffee and reflects on what has happened to Steinberg. Even here, in profitable Store Number Four, the company's larger struggle for survival has taken its toll. The supermarket division has been in trouble for a long time. Over the years Fletcher has seen layoffs, threats to close the stores, and showdowns with the union.

He started at Steinberg at the age of seventeen when the company was the undisputed king of the Quebec grocery business. Now, it was number three. "When you work twenty-four years for a company and you hear about people losing their jobs, it's a shock," he says.

During 1988 to 1989 Steinberg was the subject of takeover rumors, shutdown rumors, and everything in between. "The staff was really, really concerned," he says. "They'd put in a lot of years of service. Many of them were career employees, myself included. It was like the end of a dynasty."

Some of his employees refused to believe the stories and rumors that Steinberg would be sold. Some figured the company was only trying to scare the union into making concessions. Others, hearing that Steinberg's competitors in Quebec might buy the supermarket chain, said, "What's the difference if we work for Provigo or Métro-Richelieu?" But those were the militants. Most of the employees were worried where their next cheque was coming from. Nobody was really safe."

It was a confusing time for Fletcher, with new rumors flying every day. "People were always coming up to me and saying, 'What's the real story?' I'd tell them to read the papers."

As the company's demands for union concessions increased during 1988, the employees felt hurt. "The general feeling I had from employees at this store," Fletcher says, "was that they weren't ready to give things up. For example, the night staff are not militant, but they're an excellent team of workers, in terms of their output. They said, 'Yes, we're better paid than the competition, but they don't pack as much as we do. We work harder, we pack 300 cases a night.' They took it personally. They felt they were being lumped with a bunch of people who don't work as hard."

The concessions, in the end, were substantial for the full-time employees. The work week jumped from thirty-seven hours to forty hours in 1988, for the same pay. "Some of them felt they gave up a lot," Fletcher says. "They work three extra hours and they aren't paid for it. Initially, that had an effect on morale."

When the company was finally sold to Michel Gaucher in 1989 Fletcher felt a deep sense of loss. Store Number Four had a long and colorful history, intimately linked to the Steinberg family. The store opened in 1930, one of the first expansion moves that Sam Steinberg made. Sam and his young wife Helen moved into an apartment upstairs and Helen worked as a cashier at the store. Her brother, Lawrence Roth, was the store's first manager.

Mike Aronovitch, who later became the Steinberg family physician, was one of the first employees hired at Store Number Four, for the princely sum of $16 a week. He remembers spending hours carefully mounting fancy displays of fruit in the window. There were no shopping carts or self-service in those days. If a lady wanted a dozen apples, Aronovitch filled a bag for her. "The whole store was a grocery counter on one side, a display on the other," he remembers. "The phone was ringing all the time. You brought goods in, displayed them on the stand, the phone would ring, you'd take the order, make it up, put it in a box with the bill, and it would be shipped out and delivered." He worked from 7:00 a.m. to 9:00 p.m. and after work he oiled the wooden floors.

Store Number Four remained one of the company's flagship supermarkets over the years. Sam's daughter Mitzi worked there as a teenager, packing fruit in the summer time. Helen Steinberg, who lived just up the hill in Westmount, continued to shop there all her life and Graham Fletcher came to know her well.

During the takeover battle, most of the employees of Store Number Four had hoped that Steinberg would be sold to Oxdon, because Oxdon had promised to spin off the grocery operation to Loblaw Companies Ltd., the big Toronto-based supermarket chain. The employees figured they'd be better off with a corporate chain that knew the supermarket business rather than with a neophyte like Gaucher.

For Graham Fletcher, the real problem was not the sale of the company but the concessions the union had made to management in 1988. The agreement meant he could not hire any more full-time workers. The most he could offer a new employee was twenty-four hours of work a week. He could not adequately replace the fifteen experienced full-timers from his store who had accepted the company's offer of an early retirement buyout.

"It's increasingly hard to get people," he says. "Take a wrapper. He makes $4.75 an hour. Over twenty-four hours that's a maximum of $114. Who's willing to get off unemployment insurance or welfare to make that kind of money? Nobody wants to work for that." More than ever, Fletcher finds he is hiring recent immigrants to Canada, people who are willing to hold down another job on the side. But a lot of people he hires are here for two days and then gone.

Once upon a time he could afford to be selective. By 1989 Fletcher was putting help wanted ads in the store window and in the newspapers — the first time he had ever done so. When interviewing young applicants, he makes sure they're living at home with their parents, because if they live on their own, he knows they'll never make the rent on twenty-four hours of Steinberg wages. They'll quit in a few days.

Fletcher understands why new employees are so poorly motivated and have so little initiative. They have no prospect of advancement in the store, no chance of attaining full-time status for many years. This is a reversal of everything Steinberg once stood for. When Fletcher had started at the company as a teenager, employees knew they could advance through the ranks. He had done it himself. Now he realizes that if things had been like this when he started as a wrapper in 1967, he'd never have risen to become a store manager.

12:05 p.m.: The lunchtime rush begins and the pace of business will be brisk for the next ninety minutes. Employees begin wandering upstairs to the lunchroom for their break while others punch in to work the afternoon shift.

As Fletcher takes his lunch break, he reflects on the worst hazard of the job: holdups. They are a part of life in the supermarket trade in Quebec and there's little Steinberg can do to prevent them, short of putting security guards in every store. Fletcher has seen his share of shotguns and pistols. His biggest challenge is trying to calm down his staff whenever the store is held up.

One Christmas Eve around 4:00 p.m., Fletcher was standing near the entrance of his store when he suddenly felt the cold steel of a pistol pressed against his nose. It's a feeling he wouldn't wish on anybody. He was told to lie down while the cash registers were emptied. After the gunmen had fled, he called home and told his wife he'd be a little late for Christmas Eve dinner that night, where twenty-five guests were expected. The police arrived later and asked him what the gunman looked like, and all Fletcher could say for sure was that he wore black shoes. When he finally arrived home for Christmas he found it hard to celebrate.

2:05 p.m.: The rush subsides and an afternoon lull descends on the store. Anita Knappe, the head cashier, takes advantage of the slower pace to get off the floor and do some office work upstairs. She begins to fill out employee evaluation forms for the 40 cashiers and 14 wrappers she supervises. As one of Fletcher's principal lieutenants, she helps schedule the cashiers' workdays, breaks, and lunches and handles any problems that come up.

"I'm a troubleshooter and I have to be a bit of a sergeant major too," she says. "I make sure everybody's dressed properly and there's no idle time. I also have to be an intermediary, solving problems for the customer before they get to Mr. Fletcher. I guess I'm a disciplinarian too. If there's something wrong, we try to get all the facts and talk reasonably before we have to give the employee written notice of a problem."

Knappe is not a typical cashier. She studied fine arts at Concordia before marrying and making Steinberg a full-time career. She enjoys the responsibility and she's seen it all. "I guess the worst thing that happened to me is that a customer once bit me, just took my hand and bit it," she recalls. "Another time, an elderly gentleman starting urinating against a wall, then started taking off his shoes and socks."

Knappe has the tough assignment of breaking in new recruits and shepherding them through their first stressful weeks behind the cash. "I end up keeping two out of every ten," she says. "They have to be neat in appearance, flexible in times, and precise. Personality is important — whether they get along with people. They have to be fast learners and speak both languages. At first they're very shy, but after a month they're very assertive. They have to learn how to deal with situations head-on. I tell them not to argue with the customer. If you wrapped it in a plastic bag and they want it wrapped in a paper bag, just take it easy. Dealing with the public is something they learn on the job."

Not everybody is cut out for this kind of work. "It's not an easy job, you're stuck in one place, and you're the PR for the company. You're the one the customer sees. We want you to be courteous. That's important because a lot of elderly people will take the time to say, 'Hi, how are you?' After a while you get to know people, their kids. For a lot of people, we're their only social contact."

Knappe usually comes in early to get her schedules ready — often an hour ahead of time. She worries that if she's not in the office early enough, she won't be able to solve the inevitable problems of sickness or absenteeism that arise, for the job takes a toll on the health of cashiers. "Girls develop back problems, severe headaches. If they're having a bad day and they're stressed, they might hurt themselves grabbing a heavy article. Unfortunately, absenteeism is a problem the customer doesn't understand. If they're stuck in a lineup and I tell them three people are sick, they just look at me like 'What do you mean?' "

2:30 p.m.: Knappe is still agonizing over the employee-evaluation forms. "The hardest part of my job is to remain fair and not have visible favorites," she says. "Some people are here just for the money. Others will give you that extra ten percent. Most give their best."

The full-timers make $12.50 an hour, or $460 a week, pretty good money for a two-income family but not great for a single parent supporting a couple of kids. Anita Knappe winds up as everybody's confidante, hearing all the personal problems that complicate the lives of her cashiers. "You have to work around it," she says. "It can affect their work. Sometimes I say, 'Go home, you're no use to me.' "

5:35 p.m.: The afternoon rush is well under way and the store is noticeably busier now as working men and women stop in for

groceries on their way home. Graham Fletcher and his staff are
prepared for this moment. "We try to be one step ahead of the
customer," he says. "The strawberries, the bread, the meat, we
always want to be wheeling it out fresh."

5:57 p.m.: Three minutes from closing time and customers are
rushing inside before the doors are locked. The produce manager is
already taking the fresh fruit and vegetables off the counters and
loading them onto a pushcart to store them downstairs.

6:00 p.m.: Fletcher locks the doors on the Victoria Avenue side,
then on the Sherbrooke Street side. He begins stacking the carts,
putting the returns back on the shelves, and turning the lights off
over the counters.

As he does at the end of every day, Fletcher goes up and down the
aisles with a cart, checking for items in the wrong places. Often he
finds things like packages of pantyhose with nothing left in them or
bottles of aspirin with the pills gone. Tonight he finds an $11.91 cut
of meat left in a juice freezer. A customer had ordered the cut from
the butcher's counter, then probably decided it was too expensive
and dumped it. "It bugs my ass," Fletcher says. "Who pays for that?
The consumer." When Fletcher shows the package to the butcher,
the butcher nods and remembers that the customer didn't really
seem to want the piece of meat as he wrapped it.

6:10 p.m.: The wrappers are spraying and cleaning the vegetable
counters and the cashiers are washing down the checkout belts
under the watchful eye of Anita Knappe. "At the end of each day
we make sure the cash area is clean, our stock is put away and the
last deposit is made," she says. "We make sure we have the right
staff for tomorrow and we go home."

6:17 p.m.: The last customer has apparently checked out. The
cashiers put their money into pouches labeled with their names and

seal them. When they return the next day they will make sure the seal hasn't been tampered with.

6:23 p.m.: A straggler in the store that nobody spotted suddenly turns up with a few items in her cart and wants to be checked through. One of the cashiers patiently reopens her register. With quitting time at hand the cashiers are in a playful mood. One of them squirts a bag boy with her bottle of cleaning spray.

6:29 p.m.: Graham Fletcher checks the computer. The final tally shows sales of $49,800 for the day. There weren't as many customers today as usual, but the orders were bigger.

He makes one last check of the upstairs office before heading home, then remembers something important. His wife had called earlier to say that one of the kids was having a party for the T-ball team and not to forget to bring home a cake.

The day is over, and to an outside observer it seems like a marvelous performance — a coordinated effort by employees and suppliers to keep hundreds of shoppers satisfied. But to Graham Fletcher and his staff of 120, it's all in a day's work.

Fletcher never had the opportunity to meet Sam Steinberg personally although he'd seen him at a store once or twice. Fletcher figures that if Mr. Sam were alive today, he'd be pleased at how Store Number Four performs. For while this modern supermarket, with its computers and electronics and array of newfangled consumer products, seems a world away from the grocery store that Sam's mother first opened in 1917, the foundation of the business remains the same: serving the customer. Ida Steinberg built a family dynasty on that simple truth.

It all began with a tiny store on teeming St. Lawrence Boulevard, the street known to Montrealers as The Main.

# 3

# *The Early Years*

Ida Steinberg was more than the official founder of Steinberg Inc. The tiny strong-willed family matriarch was also the source of inspiration for Sam's business genius and unwavering devotion to his family, two forces that would propel a single store into a phenomenal business empire.

She was born Ida Roth in 1884 to a dirt-poor Hungarian family of eight children: a boy, Lewis, the eldest, and seven girls. Her mother ran the household; her father had had religious training. Ida's life was difficult, marred by family tragedy and constant struggles to make ends meet. In her fifty-seven years she knew only work. Yet the hardships she endured shaped her into a tough resilient woman capable of laying the groundwork for the giant corporation that would one day bear her name.

Ida Roth was confronted with adult responsibilities early. By the time she was thirteen both her mother and her father were dead — they had died within weeks of each other, both in their forties — and as the eldest daughter she was thrust into the role of surrogate mother. She had taken a single year of schooling at that point, but the family duties she had suddenly acquired halted further studies.

As a young girl barely in her teens, Ida was hardly capable of replacing two parents for her seven siblings; she needed parents herself. It was decided that the Roth children would be split up and dispersed among various relatives. Ida was sent to live with an uncle who owned a general store in a village called Gelsa near the eastern Hungarian city of Debrecen. He put her to work in his store selling goods such as cloth and needles, unwittingly giving her her first taste of business.

In 1902, at eighteen years of age, Ida married a young baker named Vilmos Sternberg, as he was called then. The marriage wasn't exactly the culmination of a blissful romance. This was an era of arranged nuptials; the first time Ida met him was the day before they were wed. Vilmos had virtually no public schooling beyond religious education. He was a serious scholar of the Talmud. Hardly a career man — his work as a baker was sporadic — he wished to continue his religious studies. The responsibility for making a living was left to Ida. The arrangement was typical of the custom in Eastern Europe then, where the boys usually received more Hebrew education than the girls, and the girls worked. So while Vilmos studied and prayed, Ida kept busy baking buns to sell in nearby Debrecen. She used the money she earned to buy garments to sell to housewives back in her home town of Teglas.

The money Ida earned did not extend very far, especially when she began to have a family. She gave birth to four children in quick succession — Jack, Nathan, Lily, and an energetic little boy called Sam, the second eldest, born as a Christmas present to her on December 25, 1905.

Life in Hungary was often difficult and regimented for her children. Ida's eldest son, Jack, would have his knuckles rapped by the schoolmaster at the Hebrew school he attended if his lessons weren't completed properly. And there was still little money.

Soon the family would leave that life behind. Ida was doing her best to provide for everyone, but she knew that opportunities for a better life awaited her family in the New World. So in 1911, like many East European Jews who would immigrate to North America during this period, she and the family set sail for Montreal. Two of her sisters, Mary and Rachel, had already made the journey there. They had written to Ida, their letters glowing with accounts of life in "America" (the term included Canada too), a land where one could rise above poverty and where anti-Semitism, then on an alarming increase in Europe, was not a threat.

Sadly, two other Roth sisters who stayed on in Hungary would later perish in the Holocaust: their husbands had not wanted them to go to Canada. Ida's brother and two more sisters came to North

America. One, Fanny, joined them in Montreal, while the other settled in the United States, where she died at a young age.

Ida sold all her possessions to pay for the voyage. It was a long, sickening passage, the family's spirits nonetheless buoyed by their eagerness to taste life in the New World. The family was well looked after during the journey, with the ship's captain, quite taken by the Sternbergs, providing the children with oranges every day. The youngsters were adept at amusing themselves. Little Lily, a one-year-old with a mop of blonde curls, delighted in splashing about in the puddles that dotted the ship's decks. Looking for her was simply a case of finding a little pool of water.

Finally the Sternbergs reached North American shores, although ironically they almost didn't make it to Montreal, getting off the ship in Quebec City by mistake. By chance the family met an immigration officer by the name of Roth, no relation to Ida, who spoke Yiddish and Hungarian. That was indeed fortunate because none of them could speak anything else. The officer put them back on a train and directed them toward Montreal, where Ida's sisters were anxiously awaiting their arrival. Before that, however, the officer, perhaps inadvertently, had "Canadianized" their name from Sternberg to Steinberg.

Thus the Steinbergs began their new life in Canada. It started off with as many hardships as the life they had left behind, taking the luster off those golden tales of promise and opportunity they'd heard about while in Hungary. Ida, Vilmos — who also anglicized his first name, to William — and the children lived in a big unheated house on a side street down near the St. Lawrence River by the Bonsecours Market in what is now Old Montreal. Ida's sisters Rachel and Mary brought in some money working in a garment factory. It was scarcely adequate to support the family, so Ida rented out rooms in the house.

To maximize the number of rooms available for this purpose, the family was crammed into as little space as possible. "We all slept in one room; the others were rented out," remembered Lily Steinberg Rafman, tiny like her mother and with steely blue eyes and the earthy, no-nonsense manner typical of the Steinbergs.

While boarders helped fill the family purse, their presence caused the occasional *contretemps*. One of the two single Greek male boarders, for instance, fell in love with Ida's sister Rachel, or

Rae, a "gorgeous" woman, by Lily's description. It was bad all around, said Lily: "He wasn't Jewish."

Ida's sister Mary was having her problems, too. She married an Eastern European man named Cohen who at the time of their wedding had vehemently assured Mary he was single. She was understandably shocked when she discovered he had a wife and two children back in Europe. The marriage was hastily annulled but not before the couple produced a child, Sam Cohen. "That was a real tragedy," said Lily.

Money continued to be a problem, especially with two more mouths to feed: Max and Morris, born in 1912 and 1914, respectively. Things were even tougher because William was never able to provide for the family. "My father never made a living in his life, if you want the truth," said Lily flatly. He brought in only a meager income through his job as a sometime baker. For a period he worked at Canadian Pacific where he received six dollars a week. Essentially, though, he was a recluse, a religious man who taught Hebrew and rarely spoke English, who preferred to spend most of his time in a small east-end synagogue where he worked as a *shammos*, or caretaker. There he did odd jobs, cleaned, and took care of the prayer books. He found it a struggle to adjust to life in his new country and some of his relatives believe he never truly adapted.

Shortly after the family's arrival in Canada, an incident occurred that would permanently mark the children: William left. According to Lily, Ida's sisters were responsible for his departure. They were worried about Ida, a young mother with six children already and scarcely the means to provide for them. Even though a large family was the norm, she simply could not afford to have any more children. "My aunts talked my mother into leaving my father. We were already six kids. There was no such thing as contraception then. So my mother decided to split up." William departed to a dingy rooming house on St.-Dominique Street in Montreal's east end where the little picture of his children he kept on his dresser provided a fragile but precious link to his family.

Although it was an unusual arrangement for the day, the split wasn't particularly difficult for Ida. She hadn't really loved William; she hardly knew him. Lily sided with her mother in the matter but the boys weren't happy about the separation. Yet perhaps as a way of protecting themselves from the emotional discomfort of dealing with the loss, from that point on the boys acted as if their father had ceased to exist. Executives who came to the company later on were consistently struck by how the father was never mentioned. Ever.

William's departure may not have exacted a profound emotional toll on Ida, but it was difficult for her in another way. It left the entire burden of providing for her children squarely on her shoulders. Poor as she was, family cohesion was terribly important to her. She was determined that her family would not be torn apart the way hers had been after her parents died.


It was 1917. The Great War was still raging and Canadian troops took Vimy Ridge. In Montreal the turn-of-the-century wave of immigration had transformed the Montreal core into a lively, bustling place. Ida, now liberated from the hapless William, was encouraged by family members to get into business herself to make ends meet. She had picked up the rudiments of shopkeeping from her uncle and the baking business and had managed the affairs of a fairly large family. She liked the idea.

She managed to find a little store on St. Lawrence Boulevard, the cobblestoned street that bisected the city into east and west and that was known to Montrealers simply as The Main. It was the vibrant and colorful heart of the Montreal Jewish immigrant community and a cosmopolitan gathering point for a variety of ethnic communities who lived in neighborhoods on either side of the boulevard. Yiddish blended with French, English, Portuguese, Greek, and a host of other languages. The Main was home to merchants of all descriptions and also the center of the city's fast-growing garment, or *shmatah*, industry, as it is known in Yiddish.

The popular mythology is that Ida's first shop was the original Steinberg store. In fact, she ran that store on the Main for only a short time before opening another one. The space was much too tiny for both living quarters for Ida, her six children, her two sisters Rachel and Mary, Mary's son Sam Cohen, *and* the store. Luckily, shortly after opening the first shop, another opportunity came up further north along St. Lawrence, at number 4423. It had belonged to a relative in the needle trade who wanted to vacate it and move closer to Sherbrooke Street. So Ida took the store, filled it with $200 worth of merchandise and put up the sign, "Mrs. I. Steinberg, Grocer", hardly imagining then that she was planting the first seeds of the empire.

That store was narrow, deep, and tiny, not much bigger than an average living room. Like most food stores of the day, it was a full-service shop where customers telephoned in their orders. The staff took the order, made it up, put it in a box with the bill, then shipped it out the back of the store, where it was delivered by horse-drawn cart. Meat wasn't sold that way then, only fruit, vegetables, and staple grocery items such as tea, coffee, sugar, and spices. Everything, some 100 different items in all, was sold in bulk. There were biscuits in open barrels, oatmeal in massive sacks, huge crocks full of pickles. Lavish arrangements of fruit and vegetables, raisins, tinned pears, the most delicious items available in the store, were conspicuously displayed at the front to entice shoppers inside. At the back of the display was the delivery schedule, rigidly maintained. The spread was painstakingly constructed each day, with the fruit carefully polished and placed in elaborate pyramids. It was an early example of the merchandising flair that would later distinguish the Steinberg company.

The business eased Ida's immediate concerns about providing for her children, guaranteeing that at least she'd have food on the table. Living conditions remained deplorable. All ten family members were squeezed behind and above the store. They cooked on a little coal stove that also served as a heater and they slept in a crowded, stuffy attic. It was not equipped with a shower or bath so the younger children, Max and Morris, went to their Auntie Fanny's once a week to bathe, while Ida sent the others to the Montreal Swimming Pools. Ida gave them each a nickel so they could rent a towel for the obligatory shower before and after their swim. As well as serving the interests of personal hygiene, the swimming-pool visits enabled the kids, Jack in particular, to develop into expert swimmers.

If living conditions were tough, so was the Steinberg spirit. Together the family coped. If the flat was too cold, well, you wore long woollen underwear. You didn't indulge or complain. Hardship bred a feeling of closeness, of pulling together.

The little store became the centerpiece of Steinberg family life, the vehicle that would enable the family to rise above difficult conditions and, most important, stay together. The driving force behind it was Ida, an industrious one-woman show, a tireless shopkeeper who toiled long hours at the store, which operated from seven in the morning to eleven at night, six days a week. Her working day was so long that often her children saw her neither rise nor retire. Her boundless energy and capacity for work were contained in a tiny frame under five feet tall. She was so small that an employee once had to attach hockey pucks onto the pedals of her car so she could reach them.

Ida's height belied the force of her character, however. She was hard and unforgiving, and her wavy red hair parted down the center and pulled back tightly behind her head added to her severe appearance. The delivery boys may have towered over her in height, but Ida clearly ruled the roost and would brook no idleness in her store. She was not gratuitously harsh; it was just that survival meant work. There was no time for sloth.

Ida's devotion to the store paid off. It soon became popular in the neighborhood, especially among the many poor people who shopped carefully to find the best prices. Word spread across town about the store on The Main where the little woman in the white apron knew all her customers by name, let them haggle with her over prices and let them buy on credit. She was the storekeeper who surprised her customers by adding an extra apple or cookie to their bag of purchases — "for good measure", as she explained. That kept them coming back.

"Always give them a little more than they expect," she told her children. She had dozens of such proverbs, simple little home truths that brought a human touch to her style of business. They were based on two cardinal rules: first, aim for large volumes by stocking the shelves with only top-quality products and selling them at reasonable prices (it didn't matter that the profits would be low — good prices would entice customers back); and second, treat those clients right. They were paramount.

Ida's maxims were not lost on Sam, who would dish the same ones out when the business had grown a lot larger and more sophisticated than his mother's single store. Whether all the stories he told were indeed factual is open to some debate, but Sam loved to repeat them. They became part of the Steinberg tradition long after Ida had begun to take a back seat in the business, recounted so often by Sam through the years that they became woven firmly into the Steinberg corporate mythology. Many a senior company executive could recount them.

There was one anecdote, for instance, about the customer who had already racked up a significant amount of credit. One day she came into the store, ordered a few more things, paid for them, and left. Sam was furious with his mother. "Why didn't you say anything about the money she owed?" he demanded. His mother calmly responded, "I would have scared a paying customer. If I'd asked her for the money she would have been afraid to come back." There was another about the customer who paid $1.60 for a gallon of cottonseed oil — the same rate charged to a customer who bought only a half-pint. "Why charge them the same unit price?" Sam wanted to know. "Shouldn't the customer who buys a larger quantity get it cheaper?" "The woman who bought half a pint," explained Ida, "that's all she could afford at the time." No use charging her more.

Sam's constant references to his mother's way of doing things demonstrated the enormous influence Ida had on his own business style and how much he adored her. When he opened a store on the corner of Sherbrooke Street and Victoria Avenue in 1930, Sam ran a special ad section in the newspaper that included a tribute to women. He arranged for a portrait of his mother to be taken especially for the section. That same portrait hung in the Steinberg boardroom many years later, a testament to her revered role in the company.

Ida's children learned the ethic of hard work early in life. The three eldest boys, Jack, Sam, and Nathan, were scarcely in their teens when they began to do odd jobs to supplement the income of the store. For them there was no going out to play ball or shoot marbles with friends. When they got home from school they went right to work. Their friends were the family members they lived with.

Their workplace consisted of the rough and tumble streets of east-end Montreal. Soon the children developed enough smarts to carry them through the trickiest of situations. They hawked newspapers around the corner of St. Catherine Street and The Main, where turf wars were fierce and the other hawkers were a lot bigger than the Steinberg boys, especially Sam. He was always small, barely reaching five feet four inches and weighing just 140 pounds. The other kids delighted in trying to knock him off his corner to zero in on his business. But if they expected easy victory they were mistaken, for Sam was a natural scrapper who defended his territory with zeal. It was more than simply lust for a good fight that motivated him, although that was important too. He had to bring home some money. Every copy sold — a penny for *The Montreal Star* — was precious to a poor boy helping his five siblings and mother make ends meet in an unheated east-end apartment. He used his wits to sell papers, even if it occasionally meant breaking the law. When he was nine he would hop the open streetcars, quickly flog a few papers to the passengers and then jump off again before the conductor could catch him. He relished the challenge of discovering new ways to make money any way he could.

The boys also set up pins in the neighborhood bowling alley. For Sam, that job provided yet another opportunity to be shrewd and mischievous. His strategy for maximizing his take was simple. If he knew that the next bowler he had to set pins for wasn't the most generous tipper, he'd say to the kid in front of him, "Hold my place, I'll let you get ahead of me. I've just got to run to the washroom for a sec." The other kid would move up, Sam would come back, the other kid would have been cursed with the chintzy tipper, and Sam would be in line for the next, more generous one.

All of the children, of course, worked in their mother's store. It was part of an unspoken deal really: if the store helped them survive, it followed that they had to help keep it going. The children did everything, from running messages after school to washing and oiling the wooden floors and scrubbing the counters at night (Ida was a stickler for cleanliness) long after the store was closed. She taught them every last detail about the business, from serving customers to pricing to selecting produce.

Each child had specific duties. Sam became the store buyer; Nathan his assistant. The two would race down to Bonsecours Market at the crack of dawn, dashing through the long, dome-topped building to select the best produce. They were quick but dead accurate and the prices they paid were fair, so much so, that over time when Nathan became the buyer, the farmers at Bonsecours would refuse to sell any produce in the morning until he had set the price. Jack delivered groceries. Lily answered the constantly ringing telephone and took down orders, dealing with the predominantly Jewish clientele in Yiddish. The others helped out in the same way. In the early days, young Morris's specialty seemed to consist of getting into trouble. He would fuss when the customers came in and then had the nerve to demand a cut of the business. "I'll be a good boy," he would holler. "Give me a cent!" Ida just ignored him. She had no time for pampering.

The Steinberg children formed a curious collage of personalities. Jack, the eldest, was the black sheep of the family. Naturally athletic, he much preferred going for a swim to working in the store. Later on, cars and women were his principal interests. Work never figured high on his list. Often, if he were late in making a delivery, his brothers knew exactly where to find him — in the local pool hall. Nathan, round-faced and slightly plump, was affable, gregarious, probably the most outgoing of the children. He would later do public relations work for the company, a role that he embraced with enthusiasm. Stocky little Lily was hardworking and serious, with a strong personality, a blunt tongue, and a sharp mind. Of all the siblings, she was Sam's closest match intellectually. Max was quiet, introverted, and studious and Morris was happy-go-lucky and likeable.

And then there was Sam. Blessed with natural talent, drive, and a keen entrepreneurial sense, he emerged early as the brightest of the family. He seemed to have a genius for knowing what customers would want, accept, and need before they themselves realized it. Most importantly, he enjoyed the service he provided.

Sam's abilities soon eclipsed those of his siblings and he evolved as the undisputed leader of the family, even though Jack was the eldest. Sam realized this himself and had no qualms about playing the part of boss. He readily ordered his brothers around, reprimanded them, at times took advantage of them. But if he had all the brains, they offered him an invaluable quality in return: trustworthiness. It was one of the advantages of a family-run business. In the first store, for instance, there was only one qualification you needed to take the cash: you had to be family. Years later the brothers would be given high positions within the company. They weren't necessarily the most competent or capable, but that was how the company worked.

If hard work figured prominently in the Steinberg children's lives, circumstances were such that education did not. Despite the family's constant toiling in the store, money was always scarce. So, as was the case for many children of the pre-Depression and Depression era, especially those of immigrant parents, working to contribute to the household took precedence over attending school. Of all the children, only Max, the second youngest, finished school, graduating from Mount Royal High School.

The premium Ida put on work rather than education pained Lily in particular. She was in her second last grade of high school and wanted very much to return the following year to matriculate. She had two strikes against her. First, the fee was $2.50 a month, more than her mother could afford. Second, Ida needed her to work in the store. The verdict was no. "I cried for a whole day because there was no such thing as my going back," Lily remembered. But the demands of the store quickly put an end to her self-pity. She dried her tears and then came down to answer the phone. Work went on.

Another incident underscores what Ida thought of schooling for her children. One day when Sam was fourteen and a grade-seven student at Mount Royal Public School, he had a row with his teacher. She was writing up a list of figures and planned to ask the class some questions based on it. Sam, quick-minded and terribly impatient, hollered out the answers before she had finished. The teacher did not take kindly to such impertinence and ordered him to bring his mother to school so that she might know of her son's transgressions. Ida dismissed the idea instantly. She certainly wasn't going to close the store to settle a silly dispute with a teacher. As a result Sam was expelled and his formal education ended, a fact that did not distress Ida terribly. On the contrary. She couldn't have been happier. Sam could officially work full-time in her store, and she desperately needed the help. Sam's unceremonious dismissal from school was a propitious event in the history of the company, a turning point of sorts, because it allowed the youngster to unleash his talents on the business without distraction.

For his part, Sam was only too happy to oblige his mother. An aggressive, eager hustler, he relished the responsibility she accorded him, even if he did complain occasionally. (When he once asked her why he had all the responsibility, she told him, "With a good team of horses, the one in front pulls the load.")

To help make it easier to deliver groceries to customers, Sam managed to procure a "Comfort Soap" delivery cart by saving fifty of that company's soap coupons. Later, the family bought a pony named Nellie to make deliveries. Nellie, who was slightly swaybacked, was a prized possession, treated with kid gloves. The gentle handling she received often defeated her very purpose, such as the time Sam felt she couldn't manage to drag a load of produce from Bonsecours Market, from the bottom of a steep hill near the river back up to the store. So he left her at the top of the hill, hustled his little frame down the hill and lugged the heavy sacks up himself.

It was not long before Sam began to make his own business decisions. The first was to expand the shop. In 1919 the city was in the process of lifting up the cobblestones from the streets and had blocked off part of The Main to do the repair work. There was a small shoe store next to Ida's shop, and it was doing virtually no business. An agent for the store's owner called Sam and asked him to put up a "For Rent" sign in the window. Sam asked what the rent was: $60 a month. "Don't bother trying to rent it," Sam told him. "I'll take it."

He tore down the wall between the two stores and expanded both the selling space and the family's cramped living quarters simultaneously. Sam was only fourteen years old when he undertook Steinberg's first expansion.

Something seemed to click for him after that. When he learned that a store was for sale on Bernard Avenue in nearby Outremont, he quickly went over to inspect it. He surveyed the store, and with his characteristic ability to size up a situation in a flash he calculated that the store and its contents were worth at least the $1,000 asking price. He bought that store as well and dubbed it Store Number One, as if to hint that this was the beginning of something much bigger.

Seizing that Bernard Avenue store demonstrated young Sam's ability to respond quickly to changes. At that time clients were moving away from The Main toward the more fashionable sector of Outremont. Opening a store there reduced the chance of losing those crucial customers. At the same time, by putting his younger brother Nathan in as manager, a family member was looked after. That pleased Ida greatly, for she had repeatedly emphasized that the family's welfare had to be their top priority. In fact, it was Ida who gave Sam $2,000 to open that Outremont store, telling him, "Sam, you must look after the boys."

Through the 1920s Sam continued his mother's tradition of putting the best possible products in the store, most notably top quality eggs for his customers. He persuaded farmers to guarantee him fresh eggs daily by paying them a premium and agreeing to give them a special feed for their hens as well. The practice of designating the best eggs Grade A1 is a result of Sam's initiative. Of course, this cost money, but the customer loyalty the effort generated was worth it. Sam was beginning to mark himself as a pioneer in the grocery business.

By the late 1920s Sam's family included a wife, Helen Roth, who also happened to be his first cousin, the daughter of Ida's brother Lewis. Helen had come over from the Hungarian village of Tallay in 1923 at age fifteen with her brother Sam Roth. She came into one of the stores one day, and Sam Steinberg thought she was so breathtakingly beautiful that he didn't want to leave at the end of the day. He couldn't bear to let this plump young woman with the lovely flush to her cheeks out of his sight. It is said that Sam had a girlfriend at the time but dumped her forthwith to be with Helen.

Sam courted her for three years. Of course going out with the lad meant being drawn inextricably into the business. During their courtship Helen often accompanied him on his delivery rounds, first with Nellie and later in a Model T delivery truck.

The two were married in January 1928. He was twenty-two at the time; she was nineteen. Their wedding portrait shows her in a delicate white veil gathered at her ears with flowers and Sam sporting a natty bow tie and a sprig of baby's breath in his lapel. Both of them, with a hint of a smile on their serene smooth-skinned faces, look like two cherubic children, worlds away from any grownup responsibilities.

The image is deceptive. Although not long out of his teens, Sam's life at that point was full of adult concerns. His honeymoon lasted only a weekend, for by Monday he had to be back tending to the business. And his marriage to Helen brought him more family obligations than ever since her people, the Roths, now had to be accommodated. Once again, family needs were propelling further expansion. Sam formed a partnership with Helen's father, Lewis, who ran a fruit store, on Bernard Avenue in Outremont. Sam and

Lewis each got eleven shares. The Roth store, called Roth's Outremont Fruit Store, was changed to Steinberg's and became Store Number Two.

In 1929, a year after Sam and Helen married, the first of the couple's four daughters was born, Mildred, or Mitzi, as she was known. Helen became not only a devoted mother but also a source of unerring support over the years. Her role in the company would never be high profile or flashy; she was more of a "silent partner" who heard all Sam's business ideas, plans, and strategies.

Sam's family responsibilities were increasing and he responded accordingly, opening up two more stores by 1930. "I was just meeting the needs," he told an interviewer years later. His brother Nathan was in Store Number One; his father-in-law in Store Number Two. "But that's too much of a [family] load for these stores to support. So I looked for another store."

At that point Sam didn't have much capital with which to expand. The technique he employed is known today as leverage — using other people's money to pay for new stores. His trick was to obtain a thirty-day credit from his suppliers so that he could sell his goods long before he had to pay for them.

In 1930, following the death of Helen's father Lewis Roth, the shares were redistributed and the company was incorporated under Quebec law under the name "Steinberg's Service Stores Ltd.", known to most people as "Steinberg's Triple S". Sam and Helen kept control of the company, with the rest of the shares divided among other family members.

The Depression years had moved in upon the world like a heavy cloud, bringing bread lines, soup kitchens, and, for countless unfortunates, the dole. Paradoxically, in the early part of this period the Steinberg business grew. In 1931 the company opened three new Steinberg's Triple S stores. By contrast, the competing chains that had emerged by that time were feeling the pinch of falling volumes. In those days the competition included Dominion Stores, well established in the 1930s; the American chain A & P, with a few stores in Montreal but with a well-known presence in border towns like Plattsburgh; and Spots Fruit Stores, with numerous stores in Montreal. The Depression forced some firms to close unprofitable stores. Steinberg, the smallest of the major players in both sales volume and number of stores, moved in to pick up the slack the chains left. The reputation Steinberg had carved out for itself with its continued emphasis on quality products and top customer service was paying off.

The Depression era marked a significant shift in Steinberg's strategy: the conversion of the stores from their original format, from the telephone order and delivery service to customer self-service that allowed them to select groceries themselves. Sam had heard about Loblaws' move to self-service in Ontario, doing away with telephone orders and home delivery and lowering prices accordingly. So one weekend in 1933 he travelled to Ottawa with a coterie of advisers to investigate how Loblaws was doing with this new way of selling groceries. He liked what he saw and decided to try it himself, although his entry into the self-service domain was less than auspicious.

A catalyst of sorts in putting the changes into place was Michael Aronovitch, then a young medical student who worked summers and weekends at Steinberg to help put himself through university. That year Aronovitch convinced Sam to open a self-serve store on Ste. Catherine Street near the Montreal Forum, home of the Montreal Canadiens. Aronovitch reasoned that a store there would capture business from the nearby community of Verdun to the south. Sam agreed with his young employee's strategy, so he found a store, rented it, and installed Aronovitch as its manager. The shelves were open to the customers, who could select their own groceries.

The venture was a huge mistake. Aronovitch hadn't correctly gauged the competition from the Thrift store next door. Nor had he realized that the dimensions of the store were all wrong for the self-service idea. "There was only one aisle and it was just too narrow to be a self-service store," lamented Aronovitch years later, the memory still embarrassing. "That store just flopped." The company lost $35,000, the first red ink in its history, and took several years to recover.

Sam and Aronovitch discussed the problem. "We opened in the wrong place," said the young student. "To get the Verdun customers we have to be *in* Verdun." So the next year, 1934, he decided to open a store on 5107 Verdun Avenue. It was an instant hit and soon it began ringing up sales of $4,000 to $5,000 on Saturdays — figures that were unheard of in those days. But it was a pressure-cooker of an environment. The store would fill up with so many people that the front door had to be temporarily closed until the first customers admitted had left. Then a fresh batch would be permitted to enter. Inside, clerks would throw produce to each other over the heads of customers — the throngs were so thick that it was futile to try to walk through them.

Now Sam was convinced the idea *would* work. He gutted several of his stores, ripping off the Steinberg sign and in its place putting up one that bore the name "Wholesale Groceteria". He didn't want clients to confuse the self-serve stores with the full-service Steinberg stores. He eliminated shopping on credit, telephone orders, and free delivery. The new modus operandi was "cash and carry". Doing away with these services reduced his overhead, allowing him to introduce the most important feature of the new format, heavy discounting. He slashed prices by 15 to 20 percent. A box of cornflakes that sold for 8 or 12 cents in the full-service stores went for 6 cents a box in the self-service ones. In the Depression years price cuts were welcomed by consumers who flocked to Wholesale Groceteria in crowds, often waiting in long lineups to enter. But the bigger the crowds, the higher the sales.

There was a catch to all this success, though. Some customers who still shopped at the regular Steinberg stores were disgruntled that they had to pay higher prices for what they argued were the same products. Other customers, in contrast, resented having the self-service format taken away from them. One angry customer once grabbed Max, who was managing Store Number Eight, by the lapels and shook him in protest over the change.

Nevertheless, Sam's entrepreneurial instincts told him he was onto a good thing. By 1935 he had opened ten stores and all were converted to Wholesale Groceterias. Something significant was happening: for the first time Sam wasn't expanding the business in response to family demands. He was responding to a market opening with a strategy, a vision of what the business had the potential to become: something big, lucrative, and enormously successful.

In 1931 Sam closed his mother's original little shop on The Main. It wasn't because business was slowing down; in fact the reverse was true. But his mother, who suffered from angina, was working too hard and the business was outgrowing her ability to cope. Sam moved her to a store on Monkland Avenue in the western part of

Montreal, which she co-managed with her daughter Lily. The two shared an apartment above the store. Although the move was intended to give Ida a rest, she continued to work to excess, despite her family's pleas that she retire. She always vowed to retire when Lily got married. True to her word, several years later when Lily married a Montreal businessman, Hyman Rafman, Ida gave up the grocery business for good. (Lily herself bowed out after her first child was born.)

But retirement was terribly hard on her. She made needlepoint chairs to keep herself busy, but deep down she felt her life had lost its sense of purpose. She longed for the earlier days when she had something to live for: the busy little store bearing the logo, "Mrs. I. Steinberg, Grocer".

As his mother faded from the picture, Sam moved more sharply into focus, always grasping opportunities to change and improve his stores. He was forever busy painting the interior of a store, perhaps adding another counter, converting some fixture. If an employee asked why he felt it necessary to change things all the time, he would reply, "Anybody who stands still is going backwards."

One thing that helped Sam go forward was his open-minded attitude. He made frequent trips throughout North America in search of the latest industry developments and brought them home to Montreal. When he saw shopping carts in an eastern U.S. store he thought they would be useful in his stores. Another time he saw some American stores whose interiors were painted not white but in pastel colours — another good idea too, he mused. Sam usually traveled with one of his brothers or managers; he seemed to need a sounding board for all the ideas that tumbled out of his head.

Each improvement the company introduced cemented Steinberg's reputation as a retailer who built upon the latest trends in the North American grocery business. In 1936 and 1937 the company boosted sales of vegetables and dried fruit by wrapping them in cellophane, the clear moisture-proof plastic wrap that Canadian Industries Limited (CIL) had just introduced. In that period the company also introduced its first selection of private label products. Then in 1937 Steinberg christened two supermarkets, becoming the first grocer in Canada with separate coolers for meat, dairy products, and produce. The meat department had been one of the last places in stores where a customer was served by a butcher behind the counter, but then in 1943 self-service meat departments were introduced, with the cuts of course wrapped in the famous CIL film that had since been upgraded for meat to prevent it from darkening.

During the early 1940s the company began another practice that would prove lucrative in future years: it started banking land sites for possible future store sites. Sam was to demonstrate an uncanny, intuitive knack for choosing locations, although he never bought them for speculation. His intent was always to develop stores. He was so convinced of the value and power of land that once he had settled on the idea, he got all his friends to help him buy, simply to prevent the competition from getting at prime locations.

By the end of the 1930s, Ida's little fruit-and-vegetable store had evolved into an early version of the modern supermarket chain. In 1939 there were more than fifteen outlets. The stores were getting larger and larger. The company was becoming so successful that there were rumors it was backed by money from the wealthy Montreal liquor merchant, Sam Bronfman. Sam Steinberg dismissed that notion in a hurry. Not a penny of non-family money was invested in the company at that point. He would make that same boast until the early 1950s when the pace of expansion forced him to seek outside financing.

The Second World War followed, plunging Canada into a time of despondency. Whereas the Depression was a period of innovation and expansion for Steinberg, this was one of hardship and stagnation. "It stopped us when we were going full speed," Sam once told an interviewer. By that time Sam and Helen had four young daughters — Mitzi; Rita, born in 1932; Marilyn, born in 1933; and the last, Evelyn, born in 1938 — so his family felt the slowdown in business acutely.

The war meant a terrific scarcity of labor, building supplies, and food. Rationing began, and as a consequence profiteering and black markets flourished. During the war a box of Jell-O powder or a can of salmon rarely appeared on the shelves of a chain store. Such products were mysteriously diverted and later resold at vastly inflated prices. It was an era for the more unscrupulous merchants to squeeze millions of dollars out of consumers.

Sam Steinberg firmly resisted such practices. His ethical standards were high, and true to the spirit of his mother Sam still considered the customer supreme. His view was that times were tough enough for consumers as it was; he wasn't going to exploit the situation and make things worse for them. One sunny June day in 1943, he gathered family members and store managers together on the lawn at his Overdale warehouse to spell out the company's wartime policy in no uncertain terms. The government had imposed price freezes and Sam was determined to adhere to them. In Steinberg stores salmon was 19 cents a can, Jell-O was 6 cents, and butter was 29 cents a pound, just as the government had decreed. The competition could charge whatever it liked. Sam also imposed a system of double rationing, providing little rationing books, so that the same customer would not be able to purchase a scarce product like coffee twice within the same week.

"I'm not going to make money on the backs of the people," Sam vowed to them. "If any of you want black-market money, go ahead — but you'll have to quit and go work for other people. You won't get a cent out of me." Some employees did leave, thinking they could make easy money elsewhere. However, most stayed.

And so did the customers. Sam's determination to resist wartime price corruption was not just a display of integrity. It was a shrewd business tactic and it gave the company a big break during this difficult period. While his competitors jacked up their prices, Sam quietly undercut them. Customers quickly learned that while plums may have sold elsewhere for 19 cents a tin, at Steinberg's they sold for 10 cents. His stores were jammed. Sales in one store in the western part of Montreal jumped from $6,000 to $21,000 within three months.

Word about the dynamic, ethical grocery chain reached a small town hundreds of miles northeast of Montreal called Arvida, in the heart of Quebec's blueberry region, Saguenay-Lac St-Jean. There the Aluminum Company of Canada (Alcan) was turning out aluminum for the war effort in great quantities for use in munitions and airplanes. While Sam was giving his customers a break, the local grocery merchants, realizing they had a captive market, were doing just the opposite, charging sky-high prices for substandard food. The wives of company executives were frustrated every time they did their shopping and they appealed to their husbands to do something. So in 1940 the company's president, R. E. Powell decided a solution to the problem would be to build a Steinberg store there, a haven where customers could buy quality products without fear of being exploited. He made his pitch to Sam, believing in the idea so much that he even offered to foot the costs of constructing the store. Sam agreed, but he wanted a few conditions attached to the deal, including a three-year guarantee that he would turn the same profits he'd normally make in one of his Montreal stores.

The Arvida store signaled a new opportunity that was anything but easy for a Montreal-based Jewish anglophone company transplanting itself into the heart of francophone Quebec. There were boycotts, pickets outside. Loyalties in the region rested with the francophone chains and anti-Jewish sentiment was high. Steinberg was viewed as "the big Jewish Montreal firm coming to take our money," recalled Jack Levine, for decades one of Sam's principal lieutenants. Nonetheless, devotion to customer service paid off and the company continued to go forward.

One day in April 1942, during Passover, Ida Steinberg suddenly fell ill with pneumonia. Several days later the woman who had founded the Steinberg empire with her single store on The Main was dead.

The boys' father, William, was still subsisting in the downtown Montreal rooming house. The boys had been providing him with a modest stipend throughout all those years, with virtually no contact with him. He was all but incommunicado. At company and family picnics that were held through the years legions of Steinbergs would turn out — except William.

After Ida's death the relationship between William and his children finally began to thaw. William now came around to the homes of his children, who by that time had their own families, sometimes with little gifts — a bottle of homemade wine to his son Jack's family; for Jack's daughter Marsha, a little table and chairs. The boys had never felt any acrimony toward their father; he was simply out of the picture, an eccentric, lonely man.

William had wanted to teach Hebrew to his grandchildren, but he never got around to it. In William's last years, Mitzi sometimes visited him at his rooming house with her father, and the conditions she found there appalled her. The sheeting was filthy and the whole place was disgusting. She couldn't understand how her father and uncles could have allowed him to live in such conditions.

Five years after Ida's death, William died. Now that the first generation of Steinbergs had gone, the first chapter had ended. But Ida's legacy would live long into the future. As the 1950s were to show, Sam was determined to make the most of the business his mother had built, to turn her legacy into an unrivaled Quebec corporate success story.

# 4

# *Growing Pains*

B y 1950 Canada was full of prosperity and promise. The war was over, the hardships had ended, and Steinberg was poised to enter its greatest years.

The exuberance was palpable at the company's head office on Hochelaga Street, a former aircraft propeller factory in Montreal's east end. The atmosphere of vibrant optimism was a 180-degree shift away from the wartime mood, when the company's growth had been stifled by rationing, shortages, and regulations. The only thing Steinberg had been able to do during the war was bank land sites at rock-bottom prices. Now it was ready with ambitious plans to develop that land and build new stores at an unprecedented rate. The customers were certainly there: the company's refusal to gouge them during the war, as costly a decision as it had been, had built up a great public goodwill, which was ready to be tapped.

Sam Steinberg had the Montreal market virtually sown up. His competitors, Dominion and A & P, were concentrating on Ontario, and Steinberg soon became the premier grocery chain for anglophone and francophone consumers alike. Its very name had crept into common parlance, like Band-Aid or Jell-O. You didn't go grocery shopping; you went to "do your Steinberg", even if it was at some store other than Steinberg.

If the 1950s were the company's golden years, Steinberg was hardly a typical modern corporation. It was more an organized free-for-all. Sam managed the business by the seat of his pants, and it showed. Business records and minutes of company meetings were in a terrible state, the office equipment was out of date, the

Hochelaga Street headquarters were hectic and noisy. On the second floor, employees worked cheek by jowl, their desks crammed together so tightly that there was barely enough space to pass between them.

Sam didn't care how his executives operated, as long as they got results. His unorthodox management style would have made a Harvard Business School professor eat his lecture notes in frustration. Executives who came to Steinberg during the 1950s found the place so chaotic, it was almost primitive.

James Doyle, who joined Steinberg as vice-president and general counsel after a stint with Ford Motor Company of Canada, was particularly baffled by the communications style at Steinberg. "One person would say, 'What should we do with the whatchamacallit?' And Sam would say, 'I think we ought to sell it at 69 cents.' I wouldn't have the faintest idea what they were talking about." To make matters more confusing, Sam and his brothers would sometimes converse in Hungarian at meetings, leaving those executives who didn't understand the language scratching their heads.

Sam personified the electric, ambitious pace of the company. He was a whirling dervish, darting about from store to store or popping in unannounced on meetings at Hochelaga. He loved meetings, even marathon ones that lasted six or eight hours. They were colorful sessions during which Sam's top people, mainly the uneducated, self-made guys he'd taken on during the Depression, would shout each other down, their words peppered with curses.

The lack of formality worked in Steinberg's favor. It was still a private, family-controlled company, and with Sam's entrepreneurial instincts driving it like a turbine the company could turn on a dime. If it wanted to change a price, introduce a product, put a different color scheme in the stores, it had the flexibility to act quickly. And in the Quebec grocery business no one ran faster than Steinberg. There was no question that its hustle was paying off: the stores were money-makers. By 1952 Steinberg was selling $70-million worth of groceries a year and annual profits passed the million-dollar mark for the first time. Sales were so high that at the end of each day, more than a dozen clerks at the main branch of the Royal Bank of Canada on St. James Street were recruited to count Steinberg's cash deposits.

Nathan Steinberg's desk drawer was a testament to the dizzying popularity of Steinberg stores. It was jammed with requests for new stores, including one in the form of a petition signed by the mayor and every citizen of a small Quebec community. As one executive recalled, "We could put up a store in a cow pasture and it would do well." Several times the company did just that.

By 1952 Sam and Helen and their four teenage daughters lived comfortably but modestly in an upper duplex in the Montreal suburb of Outremont. Although Steinberg had become a phenomenal success and the dividends rolled in, Sam reinvested them into the business instead of channeling them into an extravagant lifestyle. At the same time he also began to consider how best to secure a future for his family.

During the war he had purchased a building lot in the wealthy Anglo-Saxon suburb of Westmount overlooking the downtown area and the St. Lawrence River. He decided it was now time to move the family from Outremont and he ordered the construction of a home on the Aberdeen Avenue site. When it was completed, the large, gray stone house was spacious and comfortable with a simple, square look that contrasted with many of the more ostentatious homes in Westmount. Like Sam himself, the architecture was unaffected. The house was spacious and comfortable, with a pleasant hillside garden for Sam and Helen to putter around in.

It was also time to plan for the girls' financial future, and Sam consulted his lawyer, the late Lazarus Phillips. A Steinberg director for many years, Phillips was a brilliant tax lawyer whose legal victories were the stuff of legend. Trained as a rabbi in his youth, he could converse with equal ease on Roman Catholicism.

Phillips enjoyed considerable political and corporate power as a director of the Royal Bank of Canada, Trizec Corp., and a number of other companies. Although he failed in a one-time run for elected office (he was defeated in a 1943 Quebec by-election by the Communist candidate), he was appointed to the Senate in 1968 by Prime Minister Lester Pearson.

Phillips and Sam made an odd couple: one was a learned man, schooled in religion and law; the other was a grade-school dropout who lived by his wits and hustle. Yet the respect and affection

between them was obvious. The Steinberg family became the beneficiaries of Phillips's financial genius. "At least half of all the money
the Steinbergs ever made was due to the way Laz Phillips set things
up for them," Doyle said.

When he was asked to arrange Sam's daughters and grandchildren's financial affairs, Lazarus Phillips decided on four trusts,
one in the name of each of Sam's children, just as he had done for
another wealthy Montreal family, the Bronfmans. The trusts
would save Sam a great deal of tax money. Yet this was the first of
many unfortunate decisions that would later haunt the Steinberg
family.

Into the trusts went the voting shares owned by the family —
shares that were never to be publicly traded on a stock exchange.
The family members signed a voting-trust agreement giving Sam
the right to vote their shares until he should die or voluntarily forgo
that right. He exercised sole voting power until the day he died. The
arrangement reflected how much faith the family had in him; it also
showed his influence over the other brothers. They had no ground
from which to challenge his power. The unspoken truth was that
despite the input by brothers and cousins, the success of the company — not to mention their own personal wealth — was owing to
Sam Steinberg alone.

In addition to devising the trusts Phillips developed several other
financial ventures, among them what developed into the most
lucrative part of the Steinberg empire: Ivanhoe Inc. The real estate
company became the principal vehicle for financing Steinberg's
rapid expansion in the 1950s, raising money by issuing mortgage
bonds that were secured by Steinberg stores.

Like many immigrants who arrived penniless in North America,
Sam considered real estate tremendously important. To him, a
piece of land was a measure of long-term security. "All Jewish
immigrants' first few dollars went into real estate," explained Martin Kaufman, a Montreal financial analyst who has tracked Steinberg for years and who himself was born of East European parents.

In the beginning Sam's land scouting methods were casual and
highly unscientific, "instinctive", he said. He used to do what he
called "Sunday morning market research". He'd get into the car
with Nathan, drive around the city and say, "This site looks good."
When asked by company lawyer John Ciaccia how he knew a piece

of land in New Brunswick would be a good site without having researched it first, Mr. Sam replied, "Johnny, I smell it." One of Sam's sons-in-law at the time, Leo Goldfarb, who played a key role in developing the real estate division, recalled that Sam picked land that looked highly unlikely — "It was in the boondocks. But it became central years later."

With time, Sam had become a bit more orthodox in his site selection. He established a market research department that not only examined consumer trends but also identified potential locations for new stores, based on new highways and subdivisions. The idea was inspired by the Boston-based Stop and Shop supermarket chain, which had introduced the first grocery-chain market research department in the United States. The plan was to have a stock of land ready for Steinberg stores as soon as new housing developments were completed.

Even though the research department introduced more formal procedures into the company, Sam's gut instincts would often prevail. He and his research director, Harry Suffrin, once had a blistering argument over a piece of land in Montreal's east end. Sam wanted to buy it but Suffrin argued that the population projections for the area wouldn't support a store. Sam bought it anyway. True to his predictions, the population of east-end Montreal mushroomed, and the store prospered.

During the late 1940s and early 1950s the company had expanded at a steady, albeit unspectacular, pace. But in 1952, with a supply of land under his belt, Sam made an unprecedented announcement: a $15-million, five-year expansion program — a new store every sixty days, for a total of thirty stores. The new stores would be vast, 40,000-square-foot outlets, over twice the size of the existing ones. The social and economic conditions were ripe for expansion. Inflation was down and the baby boom was in full swing. From 1951 to 1961 the Canadian population increased by 26 percent. Houses for those expanding families were being built in record numbers. And to Steinberg's great delight, food sales rose by a whopping 78 percent during those years.

A massive population shift to the suburbs was also in progress. It was the perfect time for a new merchandising format, the shopping center, with the supermarket as its focal point. In Sam's grand vision, the stores in a shopping center would attract even more customers to a Steinberg outlet than if it stood alone. Suburban Dorval, on Montreal's West Island, was identified as the testing ground for the first shopping center.

But getting the Dorval project off the ground wouldn't be easy. Mortgage lenders had no experience in shopping-center projects and showed little confidence in them. They certainly had no faith in the Dorval idea. To them, the site was nothing but a cow pasture out by the airport and they wouldn't finance it.

Determined to make the project fly, Sam approached virtually every brokerage house in Montreal, but he was told the same thing: a debt issue — that is, a sort of IOU from a financial institution — would be impossible if it was based on a single project. Securities firms were simply too reluctant to back a project as untried as a shopping center. They told him that he would have to raise the money by issuing stock in the company, which would eliminate his control. The very thought was repugnant to Sam. His control over Steinberg was sacrosanct and he would never relinquish it.

In December 1952, he tried another avenue instead. Steinberg went into the public money market and sold $5-million of debentures "for general purposes". This was a turning point in the company's history, because it made Steinberg "public", although it left controlling power in his hands. From then on, if Steinberg wanted financing, it had to provide business plans, sales, and earnings forecasts and budgets to the investment community. It had to put on paper where it was headed. For an entrepreneurial firm whose strategies were determined by the owner's gut instinct, this took some getting used to.

The debenture issue provided Sam with the money he needed to build the Dorval Shopping Centre and construction was completed in 1954. The project was an unqualified success, the skeptics were silenced, and Sam was vindicated. There was no turning back. Steinberg was in the shopping-center development business, and as more of the food stores were located in shopping centers, the company came to depend on public financing for its rapid expansion.

The growth would be spectacular, not only in Montreal but throughout the province. At the end of 1953, nearly all of Steinberg's 38 stores were in the Montreal area; seven years later, there were 60 stores in Montreal and 32 in far-flung places such as Cap-de-la-Madeleine and Baie-Comeau.

By 1955 Steinberg's thirst for financing was so great that it sold stock to the public for the first time, in the form of a $5-million issue of preferred shares. Then in 1958, 500,000 shares of non-voting stock was issued to the public at $17 a share. The new shares were phenomenally popular. "Customers, employees, and other investors snapped [them] up as if they were weekend specials in one of the company's Montreal supermarkets," wrote *Business Week* magazine in a 1959 cover story on the company. The stock soon jumped $5 higher than its issue price and became the darling of the Montreal Stock Exchange.

It was an especially exhilarating time if your last name was Steinberg. Sharon Steinberg, daughter of Sam's oldest brother Jack, remembered being a student at the Wharton Business School in Pennsylvania when *Business Week* came out with its feature story on the Steinberg brothers. There was a picture of her father with Sam and the other brothers on the front cover. Here was her father — the man who had grown up in an unheated flat and had raised his own family in modest conditions — gracing the pages of the most important business magazine in the United States. "That was glory," she remembered proudly.

The stock issue was "to give our customers and employees a chance to share in our success," Nathan told *Business Week*. But, as the magazine noted, less altruistic motivations were also at work. The stock sale established a market value for the shares of the family members. This was a time when some of them wanted to buy homes, which they were able to do by selling part of their holdings.

Amid the euphoria of Steinberg's rising stock price, Sam hadn't recognized the dangers of issuing non-voting stock to the public. Some of his advisers, including Morgan McCammon, then Steinberg's top lawyer, were dead set against the idea. With non-voting stock, "you had people risking their money by putting it into the business, and they had no say in how the business was conducted," McCammon said; they were at the mercy of the family when it came to decision-making. And if there were ever a takeover bid for the company, there would be no protection for non-voting shareholders that would guarantee them a price for their shares. Sam was advised to issue voting stock instead, so that all shareholders would be treated equally. But Sam had always wanted to keep voting control in the family's hands. Years later, when the family's interests clashed with those of the investing public, the existence of two share classes proved to be a fatal error.

Such quibbles hardly concerned Sam as he continued his push to make Steinberg the biggest and the best. Expansion plans continued at an even more ambitious pace and in 1959 the company announced it would build 60 new stores in 36 months.

The frantic pace put enormous strains on the company. Sam was so completely caught up in his goal to expand the business that he failed to consider the impact the program would have on his already harried staff. In his haste to build new stores, Sam often totally disregarded the decision-making hierarchy within the company, not to mention the feelings of his employees. He ran roughshod over many of them. Employees responded by leaving. Yet Sam seemed totally insensitive to the effect of his power.

In the 1950s the Steinberg team resembled a future *Who's Who in Quebec*. It was a training ground for so many executives who moved on to better things that it became known as the University of Steinberg. Sam wasn't able to keep his most talented executives. Many of them were gone by the end of the decade. A young lawyer named John Ciaccia later became a highly regarded Quebec cabinet minister. And lawyer, Morgan McCammon, went on to become chairman of the brewing giant, Molson. A bright economist named Maurice Segall, who worked as Sam's executive assistant, later became chairman of Zayre Corp., one of the largest retailers in the United States.

The defections and departures weren't the only problems Sam had to face. Rival chains such as Dominion Stores were starting to turn up the competitive pressure in Quebec. They hadn't been sitting idly by while Steinberg grew, but had been expanding too. Steinberg no longer had a monopoly in the marketplace.

To keep the cash registers ringing, promotional schemes became all-important. The company started a morning radio program called the Steinberg Good Neighbour Club. It set up cooking schools conducted by people like the well-known Québécois cook, Jehane Benoit. It gave prizes to brides and New Year's babies. One of the most popular schemes the company ever devised was the Pinky Stamp program. In 1957 Steinberg began to give customers gifts in return for every $40 worth of pink cash-register tapes they brought in. Two years later these became Pinky Stamps, similar to S and H Green Stamps in the United States. Sam's youngest brother Morris was put in charge of the project, earning him the nickname of Pinky Steinberg. It was the Pinky stamp that was immortalized in Michel Tremblay's play *Les Belles Soeurs*, in which a group of Québécois housewives sit around the table discussing their personal problems as they busily paste the stamps into their little books.

Steinberg was compelled to look for ways to beat the competition. One way, of course, was to move into other markets, such as Ontario. This wasn't a new idea. Sam had once tried to buy out his archrival, Dominion Stores, sending Leo Goldfarb to meet with the president of Dominion, Thomas McCormack. But Dominion's controlling shareholder, the late industrialist E. P. Taylor, wasn't interested. Steinberg had, though, bought several locations in the Toronto area and it had leased space in the northeast end of the city in a new shopping center called Thorncliffe Park.

Up to this point there had always been an unspoken understanding between Steinberg and the dominant chain in Ontario, Loblaws: each company's territory was off-limits to the other. In other words, as a family member once said, the day Loblaws moves into Quebec, "that's the day we'll be in Ontario."

That day came. In 1959 Loblaws bought a Quebec chain called Dionne Ltd. Sam reacted immediately. "If they're coming to Quebec, we're going to Ontario." He had already heard that The Grand Union Co., a U.S.-owned chain, had put its 38 Ontario stores up for sale. This was a perfect chance to grab a big piece of the Ontario market in one fell swoop. Steinberg made a bid, and in June it bought the stores for $10-million. Sam quickly put the Steinberg name on them, making 1959 "the most progressive year in the company's history", according to that year's annual report. In truth, the move turned out to be the first in a series of strategic blunders by Sam Steinberg.

A large part of the problem was Grand Union's chairman, Lansing Shield, a powerful, abrasive American industrialist. James Doyle, who participated in the negotiations, viewed Shield as an uncouth character who "treated Sam like dirt" in the dealmaking. What worsened matters was Sam's tendency to put "big men" like Lansing Shield on a pedestal. And in Sam's view, Shield was a giant, a leading business figure who moved in circles that included then-U.S. vice-president Richard Nixon. Shield had once accompanied Nixon to the Soviet Union to meet Nikita Khrushchev. His photograph later appeared on the cover of *Time* magazine with both men.

Doyle thought Steinberg was being overcharged and wanted to renegotiate. At that stage Shield's treatment of Sam bordered on contempt. When Sam and Doyle turned up for a meeting to discuss the problem, Shield kept them waiting in his office for several hours. Doyle fumed, but Sam quietly took it in stride. When the meeting began, Doyle, who had been in the hospital during the negotiations with Sam and Shield, began to point out the problems in the deal. Shield turned to him with a snarl and snapped, "You shut up. You weren't there."

Doyle wouldn't give up. He felt Grand Union was cheating Steinberg, and with the help of Lazarus Phillips he managed to shave $200,000 of incorrectly charged assets off the bill. Yet Steinberg's whole approach to the Grand Union deal ran contrary to his business style in Quebec. At home Sam knew sites like his own backyard. In Ontario he was in the dark. What he had bought was a chain of pathetic little stores in "a lot of crummy locations", according to one executive.

While Steinberg had developed a system of land banking in Montreal, it had never done so in Ontario. As a result the choice sites went to the competition, and by the time the company realized it should buy land there, real estate was prohibitively expensive. Nor did the Ontario supermarket chains make life easier for Steinberg. Loblaws and Dominion were not pleased about Steinberg's foray into their territory so they counterattacked by redeeming Steinberg promotional coupons at equal or even twice their value in their own stores.

For a decade the Ontario stores hung like an albatross around Steinberg's neck, losing several million dollars a year. Some Steinberg executives felt that anti-Semitism was a problem in Ontario. They wondered if customers would ever take to a store with a Jewish name. Yet Sam continued to throw pots of money into Ontario and paid a heavy price for it. In 1960 overall profits dropped for the first time in sixteen years. Over time 34 of the 38 Grand Union stores were closed down and new stores were opened in better locations, with the name eventually changed to Miracle Food Mart.

The Ontario chain became a revolving door for one manager after another who went in to salvage it. They quickly burned out. The tension of being away from the Quebec market that they knew best, and away from the support of the company, was often overwhelming. Grand Union took a terrific toll on Sam as well. He became irascible and terribly hard on his staff, forcing more senior executives to leave.

Part of the problem was that the managers sent to Ontario brought Quebec-style merchandising with them. In the grocery business, the smallest details were important. For instance, in Quebec, apples were sold by the bag, rarely in baskets. But in Ontario, basket apples were big sellers. In Steinberg's first year in Ontario, when customers could only buy bagged apples, many apple sales were lost.

Steinberg faced other troubles in the late 1960s. Although the company embraced growth as its god, consumers didn't share the view that big meant better. In 1966 they organized to protest high food prices at the major supermarket chains. A year later a Senate report criticized the big chains for making excess profits. The consumer boycott failed to put much of a dent in Steinberg's business; sales continued to grow by close to ten percent a year. But the bad publicity left Sam hurt and bewildered. His customers had never treated him like this before. They had always been loyal and he couldn't understand why they were turning on him now. The pressure and criticism worsened, as consumers began to complain about non-union grapes from California, cyclamates in food, phosphates in detergent. The grocery business had become much more complex than when Sam was a young man.

As two McGill University professors, Henry Mintzberg and the late James Waters, explained in an extensive study on Steinberg, the militancy of consumers was rooted in the fact that companies like Steinberg, which once prided themselves on personalized service, had become too big and anonymous.

Steinberg realized it could not grow simply by opening a new store here and there. It had to outsmart the competition. It needed something dramatic to recapture the momentum. In 1969 it did so in a way the competition would never forget.

What did the trick was a strategy called Miracle Pricing, brought to the troubled Ontario stores by Steinberg vice-president Jack Levine, who became president of the division after Sam's death. The idea was to slash prices by between 5 and 15 percent off some 7,000 categories of goods. To accommodate those cuts, customer service would be reduced and the advertising and promotions budget drastically pared. Levine patterned Miracle Pricing after something he'd seen in a Los Angeles-based grocery chain called Lucky Stores.

The program was first put into place at Steinberg's Ottawa store, then launched in the rest of Ontario in January 1969. Down came the Steinberg logos; up went the Miracle Food Mart banners. A few interior changes were made, usually taking just several days.

The reincarnated stores brought in results that were nothing short of miraculous. At the Ottawa outlet sales increased by 80 percent within a year. A month later Miracle Pricing was introduced in Quebec. After ten years, the Ontario stores had finally turned around.

Sam Steinberg had shown an unerring genius for three decades, but in the 1960s he began to make more costly mistakes like the Grand Union fiasco. While the Ontario stores were still sapping the company of money, manpower, and morale, Steinberg decided to launch yet another ill-fated merchandising scheme: a discount department store chain. It would eventually be called Miracle Mart (as distinct from Miracle Food Mart in Ontario).

Moving into department stores was a radical departure for Mr. Sam. He could sell lettuce and cucumbers, but what did he know about underwear and blue jeans? It wasn't a totally new idea. As far back as 1946 Sam had toyed with opening a discount department store to protect his food business from competition. In the late 1950s several discount "combination" stores had opened in the Montreal area, offering both food and general merchandise. They gave discounts on groceries to attract customers, then made their money on the other goods. Sam, always looking over his shoulder at the competition, thought his whole food business in Montreal was vulnerable and that the thing to do was to open up his own general merchandise operation.

At that time the big Kmart department store chain was making inroads into Canada, buying the best sites. So as a preemptive strike, Sam decided to move quickly — much too quickly, in fact — and leaped into the department-store business with no clear strategy in mind.

Sam realized he couldn't attempt this venture alone, so in 1961 he approached Woodward Stores Ltd., a large Vancouver-based retailer that owned both department stores and supermarkets. Sam figured the marriage would make sense and Woodward's agreed because they were anxious to break into the eastern Canadian market. The partners agreed that Steinberg would build the department stores in a shopping strip that included a Steinberg supermarket, and Woodward's would operate them.

A young accountant named Mel Dobrin was appointed general manager of the new operation. He also happened to be Mitzi's husband. In July 1961, the first Woodward-Steinberg store started up in Pont-Viau, a Montreal suburb — before the two partners had even put their signatures on the final agreement, which would not come easily.

It soon became apparent that this was an ill-suited marriage. While Steinberg wanted to expand aggressively, Woodward's advocated caution. Sam feared that many real estate operators were eager to get into the department-store business and would grab the prime locations if he didn't get there first. The Woodward's people, on the other hand, wanted to see each individual unit prove itself financially viable before they started another.

The two partners managed to start a couple of department stores that were lukewarm successes. In moving east, Woodward's was making the same mistake Steinberg had made when they moved into Ontario: they may have been experts in merchandising on the west coast but they didn't have a clue about French-Canadian tastes. They were selling little dull blue and gray coats for children, for example, not realizing how much Quebecers inclined toward color. What sold in Vancouver and Victoria wouldn't sell in east-end Montreal.

In the end no formal deal was ever signed and the venture collapsed. "Finally it came down to long conversations, mostly on the telephone, as to whether they would buy us out or we would buy them out," Doyle recalled. "And in the end I was on the phone with Sam, scribbling these conversations down as fast as I could. And Sam finally said, 'I'll buy you out,' because the stores were in Quebec. Within a year the Woodward-Steinberg name had come down and a new one went up: Miracle Mart.

Miracle Mart would be reincarnated as a discount department store, attracting enough customers to feed the Steinberg supermarkets next door. During the 1960s and 1970s, Miracle Mart expanded to 34 discount stores in Quebec and Ontario but it lost money almost every year and never gained any significant share of the market. It never seemed to make up its mind whether it wanted to be a discount chain, specializing in low-priced items, or a department store with a full choice of goods.

Part of the problem was that Sam continually staffed the stores with people from the supermarket division, even though there was a world of difference between food retailing and general merchandising. His blind spot for supermarket executives was like his blind spot for the family: they could do no wrong. Sam's son-in-law Leo Goldfarb, then a Steinberg vice-president, urged him repeatedly to get top people from Eaton's or Sears. Without such professionals, Goldfarb argued, Miracle Mart could not compete. But Sam's refusal to recruit outside talent almost ensured failure.

Sam hadn't understood the enormous difference between the two forms of retailing. In the supermarket business, inventory turns over 20 or 30 times a year, but in general merchandising a retailer is lucky if the stock turns over 5 times a year. In the supermarket customers line up at the cash and everything is moving. In the department store the pace is altogether different. Sam took some of his best food-store managers, put them into Miracle Mart, and they couldn't adjust. Several suffered nervous breakdowns.

Part of the problem, too, was that Sam didn't really want the department stores for their own sake, and so he never studied that business closely; their only purpose was to bring customers into his supermarkets. But it made no sense for Sam to invest millions into a department-store chain and then run it as a sideline, without any professional management. After the Woodward's venture failed, Goldfarb tried to convince Sam to lease the stores to Sears and let them run the operation. Sam wouldn't listen and the chain went from bad to worse.

Miracle Mart was just the start of a vast diversification scheme at Steinberg, which distanced the company even further from its basic business of selling groceries. By the late 1960s the company had added a fast-food restaurant chain called PikNik, the Oak Pharmacies drugstore chain, the Cartier sugar refinery, the Phénix flour mill and a bakery. In the next decade Steinberg invested in a catalogue showroom operation called Cardinal Distribution.

Sam, a grocer at heart, felt compelled to enter these new ventures because he believed that diversifying into general merchandising was the best way to protect the family's investment. Some of the schemes, like the sugar refinery and the flour mill, made economic sense because they put products on the company's supermarket shelves at lower cost. But others, like the pharmacies or like an ill-fated chain of Steinberg-owned gas stations launched in 1965, were outright disasters.

In the end Sam paid little or no attention to these side ventures, happy to leave his executives to worry about them. He could hardly remember where the new plants were located. Ask him about his grocery stores, though, and a fountain of detailed knowledge bubbled out.

The new businesses accounted for a small fraction of Steinberg's total sales, yet they required an inordinate amount of time and attention from senior management. Soon his executives were urging Sam to get rid of them. By 1975 the diversification program had been curtailed. The gas bars and pharmacies were sold. The catalogue showroom swirled in red ink before it was sold to Consumers Distributing. The only successful diversification move was the Pik-Nik restaurant chain, which opened outlets at most of the Steinberg-owned shopping centers.

Sam's most exotic business flop was an abortive foray into France, where he opened several supermarkets around Paris in 1966. The stores, called Supermarché Montréal, were the brain-child of his nephew Arnold, who used to vacation in France. Arnold was convinced that France was on the verge of a huge retailing revolution. A faculty member at the Harvard Business

School, where Arnold had obtained his MBA, had introduced him to a French businessman named François Beraud, also a Harvard MBA. Together they decided to launch the new operation amid plenty of hype and fanfare.

However, this partnership between a bunch of street-smart Jewish retailers from Montreal and the cool Cartesians of France was the ultimate culture clash. The two groups were as different as bagels and Brie. They could agree on few details of management policy. The biggest obstacle, in Steinberg's eyes, was that it was limited to owning 49 percent of the company under French law. Arnold Steinberg had wanted a 50/50 arrangement. But Beraud and an associate had 51 percent and they ran the business, although they were not good managers. Again, Steinberg lost money, morale, and staff trying to shore up the failed venture.

The challenge was to get the French, who for centuries had shopped in public markets, to switch to big supermarkets. The store employees needed special training to handle this new merchandising format. It didn't work. Every morning when the supermarkets opened, the displays looked good, but within minutes the stores would be in chaos. "The staff didn't know the art of dealing with people," said Arnold.

The six stores in the Paris area lasted almost eight years before Steinberg pulled out and went home. The debacle cost the company over $2-million and it also cost Arnold his reputation. Because he had had more education than many in the company, Arnold had been put on a bit of a pedestal. After the botched deal, said Stephen Jarislowsky, a Montreal investment fund manager and adviser to the Steinberg family, Arnold became "a bit of a fallen idol".


Despite its stumbling efforts to diversify, Steinberg remained an extremely successful company. By 1965 annual sales had climbed to a staggering $379-million — more than four times what they were in 1954 when the expansion program had begun — and profits had reached $7 million. There was a price to pay for success. The workers who had built Steinberg into Quebec's number one grocery chain wanted to share in the company's good fortune. Labor militancy in Quebec had grown since the death in 1959 of Quebec's anti-union premier, Maurice Duplessis. Suddenly, Sam Steinberg faced a full-blown labor crisis. His failure to deal with labor strife did much to undermine the company in later years.

Until the 1960s the cashiers, meat-cutters, and truck drivers at Steinberg were part of a big, happy family, with Sam Steinberg its self-appointed patriarch. He treated his workers like any decent father would: at times tough and demanding, but always with respect and genuine concern for their welfare.

He knew many of them by their first names. He attended their families' weddings, births, funerals. He bailed them out of personal troubles. He helped them out with mortgages; he paid for expensive operations for their children. Busy as he was, if an employee had a problem, his door was always open. It made sense that Sam should treat them that way: he had originally built the company for his family, and each new employee who came to work for him was an extension of the clan.

His approach to employee relations was paternalistic, a sort of "I know what's best for you" style. Few seemed to object. During the 1930s and 1940s Steinberg did much to foster a family spirit. Every year, on the Sunday before Labour Day, it held a lavish company picnic at a Montreal amusement park, attended by thousands of employees from all over the province. Steinberg's annual dinner dance on the roof of the Mount Royal Hotel was an occasion for hundreds more to kick up their heels. Montreal jazz greats such as Oscar Peterson and Johnny Holmes often played at the party.

During those years of harmony, there seemed to be little need for anything like a union. But in 1945 the company made the token gesture of establishing an "employee protective association". This "house union" may have had some symbolic appeal to workers, since it had no real power to negotiate wage increases. These were set unilaterally by Sam Steinberg. There was no grievance procedure and until 1962 there wasn't even a written collective agreement. Steinberg did offer its employees a medical plan, company-subsidized insurance benefits, a retirement plan, and even a profit-sharing scheme.

But by the mid 1960s, Steinberg workers were starting to gripe about their wages. A young cashier named Tom Kukovica was in the vanguard of the protest. Kukovica worked in the company's Côte des Neiges store in the northwest part of Montreal. Across the street was a Dominion Store and the workers from the two companies used to take their breaks together. They talked about a lot of things — including wages. One day Kukovica discovered that while he took home $48 a week for a 48-hour workweek, his Dominion counterparts at a smaller store earned roughly double that. Despite Sam's professed concern, he wasn't the most generous after all. Kukovica vowed to change that.

The Dominion workers were already organized under the banner of the Retail Clerks International Association. In 1962 they decided to go after Steinberg's 5,000 workers in Quebec and were successful in signing them up for a five-year trial period. The gap between the union's demands and the company's willingness to pay could not be bridged, and a strike seemed only a matter of time. On June 9, 1965, after tense eleventh-hour negotiations the day before, 5,000 supermarket, Miracle Mart, and warehouse workers went on strike for better pay and working conditions.

It was a devastating experience for Sam. The very people he had hired, supported, and cared for through the years were carrying pickets and preventing him from entering his own stores. How could they do this to him? The sense of betrayal was crushing. It was like dealing with so many errant sons and daughters.

But like the father who woos back his prodigal son rather than turns him away, Sam didn't lash out in anger at his workers. Instead he was generous, almost forgiving. In one gesture so extraordinary that company people remember it decades later, Sam Steinberg gave his workers coffee and doughnuts as they picketed outside his stores.

As the picketers sipped Sam's coffee and munched his doughnuts, they were left scratching their heads. Had they missed something? Wasn't a strike supposed to be a nasty, confrontational business? Weren't employees and their bosses supposed to be at loggerheads? But here was Sam, instead of being an intransigent bully, feeding his employees as they waved placards in his face! Not the behavior of any ordinary boss.

For a family entrepreneur like Sam, that behavior was perfectly understandable. What he was saying indirectly was: you're still my children. You've done this bad thing, but you're still my children. Arnold Steinberg did not share Sam's forgiving approach to the workers. "He should have got up there and punched them in the nose," Arnold believed. "He should have been so mad."

There were other reasons why Sam wanted to end the strike quickly. In the grocery business, every day, every hour that a strike ticked on was catastrophic. The perishable goods — which made up at least twenty-five per cent of the inventory — would spoil. Millions of dollars' worth of produce could be wiped out in a couple of days. In addition, Steinberg felt something more immeasurable was at stake during a strike — its public image. It feared its credibility would be shattered and that its customers would be lost forever to the competition. The publicity a strike generated was the last thing Sam wanted. The union sensed Sam's deep aversion to a labor dispute and in future years would continue to exploit it. It was a classic case of a spoiled child manipulating a soft parent. As Steinberg's labor relations executive Alain Bilodeau noted, "they learned that if they hit and squeezed Sam it would be in their benefit."

That first strike in 1965 lasted a day and a half before Sam capitulated. Not only did he grant the workers a big wage increase; he agreed to their demand that they be paid in full for their time on strike. Never mind that this particular union demand was a complete repudiation of a fundamental labor principle: if you don't work, you don't get paid. Anything to get the damned thing settled. The company never lived down the decision to pay the union for the day and a half it struck. The union got all it wanted. "It was," recalled Tom Kukovica with a faint smile one day in 1989, "a picnic."

The union became more powerful. In 1969 the two locals at Steinberg merged with the Dominion Store workers to form a united front: Local 500 of the Retail Clerks International. Future strikes would be just as emotionally wrenching as the first one in 1965. "Whenever there was a strike it created a funeral atmosphere," recalled Sam Gerstel, Sam's one-time executive assistant. "It was really depressing. Everybody took it so personally." For management, the behavior of the workers was always very difficult to swallow. "They might have had a clerk who was with them ten to fifteen years, and there he was throwing a rock at a store

window. That was the atmosphere. It hurt them so much," Gerstel
remembered.

Sam invariably surrendered. "He could not suffer a strike," said
Arnold Steinberg. "It was like cutting a part of his body off." A
pattern of wage settlements developed that undermined the company's financial strength and made it vulnerable to lower-cost
competitors. Sam never developed a labor strategy and never really
considered what the long-term effects of those wage settlements
would be on the company's competitiveness. Instead he practised
Management by Emotion. Eventually the labor costs grew completely out of control, nearly killing the Quebec supermarkets in
the years following Sam's death.

The unofficial labor policy at Steinberg — settle at any cost —
meant that Steinberg, which had once lagged far behind Dominion
in hourly wages, ended up paying the highest rates in the province,
and some of the highest in North America. In its boom years
Steinberg could afford to cater to union demands, but once Quebec
grocery companies like Provigo and Métro-Richelieu entered the
fray, it could no longer keep up. Those companies were basically
food distributors that supplied franchised stores. Their wage scales
and overhead costs were far lower than Steinberg's.

If emotions were a factor in settling strikes at Steinberg, so were
politics. During the 1960s, while labor was gaining more power, so
was the Québécois nationalist movement. And labor unions were
among its most ardent supporters. Sam, as a Jewish employer of
thousands of francophones, was fearful of gaining a reputation as a
tough employer or an anti-French image that would be impossible
to live down.

Another factor in the union's rise at Steinberg was the skill of
leaders like Tom Kukovica, a strong-willed native of Yugoslavia
who became one of Canada's top labor negotiators. Raised by his
grandmother after his parents died in the Second World War,
Kukovica emigrated to Canada with aspirations of becoming a
writer. He studied literature at the Université de Montréal, and to
finance his education he took a cashier's job at Steinberg in 1962.

After his very first day on the job, the combative Kukovica filed a
grievance for working overtime without pay. To boot, he complained that he was earning the cashier's rate but doing a variety of
other jobs without being paid accordingly. It was obvious to him

that working conditions were rotten at Steinberg. Two years after he joined the company he became involved in union business and his literary ambitions faded.

In 1969 the union offered Kukovica a job as a full-time representative. When Sam heard about this, he approached Kukovica and tried to talk him out of it. "Why don't you stay? You could be a store manager." But by then Kukovica wasn't interested in vague promises. He felt the company had treated him shabbily over the years. He was bitter because he had discovered that if you wanted to move up quickly through the ranks, you'd better not open your mouth and speak out. "If you were a fighter like I was, and the store manager didn't like you, they'd hide your dossier and not promote you." So when Sam tried to get him to forgo the union post, Kukovica's response wasn't exactly gracious. "You jerked me around enough," he said. "It's a little bit too late."

A lanky man with curly, salt-and-pepper hair, Kukovica regarded his union involvement as a "fight for the little guy" and he believed there was a lot to fight for at Steinberg. Wage parity with the competition became the main issue. The union was also concerned that breaks and lunch hours were not being granted properly, and that promotions were being granted without proper postings or in accordance with seniority. And Kukovica didn't like the practice of penalizing cashiers if they came up short at the end of the day.

Kukovica was a real thorn in Steinberg's side. Company negotiators found him illogical and difficult to deal with. But if he was that, he was also shrewd and knew just where to find Sam's sensitive spots. One of them was his public image. Sam hated any confrontation or demonstration that would generate bad publicity for the company. "That was his weak point," said Kukovica. "He was very shy in public. He always wanted to be seen as a caring person for his people."

Kukovica never doubted those sentiments were sincere: Sam did care for his workers and always treated them with respect. He recalled one strike where Sam came to the picket line, only to find his son-in-law and vice-president, Mel Dobrin, yelling at the picketers. Sam reprimanded him. "Listen, these people are on a legal strike. They're allowed to, so please respect them."

Sam's habit of getting personally involved in these labor disputes became extremely frustrating to his top executives. After his managers had spent hours at the bargaining table trying to settle work conflicts in a professional, objective way, Sam would simply cut his own deal with the union. His executives would wring their hands in despair. The most flagrant example was his conduct with the warehouse workers.

Every time there was a problem in the warehouse, work would come to a halt. Sam would come over and inquire what the problem was. Invariably, he'd accede to the workers' demands, then pay them for the time they were on strike. In his eccentric, paternal way, he spoiled his favorites, the warehouse drivers, rotten.

The situation came to a head in December 1973 when the 2,000 warehouse workers went on strike for three weeks. Compared to earlier strikes, this was an ugly, violent episode. This time the company's main concern was to stop Sam from giving in to the warehouse workers whenever they yelled for more. Company negotiators wanted to get the message across to employees that they weren't going to get a deal just by talking with Sam Steinberg.

But if the company was tough, the unions proved militant too. There was a standoff at the bargaining table. Then the dispute became violent. The picketers tried to disrupt service in the stores, which were open as usual (only the warehouse workers were on strike). Vandals broke store windows and threw paint at them. Court orders had to be issued to stop the picketers from interfering with customers and non-striking workers. Delivery trucks were damaged. At one point, a warehouse was set afire by a Molotov cocktail, causing hundreds of thousands of dollars in damages. Sam's house was put under security watch.

Because of the violence and destruction to property, Steinberg made the unprecedented move to bring in security people to protect the stores. The union regarded the security guards as little more than strike-breaking goons and their hiring as an act of provocation. In mid December there was more trouble on the picket line, and fifteen people were arrested.

The strike was finally settled after three weeks, and this time the union made most of the concessions. But there was no winner in a dispute like this; the aftershocks were felt for years to come. Labor relations were badly poisoned by the violence. And some believe the warehouse strike directly led to an attack on the home of Mitzi and Mel Dobrin in July 1974.

By then Sam had appointed his daughter Mitzi as general manager of the Miracle Mart department store division. He had also named her husband Mel as president of Steinberg, although Sam remained chief executive officer. In the early morning hours of July 26, 1974, a bomb exploded at their suburban Town of Mount Royal home while they and their three children slept, sending the picture window of their den cascading down like a curtain. Mitzi and Mel rushed outside to find a crowd gathering around their house. A smell of dynamite wafted through the air. Leading from the rear of the home to the street was a trail of blood.

Thirty minutes later, a man identifying himself as RCMP officer Robert Samson walked into a local hospital with a badly damaged eye, and arm and chest injuries. His blood type matched that found at the house. Samson was charged with making and planting the bomb, charges he denied during his trial. He claimed he had gone to the Dobrins' neighborhood to keep a rendezvous with an RCMP informant in connection with anti-subversive work. Samson was eventually acquitted, and no one was ever caught. Years later, there are still plenty of theories about who did it.

Although the union denied responsibility, it believed the bombing was related to the warehouse strike of six months earlier. It believed that the company goons brought in during the strike were disgruntled because they weren't fully paid for their services and wanted to retaliate against the company.

According to another theory, the bombing had nothing to do with the strike and everything to do with the mob. That theory was that a small Quebec-based grocery chain competing with Steinberg was in fact a money-laundering operation for organized crime. One of its stores was suffering badly because of competition from a Steinberg supermarket nearby. The owners wanted to come to some sort of "arrangement" on prices, according to a former Steinberg executive. When Steinberg refused to have anything to do with price-fixing, the other chain planted a bomb as a message that it was time to talk.

Whether or not the Dobrin bombing resulted directly from the labor climate at Steinberg, senior management decided it was time to ease Sam out of union negotiations. Together they convinced him they were right. His handling of labor relations had been an abysmal failure. In the end, however, with or without Sam Steinberg, nothing really changed. The damage was already done and the pattern of high wage settlements continued until the mid 1980s, when it became obvious that the supermarkets were pricing the company right out of business.

# 5

# *A Simple Grocer*

W hen Sam Steinberg was a boy working in his mother's store on the Main, he would often gaze dreamily down the two long blocks near the shop. "One day," he vowed, "I'll have trucks lined up that could fill those blocks." It was no idle fantasy but rather an early hint that entrepreneurship coursed through Sam's blood, a powerful force that forever drove him to create, to expand. He never worked for money, said his daughter Mitzi; he worked to build.

Sam realized his dream with phenomenal success. Yet despite his Order of Canada award and countless other honors, he never saw himself as the genius behind one of Canada's biggest business empires. The round-faced little man with the bushy eyebrows, the piercing gaze, and the lopsided grin considered himself a simple grocer. To the day he died he listed that as his occupation whenever he filled out a census form.

Mr. Sam was a collection of ironies. He was the undisputed master of his business and the patriarch of his family, yet outside the corporate or family milieu he was a humble, shy man who never felt himself to be a legitimate part of the Canadian business establishment. He was a public-school dropout dubious of higher learning, yet he possessed an awesome mental agility and an intuitive business sense that made him a match for the finest in corporate North America. He was a tough, often intolerant boss who could tear a strip off an employee without a qualm and then turn around and help the person with a personal problem. He could argue bitterly with a senior executive and then months later contritely admit he'd been wrong.

Sam became a wealthy capitalist who controlled company stock worth hundreds of millions of dollars. Yet he remained a simple, almost folksy man forever uncomfortable with the trappings of wealth. Making money never motivated him. Only two things in life ever truly did: his business and his family.

Sam's values and business style were rooted in his background. He was a classic product of his environment, an uneducated immigrant kid who "grew up in the streets and saw what it took to succeed," according to Max Roytenberg, an economist who worked in a variety of roles for the company in the 1960s and 1970s. Sam's business and his family were important to him because he had been weaned on both since he began working in his mother's store. In the struggling early days the two were symbiotic: one existed for the other.

Yet his early years only partly explain why he alone of five brothers and a sister managed to transform a single store into one of Canada's leading family enterprises. The rest was nature's doing. Sam was born with prodigious talent. According to Roytenberg, "He was a unique genetic accident."

Sam could be a disorganized, absent-minded-professor type who preferred to leave the detail work to others. Once he found a stock certificate in his desk at home for hundreds of thousands of shares. "Is this any good?" he asked his vice-president and general counsel James Doyle the next day, not terribly concerned if it was. Yet despite such occasional lapses, recalled Doyle, "He was the nearest thing to a genius that I've ever encountered in my life."

His thirst for information was insatiable and he soaked it up like a sponge. "It was as though you were feeding information into some kind of an old-fashioned giant computer, a Univax of World War Two," said Doyle. "All those wheels would go into motion. And almost invariably the right card would slide out at the bottom."

He could grasp the essence of a complex concept in a flash. William Howieson, former vice-president and comptroller of the company, remembered once making a presentation to senior executives on an economic theory known as "cost of capital". Most had blank looks on their faces. But Sam caught onto it right away and was then able to explain it in simple language to his bemused managers.

Sam spoke matter-of-factly, almost brusquely, and utterly without pretension. He had a special talent for speaking in parables or using anecdotes to illustrate a point. "Now listen to me slowly," he would say, his favorite preface to a story, a way of saying, don't jump to conclusions. Another favorite expression was, "If you want to milk a cow, you've got to give it something to eat." Translated, "You have to invest money to make money."

To Jim Doyle, there was only one other person like Sam in that respect, the celebrated humorist and McGill University professor, Stephen Leacock. Sam shared with Leacock the unique ability of having almost anything in daily life remind him of something else, far afield, connected only by the subjective association in his own mind. He was an inexhaustible storehouse of anecdotes, mostly based on his own personal experience.

John Paré, a former Steinberg personnel director, was struck by Sam's unique style of communicating. On one occasion he and Paré were discussing mandatory retirement. Sam was sixty-two at the time and he wanted to lower the retirement age from sixty-five to sixty. "That's crazy," Paré told his boss. "You're at the peak of your career and you want to reduce it?" Sam said nothing for a minute, then got up from behind his desk and pointed to his shoes, glossy blue patent leather with a gold buckle. "How do you know they don't hurt me?" he asked and walked back behind his desk. He had made his point: walk in a person's shoes before making a judgment based on appearances.

Another typical technique, which was really his way of learning, was to interrogate everyone he came into contact with, from his banker to his salmon broker, until he felt he'd extracted sufficient information from that person. Securities analyst Martin Kaufman remembered once getting a ride from Ottawa to Montreal in Sam's chauffeur-driven Cadillac. As the two sat in the back seat, Sam grilled him on every imaginable subject, especially the buildings and real estate lining the Trans-Canada Highway on Montreal's West Island. Who owned them? What were they worth? Sam wanted to know it all.

Sam's inquisitive nature gave him a decided edge over his competitors. Few had a more exhaustive knowledge of the business than he did. In part, he was simply curious, as well as having been influenced by his mother, who had always stressed the importance of knowing all facets of the grocery business. And he did know everything — even about his customers. Sometimes he would dumbfound a customer by remembering her name, address, and the size of her grocery bill, down to the penny, from the day she had first come into the store years before.

Unfortunately, the dazzling mental abilities of this stocky little man had not been distributed equally among his brothers. Whatever all the articles said about Mr. Nathan or Mr. Jack or Mr. Max or Mr. Morris, as they were known, the company's success could truly be attributed only to Mr. Sam. There was simply no comparison between the brothers. Sam's brothers were in a different league. Maurice Segall, a former administrative assistant, puts it bluntly. "The story of Sam and the brothers is this: the other brothers were irrelevant. Sam was the brother who carried the four their whole lives. The intelligence, drive, marketing genius all went to one man."

As a result, an unusual relationship developed between them. Sam acted more like their father than their brother, a fact perhaps explained by the absence of their own father, William, from the Steinberg household. Consciously or unconsciously, Sam became the father William never was. But then, Sam had always promised his mother he would look after the boys.

But what a father. Sam could intimidate them shamelessly, order them around, pick on them and blast them when they failed to carry out his instructions. He was intolerant and would dictate their every move, Mitzi remembered with distaste. "When he said sit, they sat down; lie down, they lay down." The brothers rarely fought back; they knew from an early age that he had it over them, just as they knew later on that he was largely responsible for their prosperity. When he gave them a tongue-lashing, they had no choice but to take it.

Operating in the shadow of Sam, being defined not for themselves but for their relationship to him, took a toll on the brothers' self-esteem. "Oh, you're Jack Steinberg," people would say. "Well, I know your brother Sam." Jack in particular dreaded dealing with Sam. Just as a child tries to get something from a strict parent by going around him, Jack would go to an intermediary, Sam's executive assistant, Sam Gerstel, if he wanted a raise or if he wanted to know about something Sam should have told him. Jack's official role was to oversee Steinberg's equipment and physical plant, and he felt constantly passed over in the decision-making process by Sam. He saw many things in the company that needed improvement but felt he was unable to get Sam's attention.

Nathan, the brother to whom Sam had always been closest, was also keenly aware of his place in life. "Natie", as Sam called him, rated perhaps the highest of the brothers in the corporate scheme of things, doing promotional work and sales, serving as senior vice-president and vice-chairman of the board. Ever since the two used to race through Bonsecours Market buying produce for their mother's store, Nathan had been Sam's right-hand man. Yet always, Sam was in control.

It seemed that only Sam's death could break his spell over Nathan. Before Sam died, Nathan could never take care of a restaurant tab in his brother's presence, for example. Sam's insistence on personally taking care of both minor and major issues bordered on intimidation. Though Nathan was deeply grieved when Sam died in 1978, he felt an almost tangible relief at finally having been liberated from his brother's lifelong control.

Executives who observed the five Steinberg brothers together fault Sam for being tougher on them than he was on any employee. He often blasted them in front of their colleagues. On one occasion, his brother Max was oddly quiet at a meeting, not participating in the discussion. Sam discovered he was engrossed in a comic book. He launched into a fiery diatribe while the others fidgeted in uncomfortable silence.

The youngest Steinberg brother, Morris, defended Sam's treatment of his siblings, saying it was just his personal style. "He could get angry at times, annoyed," said Morris, a gentle, tiny man who for most of his Steinberg days headed up the grocery buying. "But he was not difficult to get along with. We knew how to get along. People who didn't understand Sam had the wrong impression of him. He didn't bother me."

The flip side of Sam's harsh treatment of his siblings was his fierce loyalty toward them. Brotherly privilege allowed that *he* could rip into them but no one else could. Anyone who dared to speak against his brothers could not expect to advance in the company.

That devotion to family carried on into their adult years. When Max Steinberg died suddenly of a heart attack in May 1965 at age fifty-three, the first of Ida's children to pass away, Sam was deeply affected. Max, quiet and reflective, had been instrumental in negotiating company financing and real estate matters for years. While Sam, with his ebullient enthusiasm, was great at making an initial real estate call, he would become impatient with the enormous amounts of detail work that followed a deal. Luckily, Max didn't mind. He was meticulous and organized, and kept voluminous records of meetings, which he had kept in green ring-binder writing pads. But Max was more than Sam's details man. He was his friend, a sounding board, and a confidant, without whom Sam seemed totally lost. Ironically, Max's death underscored how paternalistic and downright intransigent Sam could be with members of his brothers' families. When Max's son Brahm wanted to sell some shares in his father's estate, which, like all the company's common shares, were under Sam's voting control, Sam replied, "Don't worry, I'll take care of you." Brahm waited a few weeks, but the stock was starting to go down and he was getting nervous. He called and Sam gave him the same answer. Finally, he called Sam angrily and threatened to sue if he couldn't sell the stock. The threat worked and Sam arranged for a broker to make the sale. But the incident underlined what everyone knew all along: that it was Sam's company and nobody else's.

In the company, at one time, it was said that 250 people reported directly to Sam. On the surface he seemed open-minded and willing to hear out everyone, down to the lowliest cleaning woman. But ultimately, Sam Steinberg made the decisions.

Indeed, Sam did not suffer from an undersized ego and this could show up in funny ways. During the late 1950s, for instance, the company was having trouble with some of its private label, in-house brands. The Steinberg-brand hair spray had apparently caused skin irritations. The joke in the company was that if you were bald, you must have used the hair spray. One day Sam called an all-day management meeting to solve these problems. Should the company cut back on these products altogether? Expand them? At the end, he got up to comment. "As long as I'm president of the company and I own this company, private label will get its share of space." The speculation afterwards was that the real reason Sam so vigorously defended the private label goods was that he liked to see his name on them.

Sam's ego became tied up in another corporate issue several years later when the company architects wanted to change the store logo from the script style used till then — based on Sam's signature — to one suited to a more modern store design. They found the long "S" of the logo difficult for signs. Sam resisted. This was his signature, the one he used to practise for hours on end as a child. He lost that battle, though, and a stylized "S" logo replaced it.

Sam's business style was characterized by a habit of building on merchandising techniques he'd seen elsewhere. He may not have been a truly original thinker, but what distinguished him from others is that he could refine and improve upon other people's ideas. Transforming other people's ideas and going further with them are what made him a true entrepreneur.

The Steinbergs had been on the cutting edge of merchandising since the Depression years, when they would pay farmers a dime above the market price for eggs that were delivered the same day they were laid — just so they'd be the freshest around. And by the early 1950s Steinberg stores were impressive showcases of industry innovations that today are taken for granted: electric-eye doors, Muzak, conveyor belts, and car-loading service, in which the groceries are sent by conveyer belt to a depot on the parking lot and placed right in the customer's trunk. They offered customer-operated coffee grinders first and even as basic a feature as a parking lot for their customers. They were carving a reputation for themselves as industry pioneers, and grocery people from around North America flocked to the Steinberg stores to see just what these remarkable Montreal merchants were offering. In his 1959 book, *Flame of Power*, Peter Newman wrote that interest was so keen in Steinberg that three head-office employees had to spend most of their time acting as guides for visiting U.S. supermarket executives.

Sam was masterful at motivating his employees and extracting the maximum performance from them. He inspired through example, working himself to the bone. If the boss toiled that hard, the employees felt compelled to do so as well. He could be so demanding and intimidating that there was no choice but to do what he asked.

Sam had always been like that. When Dr. Mike Aronovitch started as an employee at Steinberg in the 1930s, he spent hours preparing lavish fruit displays in the store windows. On one occasion, after the young medical student had spent half a day painstakingly dressing a fruit window, Sam came along to inspect it. "I don't like it," he said sharply. "It's no good." Aronovitch had to pull it apart and start from scratch.

That behavior does not surprise some people. There was a hard side to Sam Steinberg, which he tried to hide beneath a genteel manner. He gave you the feeling he was interested in you and what you were doing. If he agreed with you, you would be surprised at the careful attention this business magnate showed in listening to you; similarly, if he disagreed, you could be equally surprised at how roughly he dismissed you.

Sam Shuster, the company's longtime physician, remembered how proud Sam was of his toughness. "Once he fired a fellow, a big guy. And then he turned to me and said, 'Did you see me fire that guy?'" Shuster's theory was that Sam had a bit of a Napoleon complex.

He drove a hard bargain in his dealings with other businesspeople. Vendors and suppliers complained about how difficult it was to deal with him. Herb Shapiro, a former equipment supplier to the company, had installed the first computer-control system in the company's warehouse in the early 1970s. One day when the system broke down, Sam became furious, threatening lawsuits left and right. "Get your ass over here and fix it," he ordered Shapiro.

Sam was often hot-tempered with subordinates, although he could just as quickly forget an argument as start one. Leo Goldfarb, the former son-in-law who was a vice-president in the real estate division, had a number of arguments with Sam and threatened to quit several times. Sam would habitually authorize him to do a deal, then change his mind after he had given his approval. One night, after Goldfarb had angrily announced that he was quitting, Sam came over to his house and plunked himself down on the living-room sofa, as if nothing had happened. While Goldfarb watched TV, Sam pleaded for forgiveness, explaining his good intentions: "You know who I am, what I'm working for," he would say. "It's for the family, and I can't be right all the time." Invariably, Goldfarb would come back.

On another occasion, the company lawyer, Jim Doyle, had a bitter row with Sam over whether or not to give an employee a raise. Doyle stalked out in a rage, slamming the door behind him. Later that night Sam bumped into him at a black-tie reception at the Ritz-Carlton Hotel, and in an embarrassed, almost obsequious, manner admitted he had been wrong — the employee deserved the raise. Doyle was astonished that a chief executive would admit such a thing to a subordinate.

In fact, Sam was rarely quick with a raise. You had to prove to him you were worthy of one. His parsimonious salaries cost him some good executives.

Even those on the receiving end of Sam's tough style believed it was effective and considered him a shrewd psychologist. Sam would expect so much from employees that they worked themselves to a frenzy to justify those expectations. Nothing was ever enough for him. He lavished little praise on employees, instead criticizing them for minute failings. But he got results.

Sam was especially fond of his store managers, regarding them as his prize employees, not to mention his pipeline from head office to the front lines. He knew them all by first name and regularly phoned a handful of them to find out what was going on in the stores. Once in the early 1970s a rookie employee named Doug Long found out to what degree Sam valued his managers. Long, former director of communications for the company, remembers Sam calling him into his office personally and reprimanding him. His sin? He had been too slow in returning the phone call of a store manager.

On the other hand, Sam's door was always open to workers with a problem. He assisted them with financial worries, visited their relatives in the hospital or attended a funeral. If an employee's child were sick or had been hurt, Sam's secretary Anne Beaulieu was instructed to call the parents every hour to keep him up-to-date.

On one issue Sam was particularly progressive with his employees: language. He believed the workplace should be welcoming to English and French workers alike. Years before politicians launched their language law debates, Steinberg instituted a program that ensured that more French-speaking employees were hired and that they could communicate in the language of their choice on the job — right up to the managerial level. Senior management meetings were usually bilingual. Even if you couldn't speak the language of your colleagues, at the very least you were expected to understand them. For many longtime English-speaking Jewish staff members, that meant taking language courses. In the summer of 1960 Sam himself trooped off to French classes at the Université de Montréal. (Nathan was fluent: his dealings with the francophone farmers through the years had given him an excellent *joual* French.) Of course a bilingual workplace ensured that his customers, most of them French-speaking, were served in the language of their choice too.

And in a gesture that acknowledged the company's predominantly francophone clientele, management decided to remove the apostrophe and "s" from Steinberg's store logo and signs, decades before Quebec language laws would make it mandatory. "[Francophones] talked in terms of chez Steinberg, not chez Steinberg's — that didn't mean anything," pointed out Arnold, who agreed that the name of the company should reflect how the majority of the customers actually talked about it.

In return for his sensitivity to customers' and employees' needs, Sam expected loyalty to the company, and when he failed to get it — for instance, when his workers struck or when a senior executive quit the company — he felt betrayed. Maurice Segall, who left the company in 1962 to go to U.S. retailer J. C. Penney, enjoyed an intimate relationship with Sam during his seven years with Steinberg. Yet when Segall left, Sam cut off all communication with him for four years. "My departure was considered an extreme act of disloyalty," said Segall. "It was like a son had married out of the faith."

Sam's supreme goal was to provide his shoppers with the best service possible. Indeed, former employees recall his regard for the customers was almost a religion to him. He drilled into his staff the notion that there was nothing one didn't do for them. Store managers were cautioned never to park their cars in the choice parking spaces outside the stores. Those were reserved for the customers. Pity the poor employee who didn't give his all to the client; no supervisor or manager was secure from his wrath. Sam practised what he preached. One story said that he had been out driving one time when he saw a woman trudging along, laden down with bags bearing the familiar Steinberg logo. He had offered to drive her home.

The adage that the customer is always right may well have originated with Sam. John Paré found that out years before he became a Steinberg executive. He'd been shopping at a supermarket in suburban Dorval, and when he arrived home found that several items had been left out of his order. He went back to the store and complained. The protocol didn't stop at a mere apology: the store manager delivered the balance of the order and a whole roast beef to his home.

Sam never argued with a customer. He would go out of his way for his shoppers, even if it approached the bounds of the absurd. One day about a month after Christmas, he received a telephone call from a distressed store manager who reported that a customer had come in with her Christmas turkey, three-quarters eaten and rancid. The woman was demanding a refund, saying the bird had gone bad. "Give her the refund," Sam ordered at once. The store manager protested, "Well, I meant to, but it has an A & P label stuck to the carcass." Sam replied, "Look, if she wants to shame herself by making a claim on a turkey we didn't sell her, don't you shame her any more by not giving her the refund." The woman went home placated and the manager was left scratching his head at this example of customer service gone wild.

The gesture demonstrated the level of integrity Mr. Sam brought to his company. He was a righteous man who stamped his business with high ethical and moral standards. Even in the early years of the business Sam refused to let family members help themselves to free groceries from the store shelves. Once, his longtime family physician, Mike Aronovitch, and his wife attended the opening of a store in Westmount, shortly after the Second World War. As a sign of the newfound prosperity of the times, there was a pile of boxes of Viau Whippet cookies — legendary marshmallow confections covered with a thin layer of chocolate that formed a little swirl on the top. They had been difficult to find during the war. Helen Steinberg bought — did not take — a box of the cookies for Aronovitch and his wife. That was the kind of company Sam Steinberg ran.

Outside the company, he tried to be an upstanding citizen. He lived within the letter of the law and was probably one of the few in private enterprise who believed in the value of taxes. His daughter Marilyn remembered her father lecturing to them: "You must know that by paying taxes we have roads and a clean city: it's your share and it's for your country."

Sam may not always have agreed with government but he did abide by the law. When the Quebec legislature introduced its controversial Bill 101, outlawing bilingual commercial signs, Steinberg petitioned the government to reinstate bilingual signs although it obeyed the law. Even after Sam's death the company continued to follow his philosophy on language — to the chagrin of anglophone consumers, who felt betrayed enough to take action. In late 1978, 53 prominent anglophone Quebecers, including Scotty Bowman, then coach of the Montreal Canadiens and Hugh MacLennan, the novelist, signed a letter to Steinberg berating the company for removing English from its in-store signs and encouraged a boycott of the Steinberg stores.

Sam wished to take no sides. He was a merchant whose job was to cater to the needs of his customers, whatever their language.

Sam's personal moral code was as exacting as his respect for public codes. One hapless Steinberg clerk learned about Sam's puritanical side the hard way when he was caught after work in what was known euphemistically at the time as a "disorderly house" — a brothel. He needed someone to bail him out, so he phoned Sam Steinberg. Not a smart move. "Let him rot" was Sam's response.

"He wasn't a prude but he was close to it," according to Irwin Hockenstein, Sam's longtime fruit and vegetable merchandiser, who got firsthand experience with his prim ways.

Hockie was a teenager when Sam invited him to join him on a business trip to New York. "He needed to take me like a hole in the head but he wouldn't travel on this train by himself. He needed the company," Hockenstein recalled. When they got to New York the two checked into a hotel right next door to a well-known strip club called Minsky's Burlesque. To the wide-eyed adolescent, Minsky's represented an enticing world of fleshly delights. Sam, however, had no more interest in going there than he would have had in giving trade secrets to the president of the Dominion Stores. But Hockenstein — "I was seventeen years of age, my hormones were in play, I was dying to go see it." So while Sam slept, Hockie sneaked out.

There was no time for Minsky's Burlesque or other such distractions in Sam's life. Not when his wife Helen was waiting at home. Their marriage was the stuff of fairy tales, a magical liaison that was happy, enduring, and always close. Relatives say Helen, his first cousin, was the perfect wife for a man totally consumed by his business. She never pursued a career of her own or took an active, high-profile part in the business. She chose to devote her life to Sam and to the company. She gave him time, support, and encouragement. "She made it easy for him to have the space and energy he needed to do what he had to do," Sharon Steinberg observed of her aunt Helen. "In that sense, she was important. A wife who needs constant attention can distract."

Sweet, mild-mannered, and quiet, Helen was a foil for Sam's driven, competitive personality. She soothed him when he became agitated, she listened patiently when he needed a sounding board, she encouraged him to take a holiday when he became overworked. In the view of his grown children, Sam idolized her.

Although Sam was the aggressive one in the marriage, relatives regarded Helen as strong in her own quiet way, arranging family affairs efficiently and without ado. Sam was dependent on Helen in matters personal. She would do everything for him, from shopping for him to laying out his clothes. Although he was head of the company and family patriarch, in their marriage it seemed that, emotionally, Helen was the stronger of the two. The daughters recognized their father's need for Helen and their greatest fear was that their mother would die before Sam did. He would have been devastated.

But Sam died first and it was Helen who never fully recovered. She did not speak of him much, but everything in her demeanor indicated she missed him terribly. He had been her whole life. After his death she kept their Westmount home filled with photographs of him and had a lifesized photo of him at their Florida condominium.

If Helen was the perfect wife she was also the quintessential
Jewish mama, a traditional housewife who raised four daughters
and baked the best peach pies around. Sam raved about her cooking. A wonderfully corny article in *Maclean's* magazine in the
1950s recounts how Sam, after sampling the fine cuisine
throughout Europe, concluded that no dish he'd tasted came close
to Helen's cabbage rolls. When her children began having their own
children, Helen smoothly assumed the role of the consummate
grandmother. When her children went on vacation she and Sam
moved in to take care of the grandchildren.

Although she never played an official role in the business, former
employees say Helen's unofficial role was significant. She sometimes accompanied him to conferences. Malcolm MacIver, the
company's first labor relations man, remembers a tense bargaining
session in the 1960s. The company was close to a strike and the
fatigued MacIver had adjourned negotiations for the day at 1 a.m.
He called Sam at home to let him know that things had reached a
delicate point. Less than thirty minutes later, Sam — and Helen —
arrived at the hotel, where she took a very active part in the
discussions before suggesting a final adjournment for the day. It's
not every chief executive's wife, recalled MacIver, who would
accompany him in the dead of night to a hotel suite to discuss an
impending strike.

Through the years Sam kept Helen informed about virtually
every aspect of the business. This was sometimes a bone of conten-
tion for employees. Sam used to phone his right-hand man Jack
Levine every morning at 7:00 a.m., for instance, and Helen would
be on an extension phone. She would ask Levine an occasional
question, but most of the time she would just listen. When Sam
gathered his coterie of top people to discuss succession at his
Palomino Lodge in the Laurentian Mountains north of Montreal,
Helen was there cooking for the executives, and keeping track of
developments. And in her own small ways, Helen tried to keep
Sam's spirit going through the company after he died. When a fire
swept through the company's head office in the fall of 1986, Helen,
then in her late seventies, showed up at the temporary headquarters
that had been set up to make sure everyone was all right. Her
gesture of concern for the employees was vintage Sam Steinberg.

The Steinberg family was tremendously close. They went to Plage Laval beach together in the summer; they went to Palomino Lodge for holidays. There was no occasion more wonderful than Helen and Sam's Friday-night Sabbath suppers. When the daughters began to have their own families, husbands and grandchildren would gather at the stately graystone house on Aberdeen Street in Westmount for Helen's delicious cooking, some lively conversation, and, of course, Sam's stories about the business. It was a warm, comfortable home, the envy of the other relatives. "It's always been my dream to have a family like hers," said Sharon Steinberg.

If there is any crack in the seemingly blissful portrait of family life, it lies in how Helen and Sam raised their four daughters. The girls were never neglected materially. Just the opposite. It is the impression of relatives and friends that the girls were spoiled rotten. A former company physician, Sam Shuster, who went to the same dentist as the Steinbergs, recalled one occasion when Sam took young Evie to the dentist. She refused to sit in the chair. Sam tried desperately to placate her, promising to shower her with all manner of enticements — "a bicycle, anything," he had pleaded — if only she'd cooperate. Evie only wanted to be out the door.

It is not surprising that Sam was so generous with his girls, lavishing them later with clothes, cars, condos in Florida. When it came to his daughters, his pockets were deep; there was nothing they couldn't have. They would never know the kind of life Sam Steinberg had lived growing up in a crowded, unheated flat on The Main.

Friends believed that Sam and Helen neglected to pay enough attention to their children's less tangible needs and failed to impart to them the importance of education and community involvement. If you have enough money, Aronovitch said, other people do everything for you. "All you have to do is meander around and decide whether to do the kitchen over."

Indeed, unlike the offspring of heads of other family dynasties, there was little sense of noblesse oblige to motivate the Steinberg daughters to lend their names to community endeavors or social causes. Marilyn, Evelyn, Rita, and for many years Mitzi were content to be housewives. Mitzi, of course, became the exception.

She went on to earn a law degree, an executive position in Steinberg, and prominence in the Montreal business community. The other daughters were never involved in the company.

In part, Sam and Helen's way of bringing up their daughters stemmed from an overly traditional view of a woman's place in society. Their parents' view of the girls was that they would be wives and helpmates, just as Helen was. Even though Sam admired his secretaries and wanted them to take on responsibilities, he considered their jobs secondary. Their most important jobs were running their homes.

He never encouraged his daughters to go to university. Mitzi chose to get a law degree on her own, but only after she had married and raised three children. Even so, when she told Sam she was going back to law school, he was extremely upset.

How differently the Steinberg story would have read if Sam had had sons. They would have been actively encouraged to enter the business at an early age. Sam's failure to encourage his daughters to live more than a traditional existence was puzzling, given that his own mother was a hard-driven woman who had combined work with raising the family. Perhaps the difference was that Ida had worked out of necessity, strictly as a matter of survival. None of the Steinberg daughters would ever come close to that kind of life. Though they had lived modestly as children, they knew a plush, warm world far removed from their grandmother's life of poverty and daily struggle.

Sam was just too immersed in his grocery empire to push them toward university or community work. Sometimes he'd be so engrossed in his thoughts about the business that he would drive home for lunch and fail to notice his own little girls walking home along the street, waving and calling to their father for a lift.

When family and business interests conflicted, the business usually won out. When she was younger, Helen fell ill and required surgery to remove a kidney. "That's it," Sam said unequivocally, "I'm through with the business. I'm going to spend the rest of my days with Helen." She made it through the surgery, and almost immediately after, Sam plunged right back into the business, his pledge to her mysteriously forgotten. It was as if her illness had never happened.

Sam's solution to the problem of finding enough time for both family and business was to combine the two. One way was to drive the family around on Sunday afternoons to look at Steinberg stores. Family dinners were another perfect vehicle for combining family and business. To the newly initiated, the line between Steinbergs and Steinberg Inc. was at times almost invisible. Leo Goldfarb always remembered business being *the* topic in the Steinberg family. "At dinner time, at breakfast time, Sundays and holidays. If you were a part of the family and you weren't part of the Steinberg organization you almost felt like an outsider. . . . You felt like a deaf mute."

The almost obsessive, dual preoccupation Sam had with company and family manifested itself time and again. He talked business incessantly at home, yet at the office, family interests were almost inviolable, no matter how busy he was. No assistant dared ever intercept or hold a call from home without putting his or her job at risk.

Sam was a workaholic who thought sleep was a waste of time. He had few interests outside the company. He read the occasional business-related publication, perhaps an autobiography now and then. When he and Helen socialized, it was usually with business associates or his brothers. He enjoyed the odd game of pinochle, and later on in life a good golf game (although typically, he was highly competitive about his scores). Even then, he was habitually late for his games: on his way to the links he would generally stop to check out a store.

Mr. Sam also loved the Pavilion of Judaism at Expo 67, Montreal's world's fair. The pavilion depicted Judaism as a cultural as well as religious force. Sam was not actively religious himself, and the person who might have influenced him in this regard, his father, was out of the picture. Obviously, his business prevented him from having a lot of time for religion, especially since the stores were open Saturday. Yet he deeply respected all that Judaism represented and saw it as a decent moral code by which to live.

The sad part about the Expo Pavilion, said his daughter Mitzi, was that it failed to attract a lot of support from the Jewish community. The founder of the Seagram liquor empire, Sam Bronfman, opposed it, although that was no surprise since the two Sams never really did get along. Both of them were too accustomed to being sole boss.

In Sam's younger days, he did have a passion outside groceries: boxing. In fact he often said that had he not gone into business he would have loved to have become a prizefighter. He and Nathan used to listen avidly to radio broadcasts of the big U.S. prizefights. And whenever Sam attended a fight in person, he was a wildly enthusiastic spectator. Irwin Hockenstein, a former amateur boxer himself, remembered accompanying him. "I'm watching the fight and Sam's describing a fight to me that I'm not even seeing: 'Do you see where he's got him under the ribs, do you see where he hit him there. . . .' "

Sam certainly had the personality for boxing. He was an aggressive little scrapper who had no respect for people who didn't stand their ground. He loved a good fight, whether it was a battle of wits or fists. When Sam Shuster was a medical student at McGill University, he tried out for the boxing team. Sam found out about this and one night challenged Shuster to display his skills. "You think you can box?" Sam taunted him. The two began sparring with their bare hands, when suddenly Sam landed a punch in Shuster's face and broke his nose.

Yet despite Sam's remarkably decisive and confident control of his corporate empire, he could be timid and insecure outside the familiar confines of family and business. Montreal money manager Stephen Jarislowsky remembered meeting Sam for the first time at a cocktail party given by the Royal Bank of Canada, Steinberg's longtime banker. Sam stood shyly by himself for most of the evening, hardly speaking to anyone. When Jarislowsky engaged him in conversation he found him bright, likeable, and knowledgeable about his field. "He was [most] in his element with his work and his family. In the establishment world — gentile, French or English, he wasn't really ever at home."

Sam Steinberg preferred to be his own man. He would have been uncomfortable with the kind of power wielded by the Bronfmans or the Reichmanns. Jarislowsky recalled the time when Sam was on the verge of completing a 50/50 deal with the Bronfmans. But at the last minute Sam Steinberg backed out because he felt Sam Bronfman's 50 percent would be more equal than his 50 percent.

It was as if Sam could not accept that a street kid from the wrong side of town had made it into the big leagues of Canadian business. Let other corporate titans relish their success, status, and wealth; Sam felt ill at ease with them. He preferred not to be bothered with money. Often he carried so little cash with him that he would have to borrow money for a tank of gas or a haircut.

The modest man acquired a chauffeur eventually, but only because he was such an inattentive driver — he preferred to size up real estate as he drove instead of watching the road — that his family feared for his safety. Acquiring his Cadillac was another exercise in embarrassment for Sam. He felt so awkward about owning what he considered an ostentatious symbol of wealth that for the longest time he left it parked round the corner from the office so his employees wouldn't see it.

Moving from Outremont to his Westmount home in the 1950s also discomfited him. He wasn't a member of the cultured, old-money set that graced the gentle slopes of Upper Westmount. Sam Steinberg was nouveau riche, and what was worse he worked in retailing. The trade was not highly regarded in a community heavily weighted with doctors, lawyers, and other professionals.

Through the years Sam refused to take an exorbitant salary for himself, drawing less than $50,000 annually during the 1960s. That was less than what some of his vice-presidents made, although he drew considerable dividends from the company.

Sam's streak of humility made him revere others in his own industry, in business, and in government. He had tremendous respect for Antoine Turmel, the former chief executive of Provigo Inc. In fact, when Sam died his family discovered a large block of Provigo stock in Sam's estate. Years earlier Sam had shown breathless, almost boyish, excitement when he had the opportunity to meet George Eaton, head of the department store company.

Such reverence did not extend to everyone. Perhaps as a result of his mother's attitude toward formal education — a luxury for those with money and leisure, not for her family — and because of his own self-made success, Sam was suspicious of academics (though he received several honorary degrees in his lifetime). When economists once gave Steinberg executives a lecture, Sam instructed one of his vice-presidents, "Listen, it's not polite if I fall asleep in the middle of this guy's presentation. So if you see my head starting to tilt over, give me a shot like this."

For years, sheer intuition and natural ability, the hallmarks of Sam Steinberg, were enough to power the company. Later on, however, as the company grew into a full-fledged merchandising and real estate conglomerate those qualities didn't suffice. As the organization headed into the 1970s it began to surpass Sam Steinberg and his family. Yet Steinberg seemed almost frozen in time, still a family enterprise run by people with a deeply rooted emotional attachment to it. The company had to let that go, to realize it was operating in a more demanding business environment where being Number One was no longer its birthright. It wasn't enough to add an extra apple to a customer's bag to boost sales. Competition was fiercer, customers distrusted big business, labor problems weren't wiped away with easy concessions from a paternalistic boss — and a family member wasn't always the right person for the job.

Sam failed to recognize that his company had reached the point at which careful, skilled management was more important than the talents of an individual entrepreneur. He was unable to adapt, to shift gears, to acknowledge that his style of operating was becoming outmoded. Furthermore, he was getting on and, like it or not, he would have to pick a successor to face all the new challenges.

# 6

# *All in the Family*

When Helen Steinberg gave birth to her fourth daughter, Evelyn, in 1938, Sam Steinberg did not pass out cigars. He lost his temper instead. When congratulatory colleagues asked him at the Hochelaga Street office whether his new child was a boy or a girl, he responded by taking a kick at a twenty-foot stock cart. "A girl," he snapped. "Another girl."

Sam loved his daughters but he had desperately wanted a boy to carry on the family name, and most importantly, to take over the business. Instead he got four girls and, given his traditional views on the woman's role, no natural candidate to succeed him. He never encouraged the girls to participate in the company, and with the exception of Mitzi none of them ever did.

For an entrepreneur who wants to see his business continue on into the next generation, choosing a successor is a monumentally difficult task. It forces him to confront two unpleasant realities: that he will die, and that his business will go on without him. It is so much easier to sweep the issue under the carpet and hope it will solve itself. That was Sam Steinberg's approach for years. A visionary in so many other areas of his business, Sam simply would not think far enough into the future to imagine the day he would not run Steinberg.

It wasn't for lack of trying on the part of his senior executives. They dogged him to prepare for succession; the issue was on the agenda every year at the company's management meeting. Specialists gave seminars on succession and it became one of the company's most belabored items. But despite their suggestions and attempts to get him to work out a plan, Sam gave it nothing more than lip service through the years. His daughter Mitzi accused the executives of flaunting the issue in his face. Sam would get fed up and say to her, "Why don't they keep their minds on their jobs and stop worrying about succession? If they don't put their nose to the grindstone, there'll be nothing to succeed to."

Sam seemed to be going strong — his heart condition hadn't been detected yet — so perhaps he felt he had all the time in the world to make a decision, or that he'd never leave the picture. Sam procrastinated not just because the task was distasteful. It was a complex, daunting job to find someone who could come close to filling his shoes. He was a charismatic patriarch, a strong-willed personality who had fashioned the company in his own image. Who could envision a Steinberg company that wasn't run, wasn't completely dominated, by Mr. Sam?

For starters, where would he look for a successor? Should he go outside the family to professional managers? Should he look to his long-serving senior executives? Or should he stay within the family, in keeping with the tradition on which the company had been built? Even picking a family member meant conflict. From which branch should he select? For there were the families of his brothers to consider as well as his own. These were agonizing questions for Sam. It was a constant push and pull in terms of obligations to his family and obligations to the company and the employees.

In the late 1960s, although Steinberg was a full-grown business empire, its corporate culture was being shaped mainly by family concerns. It had gone public but only non-voting shares were traded on the stock exchange. The voting stock was privately held and Sam controlled every share with an iron grasp. He had gone in quest of public funds but had given nothing away. His philosophy about the relationship between the family and the company was just as it had been when he had helped his mother on The Main: the company had been created for the family and would continue to exist for the family.

The family was still the nucleus of power in the company. Key decision-making sessions took place not at company management meetings but rather at Helen and Sam's home during their Friday night Sabbath suppers. Understandably, non-family executives wondered just how much they counted in the enterprise. Ex-

ecutives like Harry Suffrin, who looked after the research department in the 1960s, would get a call Sunday morning from someone
conveying decisions that had been made Friday night. That created
resentment. What worsened things was Sam's apparent insen-
sitivity to the political aspects of the family's role in the enterprise.
Indeed, at that time so many family members were involved in the
company that it seemed awash in outright nepotism.

But how many were potential successors? At the senior level
there was Sam's brother, Nathan; Nathan's son, Arnold; and Sam's
son-in-law, Mel Dobrin, all vice-presidents. Apart from Arnold, a
Harvard MBA, none of them stood out as obvious presidential
material. Quite the opposite. There were too many family members in positions for which they were unsuited. Nor was there much
talent outside the family. "None of the men near the top in the food
end of the business were qualified to take over," said James Doyle,
Sam's former general counsel. "A lot of them were old-timers not
capable of running a big corporation. Many non-family executives
who might have been capable had left the company, believing they
had no future in such a family-dominated enterprise."

These concerns prompted Doyle to suggest to Sam that one day
he might have to sell the company. Sam didn't even want to hear
such notions. The company was created by and for the family and
that was where it would stay. That was where it belonged.

Without sons, Sam considered his next option: perhaps his sons-
in-law would resolve the succession problem; surely one might
prove to be the son he never had. He welcomed them into the
company with open arms. Ultimately they disappointed him.

There was Evelyn's husband, William Alexander. He had
worked first in the bakery and later on in Miracle Mart as a buyer.
His mien was dapper and polished; he was pleasant and gen-
tlemanly. But when it came to business, the bespectacled Billy was
ineffectual. "He's a bright boy," said Sam's brother Morris, "but he
was like a fish out of water in the company." Brahm Steinberg,
Alexander's boss at Miracle Mart, recalled that while Billy Alexander did a decent job in the general merchandise division he
wasn't good at making decisions. "He always liked other people to
help him. If someone said women's berets were to be strong one
season, he'd want to buy 50. I'd say, 'You've got to buy 500,' and
he'd shake on the spot."

William's son Jimmy maintained that his father had never wanted a position of serious responsibility in Miracle Mart but the projects he undertook were successful and he won virtually the largest bonuses for gross-profit margins within the division. He defended his father as a victim of difficult circumstances. While marketing director of Steinberg Foods he was plagued by an incompetent boss. Nevertheless, he did manage to create a number of successful product lines, including a big seller, Bon Matin bread. But there were labor problems in Steinberg Foods and those, too, worked against William Alexander. He left in the mid 1980s after some twenty-five years of service.

Len Pedvis, the first husband of Sam's daughter Marilyn, entered the company in the early 1950s, working at a variety of jobs such as butcher, cleaner, store manager, and zone manager. He was also involved in the Pinky Stamp program and had been a salesman. Cheerful and outgoing, he was highly effective in the latter job.

He had lofty ambitions in the business that he failed to realize. He had helped set up what later became the joint department-store venture between Vancouver-based Woodward's Stores and Steinberg. Sam had promised to make Len general manager of the new venture, then changed his mind after Woodward's insisted on naming its own man. Pedvis wasn't even included in the final trip to Vancouver where Woodward's executives met with Steinberg to map out a deal. Pedvis felt snubbed and quit in anger, perhaps hoping Sam would beg him to stay. But that didn't happen. Pedvis later divorced Marilyn and started his own business as a Montreal food broker. Like Alexander, Pedvis was a pleasant sort but didn't strike Sam as a presidential candidate.

Rita's husband was different. She married Leo Goldfarb in 1950, bringing into the family not only a flamboyant, high-voltage personality but also a shrewd and aggressive businessman. Sam liked Leo immediately and invited him into the company. Four years later he left the children's-wear business and joined Steinberg's real estate department, where people such as Arnold Steinberg; the future company president, Irving Ludmer; and future Quebec cabinet minister, John Ciaccia, worked under him.

Leo was a talented addition. He was bright and ambitious, and his skills at negotiating real estate deals were especially valuable to

Sam. Leo, who eventually became Steinberg's executive vice-president of corporate affairs, is credited with assembling the company's lucrative land portfolio as well as developing the entrepreneurial spirit that made the company's real estate arm, Ivanhoe Inc., truly succeed.

Within the company there were strong rumors that he would succeed Sam. But there were other pretenders too, including Sam's nephew Arnold Steinberg and another son-in-law, Mel Dobrin. Mel had married Sam's eldest daughter, Mitzi, and joined Steinberg in 1950. Like Leo Goldfarb, his star would also rise — straight, it turned out, toward the president's chair.

Mel Dobrin once said that Sam Steinberg had given him 99.99 percent of everything he had in life — including a wife. Indeed, Mitzi was Mel's path into the company and the status, fame, and wealth that went with it. When he met her in the late 1940s, his life changed dramatically.

He was born Mel Dobrinsky in 1923, the son of a Russian immigrant family of six children. His father worked as a tailor and his older brother Ben found a job as a commercial artist at Steinberg, where he would spend fifty-one years of his life working in the advertising department. During the Second World War Mel was a navigator in the air force, flying thirty-two bombing missions over Europe. He studied accounting at McGill University, and although he never finished his degree, seemed destined for a quiet career as a bean-counter.

It was brother Ben who played Cupid for Mel and Mitzi. Mel, a great sports fan, showed up one day at Ben's home with two tickets for a basketball game at McGill University but had no one to accompany him. Ben thought Sam's daughter Mitzi would make a good companion and suggested he call her — with only the warning that "she's a little short."

Mitzi accepted the invitation and the courtship began. The two went skiing in the Laurentian Mountains north of Montreal, spending ever-increasing amounts of time together. Suddenly, they were engaged. Ben called Sam and asked what he thought of his kid brother. "He's a nice boy," said Sam of the future president of his company.

In 1949 Mitzi and Mel were married in an elaborate wedding in the Normandy Room on top of the old Mount Royal Hotel, today a ritzy condo and shopping project, then one of the city's most prestigious hotels. Mel, who had shortened his name to Dobrin, took a job at Steinberg, starting out in the stores rather than crunching numbers in the accounting department. Ironically, given his background, it was an area he now wished to avoid.

Mel learned everything there was to know about the stores, taking the cash, working in the dairy, grocery, packing, and the meat departments. He rose steadily through the corporate ranks; then Sam named him vice-president and general manager of the Miracle Mart division. In 1962 he was elected to the company's board of directors. This was not a man whose career was in doubt. From day one he was a man being groomed.

But Sam also liked son-in-law Leo Goldfarb who, by coincidence, was Mel's best friend. It was Mel and Mitzi who first introduced Leo to Rita Steinberg. When Leo asked Mitzi if he could take Rita out, Mitzi was more than a bit skeptical because Leo, dashing, with dark, movie-star looks and fistfuls of charm, had a reputation as something of a Don Juan. But soon they were going steady and a year after Mel and Mitzi's Mount Royal Hotel wedding, Leo and Rita tied the knot at the same place.

Sam and Leo became close, travelling frequently together, and Sam liked to confide in his son-in-law. On a trip to Vancouver, Sam decided rather impetuously that Leo was the right man to succeed him. "I would like to give up the reins of the business and I would like you to take over," he told Leo. "But how do I do it? Mitzi is the oldest and Mel is the oldest married son-in-law." Sam was in a quandary. He knew he'd have a big fight on his hands if he named Leo. How would he break the news to Mel and Mitzi?

Leo and Mel couldn't have been more contrasting personalities. Mel was pleasant, quiet, capable and careful, an excellent administrator and organizer. But he was not the charismatic entrepreneur that Sam Steinberg was. He suffered, as family physician Mike Aronovitch put it, from the "Accountant Personality".

Leo, meanwhile, was cut from the same cloth as Sam. He was a gregarious, entertaining man who would have his real estate colleagues bent double laughing over his imitations of the personalities within the company. Leo was a quick decision-maker, with the dynamic, visionary toughness to head a company like Steinberg.

Mel was slower and liked to delegate. But he enjoyed several crucial advantages over Leo. First, he was a solid family man whose values appealed to Sam's wife Helen. In matters such as these, her influence weighed heavily. Second, Mel was married to Mitzi. When she heard Leo was in the running for the presidency, she effectively extinguished any chances he might have had.

Sam knew Mitzi would be a force to be reckoned with on this question. He told Leo of his dilemma then dumped the task of informing Mel and Mitzi right into the young man's lap. He wanted Leo to explain to Mel that while he, Leo, would become president, Mel would still have a senior role to play in the company. It was an unimaginably awkward situation, especially since Leo and Mel had been friends since boyhood. Leo still doesn't know why he agreed to do Sam's dirty work for him. But he went one night to the Dobrins' home, and in their furnished basement the discussion turned to the future. Finally Leo sucked in his breath and told them that Sam wanted him to become president "so we can move into the second generation of the family".

The Dobrins were not amused. There was no way they would stand for that arrangement, they informed him. Leo quickly backed off. "I'm sorry I came over," he said. "Let's forget about what I said. That's the end of it."

Mitzi Dobrin does not recall that meeting. What she does remember is that her father never felt completely at ease with Leo, but viewed him as a "smooth negotiator". According to her, there was never any contest between the two spouses because Sam never considered Leo a serious candidate. Unfortunately for the latter, the meeting was the beginning of the end of his days at Steinberg. The unpleasant encounter convinced him that there was no place for him at the top of Steinberg Inc.

At the same time, Leo was going through turbulent times in his personal life. His marriage to Rita was on the rocks; there were whispers that he was seeing another woman. What made it even more painful was that his wife was suffering from cancer. Leo feared the marital conflict would extend into his professional life: the last thing you did was ditch the boss's daughter. And Rita ensured that Sam was kept well informed about the latest upsets.

Sam was unable to prevent these personal troubles from intruding into the boardroom and Leo soon saw the writing on the wall.

He left in May 1968 after fourteen years with the company. A year later he divorced Rita.

In the meantime the succession issue remained as unresolved as ever.


On a raw gray winter's day in March 1969, Sam Steinberg and his fifteen senior executives began a three-day retreat at Palomino Lodge in the Laurentians just north of Montreal. The subject once again was succession. Sam was sixty-four years old and was stepping aside into the newly created post of chairman. He could no longer ignore the task of choosing his replacement. The company needed a president to succeed him — the first president other than Sam in its long history.

At Palomino, the executives established a list of qualities the new president would ideally possess. The list sounded like a portrait of Sam Steinberg: the candidate would have to be knowledgeable about the industry, a man with drive and vision, one with high ethical and moral standards.

The conference was a way for most of the men around the table to express, no matter how obliquely, their own personal ambitions. Most felt they would make good candidates for Sam's job. But in the end, there were really four serious contenders: Arnold Steinberg, James Doyle, Jack Levine, and Mel Dobrin. Irving Ludmer, just thirty-three at the time, realized the others thought him too young to be considered.

Part of the session was captured on film by producer Arthur Hammond of the National Film Board. He had unrestricted access to the meetings and his documentary, *The Corporation*, provides a valuable record of what transpired.

The executives used the session as a forum to air their beefs about how the company was being run. Jack Levine, then vice-president and general manager of the Quebec division, felt the corporation was vague in articulating its goals and insisted that the new president must be able to tie all sides of the business together. He was concerned about the lack of uniform direction in the company. The Ontario division was on its own, losing money; Miracle Mart was dragging down the Quebec division. Irving Ludmer noted that there was no professional management style in the company. Arnold Steinberg said huge investments such as the $4-million that had gone into the restaurant division were being made without a comprehensive decision-making plan.

The discussion grew candid and impassioned, reaching a crescendo over the issue of nepotism. Ludmer piped up and, with a glint in his eye, told the group how he saw things. "The standard joke is that the key decisions are not made at the management committee or with the president but at the Friday night supper." Responded Sam: "I just want to ask you one question: Is it your charm or ability that got you where you are now?"

Beneath the ripostes a serious question had been exposed: just where was the power in the company then — and where would it rest in the future? Mel, who had been curiously silent for most of the discussion, offered a contribution. "I'm the only relative who attends the family dinners," he protested, adding that he'd never seen other family members such as Arnold and Nathan there. The irony of his response was apparently lost on him at the time.

To James Doyle it was clear where the locus of power lay. He said the presence of non-family members on the management committee was mere tokenism. He likened it to having "Negroes in the Cabinet" where membership was "more for show than for performance".

Henry Mintzberg, a McGill management professor and expert on Steinberg, speculated there was a sort of hidden agenda to prevent Mel Dobrin from being named president, or at least to send Sam the message loud and clear that he should open the company up beyond family members. But Sam, who had remained uncharacteristically quiet throughout the discussion, spoke up after the family dinner comment and reminded everyone who was boss. "I don't need to have the family get together. One man has 100 percent control of this company. I don't have to ask anybody. I don't need anybody's approval."

On August 1, five months after the Palomino conference, he made his point even clearer. Melvyn Dobrin took over as the new president and Sam became chairman and chief executive. In the battle between non-family and family management, nepotism had triumphed.

As he called in the executives who had attended Palomino one by one to explain his choice, Sam admitted the role of the "family factor". His candor did not assuage their disappointment. For one executive, the words are still sharp, clear, and shocking, even twenty years later. "This is not the most qualified person we're selecting, Mel Dobrin," Sam told him. "It may be in the best interests of this corporation to have a professional manager. But I've had so much fun building and running this business that I wouldn't deprive my family of running it." By naming Mel president, Sam showed he would never waver from his view that family would always run the business. Sam was not emotionally capable of having it any other way.

There was speculation that another reason Sam ceded to Mel was pressure from Mitzi. According to Jack Levine, Mitzi told her father that if Mel didn't get the presidency she would move to Toronto, so Sam of course caved in and gave it to him. Mitzi dismissed the rumors, but the news of Mel's appointment came as no surprise to her.

She had long known the outcome of that Palomino session. When she was a child of twelve her father sat her down to discuss the business with her, as he did many times. The topic that day was succession. "There have been some opportunities to sell the company," he told his young daughter. "But I refused. I want it for your husband."

When Mitzi married Mel, Sam had his successor. It wasn't as simple as that, of course. Mel happened to possess the qualities Sam valued, chief among them trustworthiness. So Mel's appointment was a fait accompli from day one. It became his birthright. Mitzi admitted that her father couldn't have cared less whether Mel was the best person for the job. "I don't even think he even thought about who the best person was," she said. "Mel was the oldest daughter's husband. It was family."

Predictably the spurned executives who didn't belong to Sam's branch of the family were unhappy with his choice. To one company executive, Max Roytenberg, the ideal successor — the only candidate who could have saved the company from its later troubles — was veteran Jack Levine. Ironically, Levine was given just that task — saving Steinberg — some nine years later, when Sam suddenly died. But by that time, the organization's problems were so deeply entrenched that even he could not repair them.

The outcome of the Palomino session demonstrated to Arnold Steinberg that keeping the company "in the family" clearly meant not just in the Steinberg clan but within Sam's branch alone. Mel's appointment was difficult for Arnold to accept at first, for he had strong ambitions to run the company and Sam knew it. But Sam had some reservations about his Harvard-educated nephew. Arnold had acquired a patina of learning and sophistication that was terribly foreign to the street-wise Mr. Sam. Arnold knew all the important people in the world of high finance but Sam believed he didn't know how to get things done. As Mitzi Dobrin saw it, "Sam knew Arnold liked caviar but he didn't roll his sleeves up" and really pitch in.

There were many times when Sam would tear a strip off Arnold in front of other executives and the soft-spoken nephew would stand there helplessly and take it. In particular, Sam blamed him for the company's failed supermarket venture in France, the ill-fated Supermarché Montréal. "What really sealed his fate in my father's eyes," said Mitzi, "is that he came back from France by boat, first class. And my father said, 'That's Arnold.' "

Leon Danco, an American family business expert, emphasized in his book *Beyond Survival* that if a family enterprise is to make it into the next generation, the choice of a successor must be based on the future needs of the company and "not a replay of the requirements of the past". Sam Steinberg was interested only in replaying the past. He viewed Mel as an extension of himself, as an ally through whom he could continue to retain real power in the organization. It didn't really matter that Mel lacked his father-in-law's entrepreneurial instincts, leadership abilities, and charismatic personality. His real function, explained Henry Mintzberg, was to act as a kind of trustee of the family heirloom while Sam continued to run the show.

When Mel became president, Sam still made every call. He phoned in every day and would often pop into the office. Even when he was on holiday in Florida he would phone Mel four or five times a day. Mel Dobrin wielded no significant power in the company throughout his entire time there. Employees sometimes wondered exactly what he did all day; he seemed to make no important decisions at all. One Steinberg executive remembers being summoned by Mel for "an urgent meeting". What did the boss want? To get rid of an exercise machine that didn't fit into his new home.

Shortly after Mel was named president, Jack Levine was appointed executive vice-president of retailing and was given the same salary and job description as Mel. It was a subtle reminder that Mel was president in name only. Nonetheless, this dilution of his power didn't seem to bother him. "Mel is a very secure individual," said Mitzi. "He's very confident in what he does because he does it right." If Sam's involvement did not emasculate the new president, it did occasionally irritate him and continued to create confusion throughout the company. Too often, it seemed, the left hand of the company did not seem to know what the right hand was doing.

Mel Dobrin's appointment may have resolved Sam's worry over how to keep the company in family hands but for other executives it confirmed their fears that the company was still rife with nepotism and that it would continue to remain a comfortable enclave for the Steinberg family.

In consequence, Steinberg suffered a brain drain of highly talented executives with unquestionable presidential potential. Morgan McCammon, who acted as company real estate lawyer in the 1950s, was one of the presidential aspirants who left Steinberg because he felt he couldn't wait forever for a promotion. He joined Molson Breweries, a company that carefully limited nepotism. He later became president.

Sam seemed upset when he heard of McCammon's appointment, once telling his former executive sarcastically, "Well, it took you long enough to become president there, didn't it?" McCammon replied, "Do you think it would have happened any faster at your place, Sam?"

William Sherman was another casualty. He rose from clerk in the fruit department to executive vice-president, a post that suggested he was in line for the presidency. It was not to be. Sam summoned him to his office one day and informed him he was being removed from his post to make room for a family member.

Sherman went to Steinberg's rival, Loblaw Companies Ltd., where he headed its Ontario division in the 1970s.

Maurice Segall was another who left for bigger things, later becoming chief executive officer of a huge U.S.-based retailer, although he claimed it was not because he felt his ambitions were being stifled. Irving Ludmer, who would figure prominently in Steinberg's denouement, also saw a dead end ahead and left in 1971 to form his own real estate company.

Mel remained president until Sam's death in 1978. Then he was bumped up to chairman and Jack Levine became president. By many accounts, the legacy of Mel Dobrin was mediocrity. A number of executives spoke of his pleasant character but were hard-pressed to identify any discernible impact he had had during his reign. He kept his distance from the day-to-day operations and he delegated.

His years were marked by a lack of strategic direction. Arnold Steinberg recalled that under Mel, direction did not come from the top but from the middle or bottom. "In many cases, Mel was simply bypassed and not necessarily unhappy about it." He gave no evidence of leadership. "There was never a meeting that I can recall in all those years where he initiated a strategic direction for the company," said Arnold, "and it suffered as a result." Under his stewardship, the company had a "bottom line mentality" that stressed profits rather than investment. Few new stores opened; few were renovated.

Mel's management style was a world apart from that of his father-in-law. While Sam was strong-minded, domineering, and combative, Mel was pleasant, diplomatic, a consensus maker. Sam was involved in every aspect of the supermarkets; Mel was distant, hands-off. "He hid behind committees," said Sam's nephew, David Steinberg. When Sam was president, he used to pop in unexpectedly on meetings at the Hochelaga offices and start peppering executives with questions. Mel did nothing of the sort. Sam used to visit his stores religiously, on his way home from the golf course, from work. Mel was not a common sight in the stores. David Steinberg believed that if Mel had had his druthers, he never would have taken the job; he took it solely out of obligation.

If Sam so badly wanted the company to flourish after he was gone, why did he select a successor who was clearly not up to the challenge and who possibly did not even want it? Perhaps Sam felt that no one could do as good a job as he could, so at least it should be left with family. Sam's nephew Brahm Steinberg remembered discussing his uncle with a psychiatrist friend. The psychiatrist believed that a powerful, ego-driven chief executive often prefers to leave his business to somebody weaker so that, later, people will say that only the boss could handle the job.

In Sam's case, keeping it all in the family was probably his principal motivation, almost an obsession. It was almost as if Sam was afraid someone might steal his company.

Family business experts acknowledge the difficulty Sam faced in naming his successor. The family business isn't a sandbox that everybody can play in, says U.S. author Leon Danco. The founder must decide what the entrance rules are going to be. David Gallagher, a Toronto-based consultant and managing director of the Canadian Association of Family Enterprise (CAFE), observes, "If you're going to have unmitigated nepotism, you might as well sell the business, and sell it while it's worth [something]."

A family entrepreneur like Sam must stop believing that his family shares his business genius, says Henry Mintzberg. "Children shouldn't run companies just because their parents did. It's like [Russian] roulette. You put bullets in the chamber, sometimes it fires, sometimes it doesn't."

Evidence from similar cases, and the advice of expert consultants in this area, suggest that Steinberg's biggest blunder was its failure to hire professional management from outside the family. But how would anybody have convinced Sam Steinberg to hire an outsider to run the cherished family business? The Sam Steinbergs of the world are awfully stubborn about their approach to life, Gallagher said. That's what got them to where they are — their narrow, precisely focused vision, their single-minded, unswerving view of their objective. After thirty or forty years of following their own opinions, they do not suddenly abandon that habit and start to heed other people's advice.

Some family-owned business empires have managed to deal successfully with these issues. The Eatons, owners of Canada's preeminent department-store chain, have a policy whereby employees, not family members, vote to determine which member of the Eaton family should assume the chief executive's mantle. Nothing counts but competence and respect from the employees. The Molsons, owners of Canada's oldest brewery, have had a long-standing tradition that only one junior member of the family is active in the business at any one time. Other Molsons have to make their mark elsewhere.

At the Montreal jewelry empire of Henry Birks & Sons Ltd., a policy stipulates that if you are going to own voting shares in the business, you must be active in it. That policy was enforced in late 1989 and early 1990 when two of the three controlling shareholders, Barrie and Thomas Birks, sold their shares to the eldest brother Jonathan, leaving him with all the company's voting stock and them without their jobs.

Other consultants point to enlightened families whose formally stated policy is that none of the offspring will work in the business unless they have proven themselves elsewhere, outside the family, first.

But in many cases there is just no one in the next generation of family capable of doing the job. This is a very difficult pill to swallow. But according to Herbert Siblin, a Montreal management consultant, "with wealth and affluence, many families don't generate the inner drive in their children in business." What's more, the qualities it takes to found a business are different from those required to keep it going. There comes a time when entrepreneurship must give way to a more professional style of management.

Unrestricted nepotism can place family members in a very difficult position. "One can see lots of children in successful businesses who are living in gilded cages," Siblin said. "They hate what they do, at least they're bored, they're under great stress." And — the ultimate irony — they do *not* necessarily bring unity or share identical visions, which is why the founder avoided hiring outsiders in the first place. According to CAFE's David Gallagher, family members often come in with totally different agendas. Once the founder dies, the squabbles begin: everyone has a different idea of what should be done.

Sam's failure to heed such advice took its toll after his death. The squabbling between the surviving family members and the professional managers increased and the company drifted, rudderless, into the 1980s.

Decades ago, when Leo Goldfarb was still active in Steinberg, he took a trip to Vancouver with Sam. They briefly discussed nepotism. "I told him, 'You can't put every member of the family into the business at the top. The best investment we can make is to get some key people at the top. The family will benefit from what these people will do and we'll develop an organization. Otherwise you'll destroy the business.' "

Sam's response still reverberates, clear and sharp, in Goldfarb's mind. It chilled him. "That business was built specifically for my family," Sam told him. "Anybody who wants to come in, there's an open place for him. If the business is destroyed as a result of that, so be it."

His words very nearly became prophetic.

# 7

# Death in the Family

It was 1970 and Rita Goldfarb was ill — again. A year and a half earlier, following the detection of breast cancer, the second eldest of Sam and Helen's four daughters had undergone a mastectomy. It had been an apparent success and Rita had felt fine, but now she felt frighteningly severe pains. She gathered her courage and went to the doctor, who confirmed her worst fears: the cancer had invaded her liver and she had three months to live. This news came shortly after her marriage to Leo had crumbled.

Rita's family sprang into action, trying to find her the best medical care possible. They flew her down to a cancer congress in Texas to visit a specialist; they visited the Sloane-Kettering cancer institute in New York. During the illness Helen stayed in her home every day, cooking and caring for the three Goldfarb children, Eileen, Robert, and Gail. All the while Rita, who had once told her sister Mitzi that she knew she would die of cancer, tried to deny the gravity of her illness. "It's not malignant," she said valiantly as she arrived at the Texas congress. She tried to keep up her appearance. But nothing, not positive thinking nor the finest medical care money could buy, could help her. In 1970 Rita died at the age of thirty-eight.

Her family was shattered by her death. Sam was especially affected, not only emotionally but spiritually, his religious faith seriously rocked. He could not understand how a loving God would take away his girl when she was just thirty-eight. A child wasn't supposed to die before her parents did; it wasn't right.

Marilyn believed her sister's death marked the beginning of his eventual deterioration.

It was a bleak way to begin the decade, such a contrast from the heady and hopeful way the 1960s had begun. Yet Rita's death was only the beginning of the darkest period for the Steinberg name.

By now, Mr. Sam's daily presence in the company was fading. His son-in-law Mel Dobrin was president and Sam was leaving more of the company's everyday business affairs to management. He spent more time on the golf course and at his place in Bal Harbor, Florida.

Yet although Sam became distanced from the minutiae of the company, it was clear he never really retired. The standing joke was that if you wanted to know whether Sam was coming in on a particular day, you just had to note whether the executives had their best suits on. If a major decision had to be made, he was still involved. Like that of an absentee landlord, his influence pervaded the company even from afar. His executives knew that when push came to shove, they would have to run to Sam for approval on the important matters.

Even so, at times Sam's gradual removal from the daily affairs of the company gave his executives a false sense of security. They discovered how heavily they relied on him when they tried to hold back details of a particular problem, wrongly believing they could handle it themselves. One time when they didn't keep Sam informed, they paid for it heavily. The company's Cartier sugar subsidiary wound up losing $9 million in 1972, after executives failed to brief Sam properly on their complex "hedging" operations in the sugar market.

It was only natural that even in retirement Sam would not sever ties with the company that had been his lifework. Another reason why he kept his hands on the controls was to avoid facing the inevitability of his own mortality. By staying involved in the company, he kept up the charade that he could run the show forever.

Sam's age was beginning to show. In the last years of his life his behavior became increasingly erratic. Once he sneaked up on a clerk who was piling boxes to make a display in one of the stores. For some reason Sam didn't like it and he knocked it all apart. His physical health was getting worse, and much as he tried to ignore it, he had a heart problem. In 1976, the year Montreal hosted the summer Olympics, Sam attended a soccer match at the Olympic Stadium when suddenly he was stricken by a sharp pain in his chest. He waited a bit. It passed and he finished watching the game. The incident frightened him into paying a visit to his doctor. The doctors diagnosed angina and suggested a bypass operation. Sam shuddered. What if he was left an invalid? The mere thought of becoming a sick man who had to be looked after was appalling, a tremendous affront to his treasured personal dignity. In part, it was mere vanity. He had always insisted on being properly dressed and well-groomed. So instead of surgery, Sam watched his diet, took his pills, and vowed to take life easier. Helen's luscious desserts made it difficult for him to discipline himself far.

Of course, Sam could never take things *too* much easier. Although he had slowed down his fierce creative drive still burned and that meant there were new business ventures to try. On May 2, 1978, Steinberg opened its first "super-combo" store in Rosemere, north of Montreal. It was a giant store where you could get hardware and groceries all in the same 60,000-square-foot lot, and he was terribly proud of it. It would be his final display of entrepreneurship.

On May 23, Sam was in his warehouse giving out length-of-service pins to employees who had missed the banquet several days before. That afternoon he suffered chest pains severe enough for him to call Marilyn, who in turn quickly placed a call to Mitzi to say their father was not well. Marilyn recalled that her sister was tied up with something that day, so she rushed over herself to drive her father to Montreal's Jewish General Hospital. Nobody knew how seriously ill he really was, least of all Sam. He didn't believe he was going to die. But a day later he did at the age of seventy-two.

His sudden death stunned the family and the company. Normal life was suspended for everyone. Sam's brother Nathan, his lifelong confidant and soulmate, had just arrived at the hospital that day to visit him but it was too late. As he rushed out of the hospital elevator he ran into Helen, who said quietly, "We lost Sam." The news broke him. Helen, Sam's wife of fifty years, never totally recovered either. Evie, in Florida at the time, flew home in the private jet of Charles Bronfman, who had had it sent down specially for her.

The news sent shock waves through the company, as employees mourned their boss and surrogate father. But through their grief, the employees honored the man in their own small ways. One worker cut short a vacation to come back in time for the funeral. Two drivers, Maurice Maisonneuve and Henri Audet, collected $261.50 from the warehouse drivers, a group that Sam was particularly fond of, to donate to the Heart Foundation. This was not the death of just any boss; it was a death in the family. The man who knew his workers by their first name, who visited them when they were sick, who considered himself one of them, was gone. From the grocery stores to the executive suites, the sense of loss was profound.

Tributes streamed in from across the province, from anglophones and francophones alike. Pierre Laurin, then head of Montreal's respected business school, École des hautes études commerciales and who ironically played a role in the takeover battle for the company a decade later, wrote in *The Gazette*, "I am proud to share my title of 'Québécois' with Sam Steinberg."

The funeral was held at Westmount's Shaar Hashomayim Synagogue, an unusual move in view of the synagogue's holiness. A Jewish funeral was usually held at a funeral parlor, but the family feared there wouldn't be enough room at the funeral home and they were right. Between 1,500 and 2,000 people showed up that brilliantly sunny May day to pay their respects to the little man who had so touched their lives. There were the Steinberg family members, of course, as well as dignitaries from government, politics, and business. Seagram's heir, Charles Bronfman, attended, as did Senator Leo Kolber, Montreal businessman Paul Desmarais, and then federal Liberal cabinet minister Monique Bégin, who had once worked in the personnel department of Steinberg. The supermarket workers turned up by the hundreds, dressed in their uniforms as a show of respect.

It was so hard to come to terms with Sam's death. How could a man like Sam, forever on the move, his mind always racing miles ahead of everyone else's, be dead? You didn't associate Sam with death. He was too lively; he never wanted to slow down. Of course he was the life of the company, too, and after he died it became pervaded by a sense of aimlessness, emptiness. It was as if the soul had left the company. The question on everyone's minds became,

What do we do now? Indeed. Although trouble had been mounting before Sam died, his charismatic presence had always reassured people that somehow the problems would be solved. Now he was gone, without having groomed a successor.

Mitzi Dobrin and her husband Mel, then president, were as unprepared as everyone else for Sam's death but moved swiftly to fill the void. Barely two weeks later, Mel became chairman and chief executive while Jack Levine, Steinberg's executive vice-president of retailing and a forty-year veteran of the company, was named the new president.

The quick appointments helped to convey a sense of continuity and competence to the outside world, even if on the inside Steinberg was a mess of grief, confusion, and unease. To a degree, the image was successfully maintained. Consumers still perceived it as *the* Quebec grocery chain and "doing your Steinberg" was still part of the everyday language. The competition raided it regularly for ideas and for staff.

But one didn't have to scratch the surface too deeply to realize what an illusion it all was. At the time of Sam's death the company was just coasting, its revenues rising only with inflation, and paying little attention to such things as maintenance and training programs. By July 1978, the end of its fiscal year, sales were off at Miracle Mart and Cartier Sugar, there was a loss at its catalogue showroom company Cardinal Distribution, and profits in the Ontario Miracle Food Mart stores were down. The company was on the fast track to disaster and for the first time there was no Mr. Sam to rescue it.

As the new era began, the biggest challenge to the company was its Quebec grocery business, its very backbone. By 1978 the familiar corporate chains — Steinberg, Dominion, A & P — no longer dominated the Quebec marketplace. Two companies, Provigo and Métro-Richelieu, had muscled in on previously sacred territory with a different format that would eventually knock Steinberg, once the Quebec leader, back to a humiliating third place.

Provigo and Métro-Richelieu were essentially food wholesalers that supplied independent grocery stores at cost plus a management fee. In return for operating under the wholesalers' names and benefiting from their marketing support, the independents turned over a cut of their sales revenues. The wholesalers could keep their labor costs low and could then pass their savings on to the consumer. This was the way of the future in Quebec's competitive grocery business, far more cost-efficient than the cumbersome system of corporate-owned stores Steinberg operated.

Provigo was created in 1969 following the merger of three small regional food wholesalers — Couvrette & Provost, which served Montreal and Ottawa; Denault, which covered Sherbrooke and Trois-Rivières; and Lamontagne, with Quebec City, the North Shore, and Saguenay-Lac St-Jean. The new entity also had the backing of Quebec's powerful pension-fund manager, the Caisse de dépôt et placement. There was considerable skepticism as to whether three small companies could operate successfully as one, but Provigo was growing faster than it had predicted itself, and by 1978, sales had shot up to over $1-billion.

Métro-Richelieu evolved out of a series of cooperative buying groups. In 1976 Métro and Richelieu, two wholesalers owned by their retailers, had merged. They operated on a cooperative system of one retailer, one vote. (In 1982 Métro and Richelieu merged with Les Épiciers unis, another Quebec City wholesaler owned by its retailers.)

After some years flying under the banners of Provigo and Métro-Richelieu, the series of mom-and-pop stores scattered through the province were becoming a powerful competitive force for Steinberg. The stores were owned by individual entrepreneurs, and now that they had the backing of marketable names they were hungry to give Steinberg a run for its money.

This was the backdrop against which new president Jack Levine took over. Like so many of Steinberg's executives, he was a Horatio Alger figure who began in the company as a poor, uneducated kid with humble roots. By dint of sweat, dedication, and dogged determination, he had managed to rise from stock boy to company president.

Levine joined Steinberg in the 1930s when he was seventeen. These were the Depression years, when youngsters shelved university plans to work and support their families. He began at a fruit store on Sherbrooke Street, the hours endless and the pay just $15 a week. On Fridays, he would stay till 10:00 or 11:00 at night and his Saturday shift would sometimes end at 1:00 a.m. Sunday.

There was no time for a personal life, as Levine found out shortly after he started. On a sunny Saturday afternoon, Sam had called him in to take stock at another nearby store. Levine didn't want to go because he had arranged to take out a girl on a picnic. Sam said not to worry, the work would only keep him about two hours. But Levine was detained and missed his date, who spurned him forever.

Despite that painful beginning, Jack Levine developed an enduring friendship with Sam Steinberg. It was an unusual liaison, at times almost a love-hate relationship. Early in his career with Steinberg, Levine demonstrated that he was not one to be pushed around. One summer soon after joining the company, he had his first "serious" discussion with Sam. He was sitting outside the store eating his lunch and reading when Sam came by and demanded to know what he was doing. Levine told him without flinching, "It's my lunch hour." Sam responded: "Don't you ever sit outside! People will think we're closed!" "But it's my lunch hour," he repeated. "You can't tell me where to sit." Rejoined Sam, "Oh yes I can. You're working for me, and the impression you're conveying is all wrong." That was one of the first of many heated discussions they would have over the years. In a way Sam liked that. The more you challenged him, the more he respected you.

As a manager, Jack Levine was a strange, complex character whose subordinates often found him difficult to deal with. He could be confrontational, irascible, intense. Employees learned that the barometer of his moods was his pipe. If it lay packed and resting on his desk, his mood was good. If he was chomping on it intently and it belched out smoke, fireworks were ahead.

He was often clumsy with words. His former colleague Max Roytenberg remarked, "He had difficulty putting words together in a stream we'd accept as the way to converse. There were malapropisms, unfinished sentences, elliptical communication." Feedback was almost never provided; certainly praise was never offered. Levine related best with the people he grew up with — the boys of the street, the men who shared a common background with him and with whom words weren't always necessary.

Whatever his social shortcomings, the family felt Levine had earned the position of president. In his many years at Steinberg he had taken risks, delegated responsibility effectively and had got things done. He worked his staff to death but they respected his own capacity for hard work, his ability, rough-hewn though it was, and, above all, his loyalty and single-minded dedication to the company. Levine put in long hours and like Sam, he traveled around North America in search of innovations to make Steinberg the best it could be. He was tremendously motivated to learn, perhaps to compensate for his own modest background. He taught himself about virtually every aspect of merchandising and came to be regarded as one of the top food retailers in North America.

Levine brought a sense of vision to Steinberg. As divisional manager he made a point of hiring university graduates, something of a precedent in a nickel-and-dime environment where life was rough-and-ready, educational levels were low, and performance meant everything. That was progressive thinking for someone with no university education himself. It certainly was a contrast to Sam, who never fully trusted those with a college degree.

Levine brought his interest in personal self-improvement to the company. His pet area was behavioral science and he introduced the company to such concepts as "re-evaluation counselling" and transactional analysis, which stressed the nurturing and development of the individual psyche as the key to a happy corporation. This was radical, touchy-feely stuff for a company built by down-to-earth, unpretentious people who believed the tools for corporate success consisted of a good gut instinct for business and a lot of sweat and toil. Jack's methods raised more than a few eyebrows and some dismissed them as gimmickry and silly psychobabble.

However, there was far more to Levine than a yen for 1970s pop-psychology schemes. When it came to merchandising, his feet were planted firmly on the ground. He was the brain behind a number of key programs, most notably the "Miracle Pricing" scheme Steinberg had introduced into the supermarkets in the late 1960s. The program slashed prices by getting rid of expensive advertising budgets. It was a miracle in more than name, credited with bringing the company out of the slump it had fallen into by the late 1960s.

Miracle Pricing, first introduced in Ontario, was an enormous success. When it was imported to the Quebec supermarkets, the results were just as spectacular. As Steinberg had anticipated, the program took a toll on its profits in fiscal 1969, but they rebounded and increased by a whopping 58 percent the following year to over $9-million. Sales reached a record $679-million.

Although such accomplishments had demonstrated to Sam that Levine was a prize asset in the company, the relationship between the two men was not always peaceful. They were two headstrong, stubborn personalities and they had definite differences of opinion and some explosive fights. Sometimes Sam would win, sometimes Levine. Shouting matches were common but Levine knew other techniques besides raising his voice. He was deft at getting what he wanted, even from the strong-willed Sam.

Levine's most crucial characteristic was his devotion to Sam, which was as strong as that of any family member, sometimes even more so. It was Jack, not any of the children, who had organized Sam's seventieth birthday party in 1975. It was Jack who put together Sam and Helen's fortieth-anniversary celebration in Florida.

For many years Levine saw himself as the Number Two man in Steinberg, even when technically he might have reported to someone else. For his part, Sam respected Levine tremendously because of his strong convictions and his boldness in expressing them. Sam liked that sort of directness in a person. Levine had spent many years at the divisional level of Steinberg, but during the 1970s he started moving up the corporate ladder in earnest. By 1971 he was promoted to head office as executive vice-president of retailing. At most companies that meant you had a good shot at the presidency. But as senior as he was, he was not a member of the Steinberg family. When he was bypassed for Mel Dobrin after the 1969 Palomino retreat, he decided to drop all remaining presidential ambitions. He even told Sam Steinberg that whenever Sam passed away, he would likely retire but would agree to act as a consultant.

So when Sam died in 1978 and Mel was bumped up to chairman, Levine accepted the presidential appointment almost reluctantly, more as a favor to his late friend than out of any desire for the position. He just didn't have the heart to say no. Apart from Sam, Jack probably knew more than anybody in the company about merchandising. But his agreement to stay on was based on one condition: that he would have full support from Mitzi Dobrin.

Their past was rocky, and besides he knew where the power really was in the company now.

The trouble between Mitzi and Jack had begun in 1973 when Sam brought his eldest daughter into the company to run the Miracle Mart department store chain. Jack, never one to couch his opinions in gentle terms, had told Sam point-blank then that the decision was a rotten one. Later he told Mitzi herself that she didn't know how to handle people and that Miracle Mart was suffering as a result. He was taken aback by her response. "She said, 'What are you talking about? I was captain of my golf club.'" Mitzi never forgave him for his objections. On another occasion Jack approached Helen Steinberg in Florida and told her, in confidence, that Mitzi should never be allowed to become company president. Helen related that conversation to Mitzi and the antagonism between them worsened.

With such a history behind them, it was not surprising that Levine and Mitzi should spar once he was named president. He later claimed the promised support from Mitzi was never forthcoming and in fact lacked in all respects. Mitzi disputed Jack's perceptions, affirming that her husband Mel supported him but that Jack was too much of a one-man show who failed to nurture his staff and who continually suspected her of trying to unseat him.

It all made for a presidential tenure that was "lousy", in Jack's words. Here he was, a man who had been Sam's right-hand man for years, and now, as president — a position he took just for Sam — nobody was taking him seriously. People bypassed him when they wanted financing or approval on decisions. The truth was, nobody viewed him as a bona fide president. He was merely a caretaker with no real influence or authority. It was an interregnum, a time where everyone was waiting for a new God, another Mr. Sam, and Levine was perceived as someone just marking time until that figure could be found. Executives jockeyed for position and waited for life "After Jack Levine".

It was a particularly difficult time to be president because it meant bearing the enormous burden of filling Sam Steinberg's shoes. Three years after his death the patriarch had hardly faded from memory. Mr. Sam's presence was still felt everywhere. People used his name to protect themselves or to prove a point, arguing, "Sam would do things *this* way. . . ." It was a company beset by chaos, a place where the improvisation, indecision, and lack of direction hit you like a blow to the face.

If nobody gave a damn about Jack Levine, people did care about Mitzi Dobrin. With her powerful multiple roles as the founder's daughter, the chairman's wife, and a controlling shareholder of the company, it was worth cultivating her friendship and approval if one harbored ambitions. One person who did so was Gerry Spitzer, executive vice-president of food retailing and a long-time company employee. He wanted to be president and for a time rumor had it that Mitzi had promised him the job. It was certainly Spitzer's perception that he was a candidate, and soon junior executives began cozying up to him. In Levine's mind, however, Spitzer was too close to Mitzi and not presidential material.

While Spitzer and others tried to curry favor with Mitzi, she and Jack continued to be at odds. Some employees felt that, deep down Mitzi resented Jack's abiding friendship with her father. Senior management committee meetings became a forum for cutting exchanges between the two and general quarreling. She remembered once questioning a shocking report by the audit committee that sharply criticized the receiving practices in the food warehouses, and asked if it was accurate. Jack snapped, "You look after your Miracle Mart. Don't question this report." One senior executive became so disgusted by the meetings, which he termed "institutionalized futility", that he stopped attending them.

While the politicking continued, other aspects of the business were neglected. The message in the company's 1978 annual report read, "In [Sam's] business philosophy, change was the one sure constant in business life; complacency was the deadly sin." Now, it seemed as if the deadly sin was firmly rooted in the company. The decision-making process was pathetically disorganized, sidetracked by the internal wrangling, with no one taking responsibility. Store renovations ceased. Management appeared to concentrate exclusively on profits, ignoring not only key needs within the company but the changing marketplace outside. They completely lost sight of what was going on outside Steinberg, as if they were locked away in some ivory tower, high above the real world.

The company may have been able to get away with ignoring the competition in the fabulous sixties, but not in the late seventies and early eighties when the complexion of Quebec's food industry

changed so dramatically. The assumption that things in Quebec
would always be as they were in Ontario, where independents were
content with their tiny portion of the food market, did not hold.

During the early 1980s, Provigo and Métro-Richelieu continued
to take away big chunks of market share from Steinberg. Provigo
scored a big coup in 1980 when it bought 87 of the 89 Dominion
stores in Quebec. With almost all of those supermarkets in
Montreal, Provigo had, in one fell swoop, gained a huge foothold in
the market that for years had been dominated by Steinberg. And by
the early 1980s the unthinkable had happened: Steinberg had slipped to third position in Quebec after Provigo and Métro-Richelieu.
Expansion in Ontario was stalled and at Miracle Mart the problems
mounted.

The listlessness, the jockeying for power, and the performance
problems were clearly side-effects of Sam's death and his failure to
prepare the company for life without him. Steinberg after Sam was
a company in search of a new leader, a new identity, and a new
mission just as the whole grocery industry was being turned upside
down.

In 1982 Jack Levine announced his retirement, and once again the
company had to find a new leader. As it turned out, Gerry Spitzer
did not become the next president. Instead, for the first time in
Steinberg's history, management decided to look outside.

The decision marked a significant turning point for the company. It was an acknowledgement that Steinberg had grown so big,
with $2.8-billion in sales in 1981, that it could no longer be run in
the entrepreneurial, family-business style of Mr. Sam.

Steinberg was still very much a family enterprise, however.
Family members still owned the voting stock, they still occupied
key management positions, and they still made the key decisions.
The choice of the company's next president would be made exclusively by Mitzi and Mel Dobrin. Jack Levine and the company's
board of directors wouldn't even find out about it until after the
fact.

The Dobrins enlisted headhunters to help them in their search
for a supermarket executive with presidential experience. Finally,
in October 1982, Mel Dobrin announced the company's selection:

Peter McGoldrick, the fifty-three-year-old chairman of a small Virginia food-store chain. He was given a five-year contract to turn the beleaguered company around.

He cut an impressive figure. Peter McGoldrick was a tall, friendly, hail-fellow-well-met character with a deep resonant voice, and plenty of "presence". Given his charm, together with the seriousness of the company's situation, employees at corporate headquarters were ready to accord him respect. He was perceived as a good manager with the toughness to take on the unions, which were gaining more power. When he was introduced at a senior management meeting, those who were present remember him as supremely self-confident and outgoing. And if his Montreal employees liked him at the start, McGoldrick liked Montreal back — particularly its nightlife.

He was greeted warmly and with great anticipation. Perhaps he would be the one to stop the company's downhill slide. He wasn't perfect; his colleagues described him as having high blood pressure and an Irish temper. Furthermore, he had no knowledge of the Quebec food industry and spoke no French. But whatever his flaws, Peter McGoldrick offered hope.

The honeymoon ended abruptly. The politicking at Steinberg was still intense and instead of starting to pull together, the middle managers kept up their infighting. Everyone wanted to carve his place in the new administration. Knives were flying high. Those who thought *they* should have inherited the presidential mantle undercut McGoldrick while others let him know who the real bosses were: the Steinberg family. If he had their respect at the beginning, it was short-lived. "He was not given the proper tools to turn Steinberg around," recalled one executive who lived through that troubled era.

McGoldrick met his Waterloo when the company hatched an ill-considered scheme to give customers five-percent rebates on their grocery purchases. The plan was conceived at a time when Steinberg was limping badly. Sales in the Quebec division, which once topped $28-million to $30-million a week, had tumbled to less than $24 million a week. Morale sagged along with the business figures. During those times of struggle, a young Steinberg executive named Marvin Biltis had gone to Harvard University to take an advanced management program. When he returned, he was flushed with excitement. He had the quick fix, the magic potion Steinberg craved to turn its fortunes around. Biltis's idea was to give 5-percent rebates to customers on their grocery bills in the form of coupons like those at Canadian Tire. To compensate for the lost revenue, he advocated the company should stop all its weekly specials. Giddy with excitement, Biltis had it all figured out: by stopping the weekly specials, the company would save 4 percent. So the bottom line was, the 5-percent scheme would really only cost 1 percent, while attracting throngs of new customers to Steinberg. The reasoning was that they could move prices back up again after the program had increased their market share.

Biltis figured the competition would be shellshocked, just as it had been during the late 1960s when Steinberg unveiled its Miracle Pricing program. Weak, poorly organized, and with little buying power in those days, the independents had barely flinched when Miracle Pricing came along. Because Steinberg hadn't turned the makeover into a splashy event, the chains, too, had largely ignored it, refusing to perceive it as a threat. So the stores had thundered ahead, unchallenged, for almost two years. The prices were so attractive that even the wives of Dominion Stores executives shopped there, their loyalties evidently resting with their pocketbooks.

The competition's failure to heed Miracle Pricing caused the Dominion and Loblaws chains to suffer substantial drops in sales and market share. Only in November 1970 did Dominion finally respond with its own discount selling. It then conceived its famous "Mainly because of the meat" slogan. Steinberg hit back with its "Monsieur Pierre" butcher campaign.

But the plight of the chains was nothing compared to the independent stores, which were savaged. According to Mintzberg and Waters, in two years almost 1,700 Quebec independents — almost 16 percent of them — had to shut their doors.

The architects of the 5-percent program believed this would happen a second time around. As it turned out, the concept was seriously flawed. Its creators glossed over the possibility that the 5-percent program might fail to bring in the necessary sales volumes. The comptroller in the Quebec division said there was no way it would work. Despite their doubts, the executives who raised concerns were not given a hearing. They were told simply that all the details had been worked out.

More importantly, Steinberg seriously underestimated the competition. The independents were better organized and able to react. They also had long memories. They had never forgiven Steinberg for the Miracle Pricing debacle and would not make the same mistake twice.

Nonetheless, on March 2, 1983, the program was unveiled: customers received discount coupons, or "Steinberg money", entitling them to five percent off their next purchase at Steinberg. The coupons had been printed in secrecy and every effort was made to prevent information leaks. Steinberg clearly expected a dramatic impact from the announcement.

To say the program was disastrous is an understatement. Steinberg coupons had barely hit the street before the competition responded, touching off a full-fledged price war. The Métro-Richelieu chain immediately announced it would match Steinberg's discounts. Its president, Jean-René Halde, even went so far as to phone reporters at Montreal newspapers himself to ensure the message got out. Métro-Richelieu didn't even take the time to issue coupons, simply stamping customers' cash-register tapes so that five percent would be refunded to them on future purchases. The very next day, Provigo responded with a deeper discount of six percent, in cash. "This will be in real dollars," declared the president of Provigo, Pierre Lessard.

Supermarket-industry analysts were horrified at what was taking place. No grocery chain was making enough money to trim its prices by 5 percent and still stay profitable, least of all Steinberg, then hobbling along in third place behind Provigo and Métro-Richelieu. The most profit before taxes that a typical chain could hope for — and this is true even today — was between 1 and 2 percent of its sales. Steinberg's pre-tax profit at the time was 1.8 percent. The 5 percent rebate meant it was losing $3.20 on every $100 of sales. It had to increase its sales astronomically to make the program pay off.

Owing to the nimble response of its competitors, Steinberg never succeeded in stealing away their customers or in boosting its sales sufficiently to pay for the program. Three months after announcing the program, Steinberg bailed out, and shortly thereafter the competition followed suit. Analysts estimated the price wars cost the Quebec supermarket operators $50-million in pre-tax profit. The damage to Steinberg was heaviest: about $18-million in pre-tax profit.

Steinberg had not only lost the war and huge sums of money; it lost prestige. Company morale hit rock bottom, especially on the front lines. It was like one more tug on a spring that had already been stretched to the snapping point. Sooner or later it wasn't going to spring back. The eager and optimistic masterminds of the program, Marvin Biltis, Gerry Spitzer, and Guy Massé, vice-president of marketing, became its casualties. Biltis and Massé were both demoted and Spitzer later quit.

The one who really took it in the chin, of course, was Peter McGoldrick, who had given the 5-percent program the go-ahead. Inside the company the coupons were mockingly referred to as "McGoldrick Money"; outside, the press was merciless. The Montreal *Gazette* published a caricature of McGoldrick flapping around like a turkey. This disaster was the last blow the beleaguered president needed. During the past year there had been costly strikes at the Montreal supermarkets and at some Miracle Mart stores. The company's big bakery shut down for good. McGoldrick's wife Mary was also seriously ill. His whole life seemed to be crumbling around him.

But the corporate world is an unforgiving place, and in early March 1984, just seventeen months after signing a five-year contract to resuscitate Steinberg, McGoldrick tendered his resignation and a settlement was reached on the unexpired portion of his contract. Shortly after, he and Mary returned to the United States. To this day, his brief reign is still regarded as a fiasco. Under his leadership, profits plunged to $13.4-million in 1983, their lowest since 1975. The only reason Steinberg continued to make money was the financial contribution it received from its profitable real estate subsidiary, Ivanhoe Inc.

Because McGoldrick left on such a dismal note, many lost sight of any positive contribution he made to the company. But Gaetan Frigon, a marketing executive who worked with McGoldrick, pointed out he turned the Quebec division into a better-managed place. Former treasurer Bill Howieson, too, offered a more balanced assessment of his performance. "Actually, McGoldrick did not fail miserably," he said. "He did a superb job in the Ontario division. He was beginning to do quite a good job in the Quebec

division. Given time, he would have done a great deal for it."
McGoldrick never got the chance. The five-percent scheme was
such a public corporate gaffe that it eclipsed his other accomplishments and permanently destroyed his credibility.

Looking back, executives who worked with Peter McGoldrick
said he was at a disadvantage the moment he walked through
Steinberg's doors and that it was only a question of time before the
company would destroy him. He walked in cold, unfamiliar with
both the idiosyncrasies of the wider Quebec marketplace and the
quirks, personalities, and curious set of rules by which Steinberg
was run. He was dangerously unaware of Mitzi Dobrin and her
personal ambitions and when he did find out, it was too late. He
had no way of preventing her from making life miserable for him.

Bill Howieson believed McGoldrick was simply the wrong man
for the job. "He was good at working out operating programs. He
was just at the wrong level. If they had appointed Peter as executive
vice-president of food operations under a strong leader, I think he
would have been a big success. But he just didn't have the subtlety
to be the president in that company."

Five years after his disastrous experience at Steinberg, the
wounds are far from healed for McGoldrick. The memories still
sting and he refuses to talk about his Steinberg days. Back in the
U.S., he tried different business ventures with little success. In 1989
his wife Mary died.

After McGoldrick's depature, Steinberg's market share continued to decline. The world outside the company was changing,
consumers were demanding different products, the competition
was becoming increasingly intense and wiser to Steinberg's maneu-
vers. It was all too much for the company to cope with. Steinberg
was slipping deeper and deeper into trouble and badly needed a
new leader. But nobody inside, it seemed, had the ability to save it.

# 8

# *The Son Sam Never Had*

Peter McGoldrick was gone but the damage to Steinberg had been done. Mr. Sam would not have believed that the empire he built so painstakingly could crumble so quickly after his death.

Into this desperate situation stepped a new president, Irving Ludmer. He had returned to Steinberg in 1983, after a twelve-year absence, to run its real estate subsidiary, Ivanhoe Inc. Now, in the spring of 1984, he was offered the job nobody wanted — president of a company that was steering straight for disaster.

Ironically, Ludmer had left years earlier because he saw no future for himself in a company dominated by family members. He had criticized the nepotism at Steinberg. He'd complained to Sam that the key decisions were made at the family's Friday-night suppers and urged that more professional managers be hired from outside. Ludmer had quit in 1971 because he was too ambitious and talented to play second fiddle to Sam's sons-in-law.

But twelve years later, after making a fortune in real estate, he came back to Steinberg, lured by a lucrative contract at Ivanhoe that gave him a piece of the company's real estate deals. And when Peter McGoldrick left the president's job in disgrace, there was nobody else for the family to turn to but Ludmer. The bright young man who had charmed Mr. Sam years ago was named president of Steinberg on April 16, 1984, at the age of forty-nine.

His appointment would prove to be the most significant event since Sam's death. Ludmer engineered a turnaround at Steinberg that few would have believed possible. He faced, and survived, a combination of crises that would have hobbled most other chief executives. He whipped the company into the kind of shape that finally enabled the family to cash in their holdings for an enormous sum.

Yet over time, this bright and strong-willed executive would profoundly alienate the Steinberg sisters who owned the business. As with McGoldrick before him, the family's goodwill toward Ludmer would quickly deteriorate into recriminations. The "problem of succession" was no longer just Sam's problem but the family's, and they seemed unable to solve it. Perhaps there could be *no* solution as long as any Steinberg was in the company.


Steinberg was in Irving Ludmer's blood. Even after he had left in 1971 to become a successful developer, he never lost his affection for the company or for Mr. Sam. The relationship between the two had been a special one during Ludmer's first tenure at Steinberg. People described him as the son Sam never had.

When he came back as president, more than one employee believed the company had found a clone of Mr. Sam. In some ways, they were right. Irving Ludmer and Sam Steinberg both came from humble, immigrant backgrounds and both were headstrong personalities. There were even physical similarities: they were small men, barely over five feet four. Each had ears that seemed to protrude at right angles from their heads, like antennae. Each had piercing eyes that sized up a business situation in a flash.

But while Sam was a shy man without any formal education, Ludmer was a fast-talking wisecracker with a university degree in engineering physics. He showed off his education, referring to Beethoven and Einstein as his cultural heroes. There was a slick side to him that the more naive Sam never had, and it made Ludmer an outstanding salesman. Perhaps because he'd worked so many years as a dealmaker in real estate, Ludmer was a street-wise kind of guy who relished the rough-and-tumble corporate world. One of his favorite expressions was, "You never have a deal until there's ink on the cheque. And then you have to check to make sure it's not disappearing ink."

While he didn't have Sam's personal warmth, Ludmer got along well with his employees. He was fluently bilingual, which Sam was not. He slipped naturally into heavily-accented "joual", the street-

French of Quebec, and could talk with the truck drivers about their routes as if he knew what their jobs were like. At a press conference, he could banter with the reporters in French without missing a beat.

To the Steinberg family, Ludmer was part dictator, part showman. "He could be the most cocky, arrogant SOB you could ever run into," recalled one family member. "He'd sit there and look you straight in the face and say, 'I'm really here for only one reason, your grandfather Sam. I grew up in this company.'" Yet within three years the family, embroiled in a dispute with Ludmer, sometimes wondered if he was lying through his teeth in order to prevent them from selling the business. He was only going to do whatever was good for himself, they believed.

Nonetheless, the family had to acknowledge that Ludmer was a superb business executive. He brought the same kind of drive to the president's job that Sam had displayed. The fierce dedication, the twenty-hour days, the relentless demands on subordinates all seemed to be fired by one desire: to preserve what Sam Steinberg had built. When Sam's old desk was hauled out of storage and installed in Ludmer's office, it was a signal to employees that the past triumphs of Steinberg were about to be repeated.

Ludmer was born in Montreal in 1935, the only child of immigrant parents. His father was a steam-presser in a dress factory who came to Canada from the Soviet Ukraine. His mother emigrated from Poland. Neither had any education. Young Irving grew up speaking Yiddish, with only the barest idea that French and English were the languages of the city. He was raised in a cold-water flat on Coloniale Street, one of those third-floor walk-ups reached only by a steeply winding outdoor staircase usually covered in snow and ice during the winter. "As a kid you sort of laughed and slid down," he remembered. "But my mother, it would take her forever to come from the top of this winding staircase down to the ground."

Inside the cold apartment, Ludmer dressed in long underwear, socks, and sweater before going to bed. "Taking a bath was an absolute nightmare because it was freezing in there. The only heating was the stove in the kitchen, and the bedroom was down the hall."

As it was for Sam Steinberg, the playground was the street, where Ludmer and his friends formed the only Yiddish-speaking hockey team on the block. Games against the French and English boys were interrupted occasionally by passing cars but the kids didn't mind.

When the five-year-old Irving went to kindergarten, he still didn't know a word of English. His boyhood friend Martin Kaufman, who later became an investment analyst specializing in Steinberg, "translated" for him. It didn't take Ludmer long to find he liked school. He excelled, particularly in mathematics, and he was always motivated to get top marks on a test.

When Ludmer was twelve, the family moved from the unheated flat on Coloniale to the more prosperous neighborhood of Outremont, near the slopes of Mount Royal. His father had saved $500 to invest with a friend in six flats. The friend lent the other $1,000 and it turned out to be the best investment the elder Ludmer ever made.

In Outremont, Irving saw grass on the lawns for the first time. He also saw bicycles that weren't locked, simply lying on people's front lawns. And like any street kid from the poor side of town, Ludmer took the first bicycle he saw, until his father set him straight. "Where I lived before, whatever wasn't locked up was yours. It was as simple as that."

Suddenly, Ludmer was the poor kid in a group of wealthy children, and he found it traumatic. The other children could afford things he couldn't. Whenever the voters' lists were posted before an election, the kids would gather round and look at all the occupations listed on the sheet. There was a manufacturer, a doctor, a lawyer — and then there was Irving's dad, a presser.

Ludmer would have to explain why it was that his father came home every night soaked in sweat after manning the steam press on a hot summer's day. He was the butt of a few jokes and it wasn't easy. Suddenly, status and wealth meant something to a twelve-year-old who, on Coloniale Street, had never thought twice about riding in a horse-and-cart with his uncle, the breadman.

Those peer pressures drove Ludmer to excel at school. He went to McGill University, where he studied engineering physics and for a while it seemed he might make a career as a research physicist. After graduating in 1957, he considered getting his doctorate at the University of California at Berkeley. But he wasn't so sure he wanted to spend the rest of his life in a lab "making bombs", as he put it. He decided to work for a year instead.

After spotting a newspaper ad for an engineering job, he sent off a letter to a post office box number and received a call from Steinberg. They were looking for an engineer for their plant maintenance department. After several interviews, Ludmer was hired in 1957 at a salary of $100 a week. His responsibility was to help look after the warehouse and bakery: not the greatest job in the world, but okay for a year.

Those were the giddy days when Steinberg was expanding rapidly and Ludmer found himself in a vibrant, hustling atmosphere. He got caught up in the excitement and the challenge, and enjoyed it. He decided to stay, figuring that even if the job wasn't nearly as challenging as solving a physics problem, it was fun and the money was getting better.

Ludmer was already starting to feel the magic of the Steinberg environment. The place operated on intuition; it was run by a bunch of street-smart guys who worked like hell and who had an enormous desire to achieve. As he looked around at the top executives, he realized that most of them were high-school dropouts who had started by hauling sacks of potatoes for Mr. Sam. It wasn't that difficult for someone as ambitious as Ludmer, with a physics degree, to get ahead.

Even in those early days, Ludmer was starting to show a brash and somewhat arrogant style, a side of his personality that would later rub some of his executives the wrong way. He was never particularly shy about displaying his intelligence. On a tour of a factory one day, an executive remembered, Ludmer acted like "a young know-it-all from McGill" who claimed he knew what all the machinery was and then got it all wrong.

Ludmer moved fast. Within six years, he was working in the real estate division with Leo Goldfarb, Sam's son-in-law. Goldfarb had met the bright young man in the company cafeteria one day and asked if he'd like to learn about real estate. Ludmer jumped at the chance.

Goldfarb was putting together land deals for Steinberg and Ivanhoe, building a real estate portfolio for Mr. Sam that was the envy of many developers. In the high-growth 1960s, the appetite for land was enormous. Ludmer, Goldfarb, and John Ciaccia, a future Quebec cabinet minister, would spend their time plotting land purchases for potential shopping centers, based on exhaustive research. They knew where the roads and sewers were being built, where the population growth would be concentrated. They would take land positions in different places in order to be there when residential development came. "We knew that if we bought bright and early enough, we probably wouldn't lose, even on the losers."

Ludmer's performance caught Sam's eye. And as Sam gained more confidence in the young man's abilities, he liked to call Ludmer up every so often and kid around, "Hey, Irving, I made so much yesterday. Did you spend more than I made?" Or he'd simply needle Ludmer. His favorite complaint was that Ludmer's mother must have dropped Irving on his head when he was a baby. Sam would say, "Did you go home and ask your mother yet? Do me a favor and call her tonight and ask her if she remembers."

The teasing and verbal jousting was Sam's way of singling out a favorite executive. In fact, the zany repartee sometimes predominated at meetings when the real estate whiz kids like Ludmer, Goldfarb, and Ciaccia made their pitch to Sam for new sites. Ludmer remembered one meeting that turned into a heated discussion, with people calling each other crazy. "We had to vote on who was crazier than whom. We ended up voting that Leo was crazier than Sam, six-to-five, or something like that."

Besides such antics, the real estate boys were aggressive, particularly Ludmer. He wanted Steinberg to be as much a real estate development company as a grocery business. In the late 1960s, he and Goldfarb went to Mr. Sam with a proposal to build five major shopping-center projects in Laval, St. Bruno, Ottawa, Hull, and Trois-Rivières. The properties were choice sites in areas that were poised for a boom. Almost any developer would have loved to get his hands on them. But when Sam saw the amount of debt he would have to assume, he got nervous. He cautiously decided it would be better for Steinberg to participate in the projects but not to develop them. Ludmer renegotiated the deals, bringing in the Bronfman-controlled real estate firm, then called Fairview Ltd., to develop the Laval and St. Bruno sites and forming a partnership with another big real estate player, Cambridge Shopping Centres, in Ottawa, Hull, and Trois-Rivières. It was a frustrating decision for an ambitious person like Ludmer. He wanted to play in the big leagues.

It was a fateful decision, too. Sam missed the opportunity to become one of the biggest developers in the country. With his choice portfolio of land, he could have turned Ivanhoe into a real estate giant rivaling Trizec. But his focal point had always been food, and in his mind the real estate was never intended to be anything more than support for the food stores.

Sam's lack of decisiveness in real estate matters infuriated Ludmer. On one occasion, Ludmer tried to sell eight or nine of the worst properties in Ivanhoe. He packaged them together and got a very attractive price from a prospective buyer. But when he took the deal to the boss for approval, Sam changed his mind. "Well," he said, "if it's worth that much to them, it's worth that much to me. We'd better keep it."

Ludmer contained his frustrations and became the head of the real estate division after Leo Goldfarb left the company in 1968. His relationship with Sam, always warm, became especially close as the two spent increasing amounts of time together scouting land acquisitions. "He let me do what I wanted," Ludmer remembered. "I was very young, I was in my early thirties. He disbanded a few committees and he said, 'Irving decides.' "

By that time Ludmer had become the driving force in Steinberg, on the real estate side and the retail side. The company was building stores at an incredible pace — sometimes fifteen or sixteen under construction simultaneously. Steinberg was the number one food chain in Quebec and Ludmer ran a large part of the show. He had control over architecture, construction, purchasing, leasing, anything to do with real estate. And as Sam entrusted Irving with more responsibility, the two spent more and more time together. They had the chance to talk on those trips around Montreal and sometimes Sam would show Irving where he grew up and how he used to scrap it out on the street corner selling newspapers, defending his territory against the bigger kids. He would tell Irving about his days as a pinboy in a bowling alley.

At other times he would confide in Ludmer, the way a troubled father might talk to a son. He'd invite Irving out for a drive to talk about the marital troubles his daughters were having or the pressures he was under from his family. Those conversations showed Ludmer how deeply committed Sam was to his family. It also became apparent that Sam thought a great deal of Mel Dobrin, because Mel and Mitzi made such a great couple and shared his family values.

(Top) Ida Steinberg: The tireless matriarch laid the foundation for the family empire, opening a tiny grocery store in 1917. (Bottom) Sam Steinberg: By the 1940s, he had built his mother's grocery business into Montreal's leading supermarket chain.

A Steinberg store in the 1920s, with Ida seated at the cash register.

The Steinberg brothers, with a portrait of Ida in the background.
*Left to right*: Nathan, Jack, Sam, Max, and Morris.

Nathan Steinberg (1951) cutting up a 150-pound apple pie as an Easter treat for children.

Sam Steinberg (1966) inspecting a model of a retailing complex with executives. *From left*: Harold Ship, architect, Emilio Gioia, president of ACI Property Corp., Sam, Leo Goldfarb.

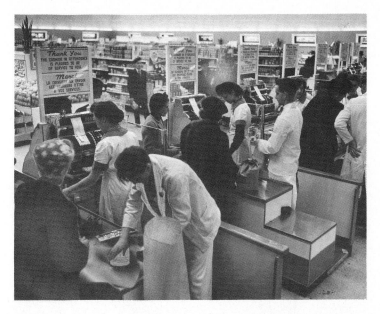

Steinberg was first grocery chain in Quebec to offer self-service.
CANADA WIDE PHOTO

Steinberg stores such as this one in the 1950s anchored new
shopping center developments. MONTREAL STAR

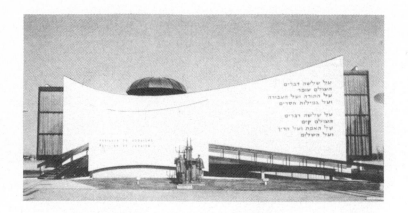

(Top) The Pavilion of Judaism at Expo '67 in Montreal. Sam
Steinberg headed the committee that developed the pavilion and
was its president. (Bottom) Sam, *left*, and Israeli president
Zalman Shazar at ceremonial opening of Pavilion of Judaism.

A family celebration, circa 1960.
*Left to right, seated,* Mitzi,
Evelyn, Sam, Helen, Marilyn,
Rita; *standing,* Mel Dobrin,
William Alexander, Len Pedvis,
Leo Goldfarb. Mel Dobrin
married Sam's daughter Mitzi,
and became president of
Steinberg in 1969.

Sam surrounded by winners of an early truck drivers' safety contest. Jack Steinberg is at front left.

Sam with daughter Evelyn at an early employees' picnic in Montreal's Belmont Park.

The Steinberg family during happier times. (Back row) *Left to right*: Mel Dobrin, Evelyn Steinberg Alexander, Marilyn Steinberg Pedvis, Len Pedvis, Leo Goldfarb. (Front row) Mitzi Steinberg Dobrin, Lewis Dobrin, Helen Steinberg, Terry Dobrin, Sam Steinberg, Billy Pedvis (on Sam's lap, left), Robert Goldfarb (on Sam's lap, right), Rita Steinberg Goldfarb, Eileen Goldfarb. MCCALL'S MAGAZINE

Jack Levine, *left*, and Sam Steinberg confer with unidentified aide in appearance before a House of Commons committee on food prices in 1973.

Helen and Sam Steinberg with liquor merchant Samuel Bronfman, *left*, and former prime minister Lester Pearson.

William Cleman, *left*, chairman of Steinberg's real estate giant
Ivanhoe, was a candidate to succeed Irving Ludmer as head of
Steinberg. Arnold Steinberg, Sam's nephew and the last top-level
executive from the Steinberg clan, tried to block the sale of
Steinberg Inc. to Michel Gaucher.

Mitzi at Miracle Mart (1977). She shook up the department store
chain, replacing most of its top management.

Irving Ludmer: The strong-willed chairman of Steinberg forced Mitzi out of the company in 1985.
LASZLO, MONTREAL

Quebec Premier Robert Bourassa, *left*, with Nancy Orr-Gaucher and Michel Gaucher at a 1987 gala. Bourassa favored Gaucher's bid for Steinberg over a rival group from Ontario.
JAMES SEELEY

Ludmer realized that the business was a way for Sam to look after his family, to give them jobs and material security, even if some family members in the company weren't terribly competent and were just along for the ride. But by the late 1960s, as Steinberg began to face increasing competition in the grocery market, nepotism was a problem quite apparent to an ambitious young man like Ludmer.

He had raised Sam's eyebrows by speaking out publicly about the problem at Palomino Lodge. He could see potential conflict. Steinberg was a public company, with responsibilities to its shareholders. They would demand better performance from the company and from the management group.

Ludmer could see Sam's side of it, too. It was, after all, his company. As the controlling shareholder, Sam could do what he wanted. If he wanted to give jobs to his brothers and sons-in-law, his nephews, and Helen's brothers, that was his prerogative. But for a fast-tracker like Ludmer, there wasn't much room at the top in a company so closely identified with family.

Besides, Ludmer wanted more money. The idea of striking out on his own began to tempt him. Ludmer told himself that the spoils go to those who are willing to take the risks. He had put together a few great real estate deals at Steinberg that were highly lucrative. Why not try the same thing for himself?

But cutting his ties with Steinberg wasn't a simple matter. Ludmer was almost a part of the family and Sam wouldn't let him go without a fight. Sam offered him more money, and Ludmer wouldn't take it. What the young man really wanted was a piece of the action on the real estate side, so he boldly asked Sam to cut him in on the deals.

He proposed a complicated scheme to Sam: Steinberg would sell him a store, taking back a mortgage on the property. Ludmer would pay mortgage interest to Steinberg of, say, $45,000 a year and Steinberg would pay *him* rent of $50,000 a year. The $5,000 difference would be income to him.

But there was more. The $45,000 was mostly interest and was therefore tax-deductible. So was depreciation on the store. In fact, not only would Ludmer get $5,000 in income but at least another $15,000 would be sheltered from the tax man. It was a lot better than a straight $5,000 raise.

But as Ludmer's agile mind spilled out the possibilities, Sam became nervous. He didn't really know what to do. He kept insisting that Ludmer take a $5,000 raise anyway, saying, "What's the matter, don't you trust me?" And when Ludmer would ask again about the tax shelter, Sam would reply, "I'm working on it."

Actually, Sam was in a quandary. He didn't want to lose his young favorite and he also couldn't give such generous terms to Ludmer without offering them to other executives in the company as well. He called his financial adviser, Senator Lazarus Phillips, and his ex-son-in-law Leo Goldfarb, who had been Ludmer's boss. What should he do about Ludmer's idea? Goldfarb said he thought it was a good idea. Sam wondered what to do with his other key men, like Jack Levine. Finally his sense of integrity and fairness convinced him to say no to Ludmer's deal.

Soon after, Ludmer left the company — another potential successor to Sam out the door. He started his own real estate firm, Ludco Enterprises Ltd., and later went into partnership with shopping-center developer Marcel Adams in a company called Iberville Developments. He became extremely wealthy in a short time. It was the ultimate job: no bosses, no regular hours, complete freedom to wheel and deal. Yet he operated conservatively, by the standards of other developers; he could have amassed an even larger fortune if he had been more of a "gunslinger". Eventually he was bought out by Adams after the two had become among the most important developers in Quebec.

It had taken him twelve years, but Irving Ludmer finally got the piece of the action he had wanted at Steinberg. Mr. Sam was dead and the company was stumbling badly. When it looked for someone to revive its real estate operation at Ivanhoe, Steinberg set its sights on bringing Ludmer back. Sam's nephew Arnold Steinberg spent more than a year trying to convince the prodigal son to return. It was a task that required not only persuasion but a very lucrative offer as well.

On Steinberg's first approach to Ludmer, negotiations dragged on for a long time. Ludmer felt that because he had his own highly successful business, the only way he would agree to return was in a joint venture with Ivanhoe. "I felt they would never go through with it," he recalled. "I really didn't see them agreeing to a joint venture with a private individual."

But Arnold persisted and brought someone in to help structure a deal. Ludmer, the mathematics whiz, must have loved those sessions. As the two sides tried to negotiate a percentage stake for Ludmer in Ivanhoe's deals, the formulae started to look like advanced calculus. Ludmer felt as if he were back in his engineering physics class at McGill.

The problem was that Ludmer needed a way to limit his risk. It was fine for him to become a twenty-percent partner with Ivanhoe in a $100-million development but he wasn't about to put $20-million of his own money at risk. After all he wasn't an institution like Steinberg. He wanted to participate in the profits, as well as some protection from a loss.

Mitzi and Mel Dobrin, who were calling the shots at Steinberg, weren't prepared to satisfy him, so Ludmer decided to break off negotiations. The whole thing had become so complicated, he was afraid he'd wind up in court with the company if a real estate deal ever went bad. That was in 1979.

Two years passed and the issue didn't come up again until Ludmer was about to set up offices for his personal company in Toronto and the United States. He needed some tax advice and went to see a brilliant young tax lawyer in Montreal, Sam Mintzberg, who happened to be Mitzi's son-in-law. Mintzberg urged Ludmer to talk with Steinberg again, promising to help. After more tough bargaining, an agreement that satisfied both parties was reached. It was a gamble that Mitzi and the other directors decided was worth taking to get one of the country's top real estate operators back into the company.

The need for someone to manage the Ivanhoe properties had become acute. The division was by far the most valuable and profitable piece of Steinberg, yet the real estate company had been without a leader for months, after the bizarre murder of its top executive, Ralph Ordauer. He was the victim of a hit man in the company's parking garage. The crime was never solved, but there was speculation that Ordauer had become unwittingly involved with criminal elements in a land deal in the U.S. that turned sour.

What's more, Ivanhoe's shopping malls and commercial properties were in bad shape, victims of a decade of neglect. After Ludmer had left Steinberg in 1971, there was no one to replace him on the real estate side. His job functions were split up and decentralized and Ivanhoe lost all the momentum it had built up during the heady days of the 1960s. "The people running the company [in the 1970s] were not real estate people," observed former Steinberg real estate executive Bill Cleman. "They were fighting for their own interests and there was a lot of political fighting going on within the company." A battle developed between the real estate and food divisions and real estate lost out.

Predictably, Ivanhoe slid slowly downhill after that, standards declined, and the company's reputation was damaged. Tenants' roofs leaked; the shopping malls needed renovation; the parking garages needed improvement. Yet Ivanhoe kept demanding market rents from its tenants. The Ivanhoe executives, imbued with the bottom-line mentality, were not prepared to take risks or to spend the money required to fix up their properties. It was no way to run a railroad.

When he came back to Ivanhoe in 1983, Ludmer was welcomed by the family with open arms. He was a frequent dinner guest of Mitzi and Mel Dobrin. Mitzi's sister Marilyn and her second husband Simon Cobrin were thrilled by Ludmer's return, viewing it as the first positive sign of a turnaround at Steinberg Inc. Investment analysts who followed the company agreed. They saw Ludmer's return as a signal that the company's sleeping real estate giant would wake up again.

Ludmer wasted little time taking charge. He immediately saw that standards had fallen and that money would have to be invested to improve the malls. Ivanhoe was the biggest real estate company in Quebec, the sixth largest in Canada, yet it was a company that needed to be prodded back to action. Ludmer brought his strategic mind to the task, questioning real estate deals that hadn't been questioned before, thinking like a good chess player, ten or fifteen moves ahead.

Irving Ludmer was barely getting started at Ivanhoe when an extraordinary call for help came from the Steinberg board. They needed a president to replace Peter McGoldrick, who had been pushed out the door. Ludmer had made enough of an impression in his few months at Ivanhoe that he was the first choice of Mitzi and Mel. They didn't want to go outside the company again, as they had done with McGoldrick.

The board also pushed hard for Ludmer's appointment. They were prepared to live with him, even if he had no previous experience as a food merchandiser. After all, Steinberg was more than just a grocery chain; it had department stores and restaurants and sugar mills and real estate. It needed a tough and visionary executive, someone who could rekindle the fire that had burned in everyone's belly when Mr. Sam was in charge.

Ludmer quickly accepted the challenge, but to the casual observer his decision must have seemed puzzling. Why would anyone want to occupy the captain's berth on the *Titanic*? Why would anyone choose to face the hopeless operating problems and the constant family politicking that had made life in the president's office so difficult for Levine and McGoldrick? There was no question in anybody's mind who was still the boss. This was a company still dominated by Mitzi Dobrin. She surely wouldn't have agreed to let Ludmer in the door if she suspected he would threaten her power.

But within a short time, it was clear that he *was* a threat. Ludmer was bright, strong-willed, and much more experienced than Mitzi. He had the full backing of Steinberg's outside directors, who'd already begun to sour on her. As president, Ludmer demanded full authority to do his job. He wasn't going to be pushed around the way Levine and McGoldrick had been. He hadn't taken the job for the money; he was a wealthy man already. The only way he'd stay was if he could call the shots.

Ludmer's arrival in the president's office was greeted with euphoria by many of the Steinberg employees who had known him during his first tenure at the company. These were people who had lived through the glory days and then been hit over the head with a shovel when things started to go badly. They were desperate. "He was the Messiah. Finally we got the guy we could trust," recalled one senior executive, who was later a victim of Ludmer's purge of head office staff. "He was here before, he was the son Sam never had. He came in as the best real estate guy in the country, bar none. That was his billing." He was a breath of fresh air. He wanted to do things. He gave the company a new direction.

On his first day as president, Ludmer swept a broom through the executive suite, cleaning out almost all the top executives in the supermarket division. If the action seemed drastic, so was Steinberg's plight. Its share of the Quebec grocery market had tumbled from 28 percent at the time of Sam's death in 1978 to 17 percent, far behind the new front-runner in the grocery market, Provigo Inc.

The first thing Ludmer had to change was the most difficult: the corporate culture of Steinberg. The company had become an overly cautious and political place where people covered their asses and wouldn't take calculated risks. The decline in Steinberg's fortunes had left the store employees surly with the customers and suspicious and resentful of the store managers; the store managers were at odds with the buyers; the buyers were unhappy with the head office supervisors. Morale had deteriorated all the way up the chain.

The problem was perhaps worst in the head office itself, where nobody seemed willing to take responsibilities. Under Mr. Sam, Steinberg had always been run from the top down. The strength of the company had been the uniformity and continuity of its management methods, which made it easy to run a hundred stores. But that wouldn't work anymore. Now, everyone from the neighborhood store manager to the mid-level executive had to be able to react very quickly to a rapidly changing market. Few put much stock in Ludmer's chances. Most investors, industry analysts, and competitors believed there had been too much hemorrhaging at Steinberg for anyone to stop the bleeding.

One stock market professional was not so skeptical, however. Martin Kaufman, a shrewd retailing analyst at the brokerage firm of Nesbitt Thomson Deacon Inc., had been a lifelong friend and admirer of Irving Ludmer since they had grown up together on Coloniale Street. They had played street hockey together, with telephone books strapped to their legs as shin pads. Kaufman knew enough to realize that Ludmer didn't need the Steinberg job, so if he was willing to put up with all the aggravation and trouble that awaited him there, Kaufman figured he must have some idea of how to turn the company around.

He paid a visit to his old friend and couldn't believe how bad things really were. The litany of problems was endless, from rust on the store counters to rot in employee morale. For example, every

store manager who needed to make a cash outlay of more than $5
— be it for postage stamps or to pay overtime — required permission from head office. Imagine a store manager earning $45,000 a
year with 100 employees under him, sales of $2-million, expensive
refrigeration equipment worth maybe another $½-million, having
to call head office every time he needed petty cash. What kind of
manager could he be? How could he ever be motivated to compete
against the independent franchisees who owned their own Provigo
stores?

As bleak a picture as Ludmer painted, Kaufman came back to
his office enthusiastic. Ludmer had talked eloquently about instill-
ing a "risk-taking" culture at Steinberg. He wanted to pour money
into store renovation so that customers would be attracted into a
Steinberg store. He had a vision of a new Steinberg, one that
concentrated on serving the customers rather than on keeping the
suppliers happy. He wanted to move the company into wholesaling, offer more prepared food in the stores, build new "super
stores" and food-and-drug "combos" to draw in new customers.

Kaufman predicted that Steinberg would be the turnaround
stock for the next couple of years. It didn't take long. Within a year
and half, Steinberg stock went from $12.50 to $50 and Ludmer
looked like a genius. The company made $73 million in 1985,
almost a five-fold increase from the previous year. Even the supermarket division made money.

As the stock market took notice, Ludmer grew wealthier. The
company had granted him options on 400,000 shares at $13.12
each and by the end of 1985 he had made a paper profit of $1-
million. (When he left the company in 1989, he sold the Class A
shares at better than $50 apiece, earning more than $10-million in
profit.) Steinberg had even guaranteed Ludmer that he wouldn't
have to pay the income tax on half his profits, just in case the tax
department ruled that they didn't qualify as capital gains.

He became both a cheerleader and a missionary at Steinberg,
getting up on his soapbox and preaching sermons about values and
excellence. "It's got to be integrity all the way," he would say. "How
you deal with your suppliers and everything. It's a whole network,
shareholders, lenders, customers, employees."

He wanted his executives to think as he did. "The first thing I
tried to inculcate was the measurement of risk, to get a feel for risk

that was shared amongst a group of executives," Ludmer said. "It's a cultural thing, you can't explain risk-reward until you share a belief about the world." What Ludmer was saying was it's okay to take a gamble, provided that you limited the downside risk on your investment and you had some idea of the potential return you could get.

He was a perfectionist and what really galled him was the shabby physical state of the Steinberg stores. The stores no longer had a retail "vocation", he said. Not enough had been put back into them. Sam had always told him, "If you want to milk a cow, you'd better give it something to eat." But Steinberg management had forgotten that. On the rare occasions when they did renovate, the end result was the bizarre reproduction of a 1950s store from Sam's heyday — clean-looking, uncluttered, and sterile. There was no imagination or contemporary look in the redesign. So Ludmer embarked on an ambitious program of store renovation and capital spending that would eventually reach $80-million a year.

Turning the supermarkets around was more than just a matter of store renovation, however. There were fundamental questions, such as what to put on the shelves. For example, Steinberg had a wide assortment of so-called private label goods that were sold under the Steinberg name and manufactured in-house or by suppliers. The company could get a better deal on private label goods because the suppliers didn't have to advertise them nationally. Steinberg was able to drop the price a bit and still make more money than on a national brand name. But private label had grown to ridiculous proportions. There were hundreds of items sitting on the shelves — everything from Steinberg soap to Steinberg shaving cream — and they seemed to be on special all the time. When Ludmer started to question his executives about this, he was told that's the way it was always done.

He wouldn't accept that answer. Too often Steinberg had stocked what the suppliers wanted, not what the customer had demanded, and that approach wouldn't work anymore in a crowded and competitive grocery market. Social and demographic forces had transformed the marketplace so much that the supermarket of the past no longer answered the needs of the contemporary consumer.

The homogeneous society of the 1950s and 1960s, when Mom had supper on the table by the time Dad came home at six o'clock, had given way to a highly segmented marketplace in the 1980s. Population growth had slowed down, the number of single-parent families and working mothers was on the rise, ethnic consumers were a new force in the market, and there was a growing preoccupation with health and nutrition. Busy two-income families were eating out or ordering in. And when they did shop at the supermarket, they often wanted to buy prepared foods.

Steinberg was facing competition not only from the franchised independents at Provigo and Métro-Richelieu with their lower labor costs, but also from convenience stores, farmers' markets, specialty food and vegetable outlets, delicatessens, bakeries, and gourmet food shops. These specialists were giving customers what they wanted, offering a wide variety of fresh produce and adding a good measure of personal service. What's more, they were earning higher profit margins, while the supermarkets were left with sales of low-margin dry groceries.

Ludmer wanted to bring service, choice, and atmosphere to Steinberg stores. If customers wanted a loaf of crusty bread, a wedge of Camembert cheese, or a pound of shrimp, they wouldn't have to go down the street to get it. He redesigned the stores to include in-store bakeries, cheese and fish counters staffed with trained specialists. Steinberg had always resisted a move to service counters because of the extra labor costs. Executives had long believed that service counters would simply widen Steinberg's wage disadvantage against its competitors. They had hoped to create a fully automated store instead. But that was an impossible dream. You could never replace personal service.

In a highly segmented market, Ludmer saw the need for several different store formats. Steinberg had opened a mega-store called Marché du Jour in suburban Montreal, an 85,000-square-foot giant modeled after stores of the same type in the United States, and its early results were encouraging. Ludmer also negotiated a partnership with the fabulously successful Price Club chain of membership-warehouse stores, based in California, which offered bargain prices on a wide variety of consumer goods.

Other challenges awaited. Ludmer wanted to franchise more of the Steinberg stores to independent owners with the entrepreneurial zeal to compete against Provigo and Métro. Along with that would come the logical next step: developing a wholesaling operation to serve the franchised stores.

The job on the food side was simply enormous, but it was just the beginning for Ludmer. Steinberg also owned a large supermarket chain in Arizona, Smitty's Super Valu, that needed constant attention. And the president had to decide quickly what to do with Miracle Mart, the junior department store chain that had been a disaster from the beginning. In 1985, he promoted Michael Kershaw, who had been with Sears Canada for seventeen years, from general manager to president of Miracle Mart, giving him two years to clean up the mess and produce a turnaround strategy for the stores. The result was a new concept — the M Store — with an accent on attractive fashion at an affordable price.

To anyone watching Ludmer attack the problems at Steinberg, he must have looked like a circus entertainer trying to keep a dozen plates spinning on rods at the same time. As soon as he got one plate properly spinning, he'd have to rush over to another to keep it from falling. Those who worked with him marveled at his talents. "He has the ability to deal with a wide range of issues that no other person I've ever met could deal with," said Bill Cleman, the former chief of Steinberg's real estate division. "He's superb in law, taxation, finance, real estate." What struck Cleman most were his formidable powers of concentration. "Every hour Irving puts in is effective. He has a tremendous retentive memory; he doesn't forget anything."

Ludmer led by example — six or seven days a week. He was up at 5:30 a.m. and in the office by 7:00. He'd go home for supper at six o'clock, taking work with him that would often keep him up until 11:00 or 12:00. On Saturday he worked at the office in the morning, then spent the afternoons visiting the stores and warehouses, where he had the same kind of common touch with employees that Sam Steinberg had displayed.

He was undaunted by crisis. Shortly after taking the president's job, he was hit by strikes in the same month at both the supermarkets and the Miracle Mart stores. Eighteen months after he took over, fire completely destroyed the company's head office — a devastating blow that wiped out all its corporate records. As flames licked out the windows of the sixteenth-floor executive office in the Alexis Nihon Plaza, Ludmer was mobilizing his management team to save the company's lifeline — its computer system. Within forty-eight hours, a backup computer in the United States had restored the company's payroll and accounting systems.

If the stress on him seemed intolerable, so were the demands he made on some of his employees. For Ludmer, there was only one way to do it, his way. A man of his intelligence and drive had difficulty accommodating other people's points of view. He did not brook disagreement readily and was inclined to be scornful of people who challenged his views, instead of dealing with their arguments on their own merit. This was interpreted as pure egotism by some of his underlings.

To others, Ludmer was simply exhibiting the traits of a successful businessman. "Anybody who becomes a multi-millionaire is probably strong-willed and has a big ego," said Al Mattison, who once worked as a vice-president under Ludmer. "Nice guys finish last. You have to have the strength of your convictions to be successful." For his part, Ludmer made no apologies for his behavior. He had strong feelings about the corporate world and how it should operate. Direction had to come from the top and the role of a chief executive officer was to establish a culture, a system of belief.

It all came down to the question of leadership, something that Steinberg had been sorely lacking since Sam's death. Ludmer was determined to move the company from its state of inertia by the force of his own will. There were half a dozen issues he strongly believed in that were so basic to his being that he would not tolerate criticism. For example, people questioned his decision to pump $80-million a year into store renovations at a time when the food market was showing no growth at all. Ludmer just wouldn't buy that argument. For him, there was simply no point in operating a second-class store because people wouldn't set foot in it.

Arguing with Ludmer was not easy, and in this way he was quite different from his mentor. Sam Steinberg had loved the cut-and-thrust of debate around a meeting-room table. He liked people who stood up for their ideas; it was his way of testing his employees' mettle. In fact, this quality was what had drawn Sam to Ludmer in the first place, this bright and brash youngster with so many opinions and ambitions. "The debate itself became the fun part," Ludmer remembered of his dealings with Sam. "And Sam loved it because he knew I was never challenging his authority or his right to make the final decision. . . . I think he changed his mind as often as I changed mine." As chief executive in his turn, Ludmer would not be persuaded so easily. He would not allow himself to be perceived publicly to be wrong.

Ludmer never patted anyone on the back or told them they were doing a good job. In 1988, 105 head office executives were fired in a massive reorganization. "They were let go because I felt these people were not up to what I would like to see in their roles," said Ludmer. "I found them negative toward the corporate culture."

He was remaking the company in his own image, hiring younger and more impressionable executives whom he could mold to his own way of thinking. None of this could have happened if Ludmer had not demonstrated his clear authority and ability in the company at an early stage. Yet it was that very success that would set the stage for a dramatic confrontation between Ludmer and Sam's daughter Mitzi Dobrin, the woman who had been the unofficial power behind Steinberg ever since Sam's death.

# 9

# Filling Daddy's Shoes

Rumors of discord between Irving Ludmer and Mitzi Dobrin began to fly around the Steinberg head office within weeks of Ludmer's appointment. According to one story making the rounds, the two had taken a five-hour plane ride to Phoenix, Arizona, on a business trip and hadn't said a word to one another the whole way.

With two strong egos vying for control of the company, life soon became intolerable in the executive suite. It seemed that every time Ludmer made a decision, Mitzi would go home and tell her husband Mel, the Steinberg chairman, about it. The next day the decision would be undone. Company executives didn't know where to turn for direction.

Mitzi admired Ludmer's abilities and recognized that he was a very capable financial man, something the company had lacked for many years. She valued Ludmer's skills at tax-planning and debt management. But he chafed under her authority and couldn't accept the public perception that she was still the boss. It was clear to him that the place wasn't big enough for the both of them.

Ever since the death of Mr. Sam, Mitzi Dobrin had been the most powerful member of the Steinberg family. She had made her presence felt throughout the company, first as the general manager of the Miracle Mart department store division, and eventually at head office as an executive vice-president. Not only did Mitzi represent the family's 52 percent controlling interest on the board of directors, but she was a tough, occasionally ruthless executive who wasn't shy about getting involved in any aspect of Steinberg business. Employees tangled with her at their peril. Until Ludmer arrived at Steinberg, she controlled the place to the point that it was jokingly referred to as Dobrin Inc.

Mitzi was tenacious and driven to succeed. During her years at Steinberg, she became one of the most powerful women in Canadian business, with a string of prestigious appointments to corporate boards and government agencies. She graced the society pages of Montreal newspapers, hosting charity balls or sponsoring cultural events. If she and Mel weren't at a party honoring financier Paul Desmarais, they would be at a reception with Mayor Jean Drapeau. When they weren't at an Israel Bond dinner with Charles Bronfman, they'd be at the Ritz-Carlton Hotel, meeting then U.S. vice-president Walter Mondale or cabinet minister John Turner or Israeli Foreign Minister Abba Eban.

She liked the attention. In Montreal's tightly knit Jewish community, she was a celebrity. She enjoyed the favorable stories in the newspapers about her rise through Miracle Mart and her efforts to turn the company around. And when a critical story appeared about the company in the press, she was known to seek out the reporter and demand to know why the story had been printed. It was Mitzi who became the company's public face. She was the one who addressed the investment analysts and bankers on Steinberg's financial prospects or was interviewed about the company's latest innovation.

That such power and influence could be wielded by so tiny a woman sometimes surprised those who met her. Barely five feet tall in high heels, with a lithe frame under one hundred pounds, Mitzi was an unlikely candidate for the role. The extravagant sweep of blonde hair across her forehead, the leopard skin coat with a Dior label, the lizard skin jacket, and the cowboy boots she sometimes wore didn't lend her the look of a typical executive.

But the gravelly voice was usually the first clue that Mitzi meant business. So were her piercing hazel eyes, eyes that reminded many people of her grandmother Ida. And when she talked business, Mitzi did her best to sound like her father, using his favorite expressions and metaphors. She gave the impression she had spent her life learning from Sam.

That wasn't really the case. Though Mitzi, like the entire clan, had grown up under Sam's dominating influence, she had never studied the business, had never been groomed for succession. She had learned everything secondhand. She didn't come to work at Steinberg until she was forty-two years old.

For many years she was close to the action but never right in it. Her judgments about people and issues were filtered through the experience of others. Later, when she joined the company and fancied herself a female version of Sam, it was obvious to the executives around her that she had no real experience of her own.

But she did possess a keen understanding of her father and what made him tick. As both his child and business colleague, Mitzi had seen both sides of his personality: the husband who was utterly devoted to Helen, and the terrible autocrat who could strike fear into everyone's heart if something went wrong or who would rake employees over the coals if they disagreed with him. She had seen the headstrong and impetuous Sam who could make his share of mistakes. And she had seen the humanitarian Sam who could be so kind and helpful to people in trouble.

"In many respects, I am like Sam," Mitzi once said in a news-paper profile of her. "I have to become very good at what I'm doing. I only enjoy myself when I do very well." Yet those who knew both would dispute that she resembled her father. Like Sam, she was emotional. However, Sam had had the ability to motivate people and to inspire them to do the best job they could do, whereas Mitzi often had problems dealing with people and found it hard to separate her emotions from rational business decisions. While she had all of Sam's aggressiveness, many observed that she had none of his charm.

Sam had never even considered the possibility that Mitzi herself might want to enter Steinberg. While he would talk about his work at the supper table and drive the girls around to the stores on weekends, it was more to vent his own obsession with the company than to train them for any future role. Indeed, Sam made a big fuss when Mitzi decided to go back to university in her thirties: that was something that a mother of three shouldn't do.

It was one of many disagreements Mitzi had with her father. In fact, they never really got along until she entered the business. As a strong-willed young girl, she wouldn't cater to Sam's dictatorial ways and tried to stand up to him. "He was intolerant," she believed. She couldn't stand the way he treated his brothers. She hated his habit of upbraiding executives in front of the family, and told him so.

Mitzi's independent streak blossomed at an early age. As a child, she had loved sports. All the other kids her age on the block were boys, so she became a tomboy, playing baseball, football, and hockey all day in the parks around the family home in Outremont. She was the closest thing to a son that Sam would get, and she was a spunky little kid. Mitzi often told the story of how she regularly played marbles in the schoolyard until seven or eight at night, well past the time she was supposed to be home. She'd bring home bags and bags of marbles, but her father would be furious that she was late. The next night, she'd do it again, showing no inclination to heed him.

She had learned early that Sam couldn't say no to his daughters very often. More than one visitor to the family home observed that the kids got away with too much. Sam really didn't have time or energy for them; even when he was home his mind was on business. "We never had a bad relationship," Mitzi said. "But it wasn't the normal father-daughter, close relationship. I was never at home and neither was he. He'd be very tired and aggravated when he came home."

The lack of attention began when the girls were small. Sam would travel often, visiting grocery chains in the United States, or attending conventions. Sometimes he'd bring Helen along, leaving Mitzi and her little sisters in the care of their uncle, Sam Roth, who would take them to a movie or to the park with a rope tying them together so they wouldn't run wild or get lost.

The girls were sent to Strathcona Academy, a public school in Outremont, and later to Westmount High School. Sam made an effort to be a good father, attending parents' day when other fathers were at the office. There was no doubt he loved his kids, but he didn't always have the time to show it.

Sam and Helen both believed that Mitzi's role in life should be one of wife and helpmate. But they indulged her curiosity about the business, taking her with them to visit the stores, letting her wander in the advertising department, where a friendly young francophone named Jacques Bouchard gave her "lessons" in French. The more Mitzi hung around the place, the more Sam's manner rubbed off on her. She heard the anecdotes about Ida and the first store on St.

Lawrence Boulevard. She heard her father speak in his colorful style, using parables to get across his points.

As a teenager she spent summers working at a Steinberg store in Westmount, her first direct exposure to the business. Sam disapproved of this; he couldn't bear the thought of his daughter working. He'd call for her at four o'clock, but she wouldn't want to leave before the other workers had finished and he had to insist that she come home with him. Unlike her sisters, Mitzi wanted to work in the stores, whether it was bagging groceries or packing fruit or dishing out candies to the kids at Christmas.

At school she practised everything from basketball to tennis for hours on end. She became involved in the Westmount High School dramatics society, not as an actress like her sister Rita but as stage manager, where she could indulge her desire to organize. She wasn't a brilliant student and her uncle Max had to coach her in math and algebra. Mitzi admitted that she played far too much. Said one of her high school teachers, "I was amazed later to find out she'd taken law at McGill. She was a bright, pleasant person but there's no way I thought she'd go as far as she did."

Nevertheless, it was Mitzi alone among the girls who had a strong drive to excel. She enrolled in university at the age of eighteen, although she dropped out two years later when she married Mel Dobrin and became pregnant. Becoming a housewife and mother, Mitzi put her ambitions on hold for a while, although she knew she could never simply be the helpmate her parents wanted her to be.

In the early days of their marriage the Dobrins lived simply, in an apartment above a Steinberg store on Monkland Avenue in Montreal's west end. Mitzi remembered having to climb three flights of stairs while pregnant. If she was the rich daughter of one of Canada's most successful supermarket magnates, she didn't act like it.

The Dobrins raised three children: a daughter Terry, and a son, Lewis, both of whom became successful lawyers in Montreal while the youngest son, Ronny, obtained his Masters degree in business administration and later went into business with his mother. The Dobrin family is close, the kind of family that Sam and Helen took pride in, especially since two of their other three daughters divorced their first husbands.

As Mitzi watched her children go to school, she realized she badly wanted to resume her education. "I felt I was stupid," she said. She was sitting at home, bursting with energy at the age of thirty-two. Even with the kids still living at home, she took the courageous decision to go back to McGill, overcoming the objections of her father and the doubts of her own family. Sam hated the idea and angrily tried to dissuade her.

It was the early 1960s, well before the feminist movement made working mothers commonplace. After ten years of remarkable perseverance, Mitzi wound up with not only a commerce degree but with a law degree as well. She was admitted to the Quebec bar and planned to work in legal aid. But her ambitions for a law career proved short-lived. After a brief stint as an intern at the Montreal law firm of Mendelsohn Rosentzveig Shacter, she would get another kind of opportunity, an offer she couldn't resist. Her father asked her to join the family business.

Mitzi was lunching with friends at Montreal's exclusive Elmridge Golf Club one July day in 1973 when Sam rushed into the dining room. The annual results of the Miracle Mart department store division had just come out and they were disastrous. Sam asked Mitzi to meet him in his office next morning, where he offered her the job of turning Miracle Mart around.

It was a shock to some, but Sam was again following his oldest and most basic instinct. Whenever Steinberg had been in trouble before and Sam needed somebody to fix a problem, he had turned to the family for help. Family, you could trust. Family wouldn't steal from you or undermine you. Family wouldn't use the power and influence of the position for personal gain. For the family, there was only one thing that counted: the welfare of Steinberg.

So when Sam Steinberg sought Mitzi out at the Elmridge Golf Club on that hot summer's day, he didn't really consider that he would be putting his daughter into an impossible position. It didn't seem to matter that this forty-two-year-old woman had no retailing experience and would be flung into a lion's den. He didn't consider how his other executives might react to the boss's daughter and the wife of the president taking over.

Sam hadn't listened to the objections of his right-hand man, Jack Levine, who had warned against bringing Mitzi into the company. Levine wanted to hire a top retailing executive from the U.S. instead. Years earlier Levine had also protested when Sam had appointed Mitzi's husband Mel to run Miracle Mart. He warned Sam he was making one of the major mistakes of his life. In Levine's view, Mitzi simply wasn't qualified to run the organization. Levine also believed it would be a terrible burden for Mel Dobrin, who had become president, to have his wife in the company. Sam had replied that he would choose whom he wanted because it was his money.

Levine knew the family better than most other executives and he recognized that Sam had a weakness about dealing with Mitzi. Devastated by the lack of a male heir, Sam began to invest his oldest daughter with qualities she didn't have. "He couldn't deal with her in any other way than to allow her to do the things she wanted to do," Levine said. Nor did Levine necessarily believe that the invitation to join Miracle Mart was all Sam's doing. He and others suspected that Mitzi had been quietly pushing for a job at Steinberg for years.

Mitzi denied that but she quickly took the job, excited by the challenge. It was the first time Steinberg had a division that was losing money and Sam couldn't come to grips with it. She figured what she lacked in experience, she could make up for in drive and energy, and also believed her training as a lawyer would help in negotiating new agreements with labor unions. She said yes to her father's offer.

It was a fateful decision. Mitzi would have a dramatic impact on Steinberg's fortunes over the next twelve years. For better or worse, she invested all her emotional energy in the family enterprise. But the company would suffer its darkest days during her tenure there. When she was finally forced to leave the company in 1985, her commitment to Steinberg also crumbled, driving a wedge between her and her sisters.

She entered Steinberg in the summer of 1973, beginning her career as a sales clerk in a Miracle Mart department store near her Town of Mount Royal home. On her first day she was shocked at what she found in the money-losing Miracle Mart operation. The place had been managed by people from the food business who had no notion of department store buying. The store was understaffed, and even the simple job of displaying the merchandise was not being done properly.

Mitzi's arrival there ruffled feathers. She pushed ahead quickly and was soon named by her father to the division's board of directors, making life uncomfortable for the recently appointed general manager, a woman named Alice King. King was a bright and capable executive with a background in auditing who had just been asked to clean up the financial mess at Miracle Mart when Mitzi suddenly showed up. They didn't get along. At one meeting, King bluntly told the Steinberg heiress, "Mitzi, why don't you get lost." Sam was livid. He said to King, "The one who's going to get lost is you."

Alice King could see the handwriting on the wall and soon left. She was "probably the best manager Steinberg ever had, but she cried uncle," recalled Henri Tremblay, the company's director of personnel at the time. She broke into tears in his office the day she explained that she couldn't take it any longer. But this was Mitzi, and who could stop her. She promptly replaced Alice King as general manager, provoking a lot of resentment among the vice-presidents. Their concern was that Mitzi wasn't really qualified, that she hadn't served her apprenticeship, that there were other people more qualified to do the job.

Sam Steinberg was probably acting out of desperation. His son-in-law was the president but he wasn't a leader. Sam realized belatedly that he had bungled the succession issue, so he reached out for his daughter Mitzi, who was bright and had just finished university. There were no other options in his mind. It was an emotional decision, certainly not a logical one.

Mitzi was smart enough, but would get no learning time on the job. She was playing in too big a ballpark, with too many people to manage. There's no business more difficult to run than a department store because it requires selling an image along with the merchandise. There are thousands of variables to play with and the image has to be consistent and predictable to the consumer over time.

The only thing Miracle Mart did consistently and predictably was lose money. In fact, Miracle Mart was the most expensive mistake Sam Steinberg ever made, losing more than a $100-million since it began in 1961 and leaving a history of trouble for Mitzi to inherit.

From the outset Miracle Mart could never quite decide if it was a department store, with a full choice of consumer goods, or a discount chain, specializing in a few low-priced items. The original concept had called for a store on one floor, so that a shopper could push a grocery cart through the aisles, as in a supermarket. But soon there were stores with two floors and three floors. The chain had no identity or consistency. Over the years, the stores chewed up managers. Sam eventually brought in a highly touted professional executive from the Hudson's Bay Co. to run the operation, but even he couldn't last.

The Miracle Mart stores stretched from northern Quebec to southwestern Ontario in regional malls or strip centers. The stores in Toronto, Hamilton, Windsor, and Ottawa were isolated from the rest of the chain so merchandise had to be trucked from the Montreal distribution center to the Ontario stores at great expense. And unlike Montreal, advertising costs in Ontario couldn't be spread over a network of stores.

There was another significant obstacle. The militant union at Steinberg had successfully organized workers at Miracle Mart — it was the first department store chain in the country to be unionized — and that left it with a huge cost disadvantage against competitors. Morale became a major problem, productivity declined, and there was constant bickering that resulted in hundreds of grievances against management every year. Later, as Steinberg's food division began to suffer, Miracle Mart was squeezed even further to help subsidize the food operation.

These were just some of the problems a green and untested Mitzi inherited. Few executives believed she could cope with the mess. But because she was the boss's daughter, everybody felt they should rally around her.

If she was looking to inspire loyalty, however, she wasn't successful. Soon after she took over as general manager, Mitzi brutally cut and slashed her way through the management ranks, firing a dozen top executives and showing the door to many merchandisers and buyers. Those who weren't fired lived in fear of dismissal. Everybody ran for cover. There didn't seem to be much thought in the way it was done. Morale worsened, and several other executives who weren't sacked soon quit on their own.

Mitzi was unapologetic about her actions, arguing that Miracle Mart would have gone down the drain if things hadn't changed fast. She claimed that people were coasting and weren't getting the job done. She did acknowledge that resentment over the firings ran high, however, and that she was under tremendous strain. "Both my husband and my father got a lot of flack," she later admitted in an interview. "It was a terrible situation. It wasn't easy."

To anyone who already knew this little dynamo, it was no surprise that Mitzi blew into Miracle Mart like a tornado, throwing herself wholeheartedly into everything as she had done at law school, tennis, or golf. Family friends recall that she spent countless hours on a driving range, perfecting her golf swing and steadily lowering her score. Her ambition at one time was to become a champion golfer. She became a devotee of physical fitness, taking up jogging initially to lower her weight and then developing such a passion for it that she would run ten miles daily. In those early days at Miracle Mart, she would get up at 5:45 a.m. to skip rope before heading to the office. Even when she moved to corporate headquarters, she'd drive herself like a thirty-year-old, climbing sixteen floors several times a day in her high heels to reach her office at Alexis Nihon Plaza.

Mitzi attacked her job at Miracle Mart with the same kind of vigor. Not only did she shuffle executives like playing cards, she devised a turnaround plan for the chain. Several Ontario stores that had been losing money were closed; slow-moving items were cut back or eliminated and buying policy was focused on basics. In apparel, where Miracle Mart did most of its volume, Mitzi abandoned the "dressy" look and substituted more basic fashions. She introduced staff-training programs to improve customer service and put greater controls on buyers. She helped introduce a new concept, the Beaucoup store, which combined a Miracle Mart and a Steinberg supermarket under the same roof.

Sam gave her a free hand. He was impressed by his daughter's tenacity and remarked on more than one occasion that she sounded just like him in a business meeting. Their relationship had taken a new turn. Instead of the confrontation that had marked the early years, there was a new understanding between daughter and father. Mitzi claimed she was still the only one who could stand up to him in a meeting, but whether he could stand up to her was doubtful. Sam seemed dazzled by Mitzi's performance and couldn't really stop her from doing whatever she wanted. A Miracle Mart executive remembered how Sam would walk into a management committee meeting and head straight for Mitzi, planting a kiss on her cheek. The rest of the committee members would stare straight ahead, wondering when the ax was going to fall on them.

Like her father, Mitzi would tour the stores, talking with the clerks and checking on the quality of merchandise on the racks. "They were scared shitless of her," recalled one former employee of Mitzi's walks up the aisle. If she spotted clerks doing something she didn't like she chewed them out publicly or threatened to fire them on the spot. She was a real contradiction at times. She could be warm, friendly, and sympathetic to her employees, yet then she could act in ways that seemed extremely unprofessional to them.

Once, at a management meeting, she presented a plan for an expensive computer study on profit margins and regally announced, "This is what we're going to do." But she soon forgot all about it and the study never took place, except in a couple of departments that really wanted it. She had ideas, without the patience and persistence to work with people and make them become reality.

There was always a group of employees trying to ingratiate themselves with her, knowing the power she wielded and the influence she could have on their careers. Besides, Mitzi was impressionable. The standard joke around the office was that she would always listen to the advice of the last person she talked to. It was a classic case of the queen having too many flatterers and courtiers. After firing so many people and replacing them with her own selections, Mitzi was left with a group of yes-men, people who told her what she wanted to hear. This was just what Jack Levine had feared when he had warned Mitzi that she didn't know how to handle people.

Professional investors in Steinberg stock were also skeptical of her. The closing of the Miracle Mart stores in Ontario prompted at least one Toronto brokerage firm to predict in 1975 that the chain would be forced out of business. There was too much competition from Zellers and other more efficient discount chains. Mitzi also claimed that her father made some bad decisions at Miracle Mart in his declining years, opening new stores in Quebec that should never have been opened.

She was determined to have an impact. She claimed that Miracle Mart made a small profit in 1975 and a bigger profit the following year, although it was hard to know for sure because the chain's financial results were consolidated with those of Steinberg. There was no doubt in her mind that things were turning around, the bleeding at Miracle Mart had stopped, and even if her enemies didn't have good things to say about her, she believed she was delivering results. A lot of people had said she would fall on her face, and she hadn't. It had taken courage for her to face the resentment, the hostility, and the intractable problems at Miracle Mart. People tried to take advantage of her because of who she was and because she was a woman. The easy thing would have been to step aside, but Mitzi was no quitter.

Sam's little girl was a miracle worker at Miracle Mart, according to the newspaper headlines. Her early success in stemming the losses in the department stores caught the attention of the corporate world, especially the Royal Bank of Canada. The Royal had been Steinberg's principal bank ever since Sam's first branch manager, a man named Matt Walters, had shown faith in the up-and-coming young grocer. Walters eventually became president of the Royal Bank, carried there in large part by the remarkable success of the Steinberg venture.

Sam Steinberg showed considerable loyalty to anyone who had ever dealt fairly with him and he rewarded the Royal with steady business over the years. Yet the bank had never asked him to sit on its board of directors. When it was suddenly desperate to find a woman to fill a vacancy on the board, the Royal decided that Sam's successful daughter Mitzi would be a natural choice and a nice way to thank Mr. Steinberg for his years of loyal patronage.

But Mitzi's appointment to one of Canada's most prestigious corporate boards might never have happened if the Royal Bank hadn't first committed a monumental gaffe in public relations. Crusty old Earle McLaughlin, the bank's chairman, had stirred up a hornet's nest in September 1976, when he announced that the bank just couldn't find a woman qualified enough to sit on the board. This was the year in which the term "Ms." made its first appearance in the *Oxford English Dictionary* and the Royal Bank and other major companies with all-male boards had been under increasing public pressure to appoint women to senior positions. Earle McLaughlin's remark was greeted with derision and disbelief. The old boys at the bank started to worry how their female customers might react to the fuss.

Soon after, McLaughlin called Mitzi and insisted on seeing her right away. She was flabbergasted when he asked her to join the bank's board and reluctant to accept. She didn't see how she could find the time, working almost around the clock, it seemed, at Miracle Mart. When Sam heard about it, he was adamant that she accept, convinced there was no better way for her to make business connections than to sit on the board of the country's biggest bank.

Once she said yes, the Royal Bank, now anxious to repair the damage to its reputation, immediately issued a press release, announcing it had found "an eminently qualified" woman to sit on the board. Under a provision of the Bank Act, she had to purchase 2,500 Royal Bank shares, costing a total of about $100,000 at the time. It was a small fee to pay for a membership in one of Canada's most exclusive clubs.

Mitzi suddenly found herself in great demand. She became a member of the federal government's Council on the Status of Women. She was the first woman in 156 years to be elected to the governing council of the Montreal Board of Trade. In 1978, she was named to one of twelve positions on the Economic Council of Canada, which advises the federal government on economic policy. In the early 1980s, she also served on one of the Liberal government's anti-inflation committees, the so-called "6 and 5" committees, that sought to bring inflation down to 6 and 5 percent respectively over a two-year period. She had become one of the most powerful women in Canada.

Mitzi's public profile made her a natural spokeswoman for the company. She was frequently quoted in Montreal's French- and English-language newspapers — and she knew the right things to say. Her father had always been a friend to French Quebec, hiring francophones well before companies were required to do so by language legislation. Steinberg's customers were French-speaking, and even when the political environment in Quebec became tense after the election of the pro-independence Parti Québécois government, Mitzi was always diplomatic. "God forbid we should alienate any of the customers," she said.

In fact, Steinberg was having trouble bringing people to head office from its Ontario stores. Some had refused transfers because they were concerned that their children couldn't be educated in English under Quebec language laws; many English-speaking Quebecers had already fled the province. Yet Mitzi maintained that nobody she knew who had fled to Toronto was happy, and she praised her home province. Some good would come from the election of the Parti Québécois government, she argued, because it would force the big anglophone firms to take a closer look at the Quebec market.

Jacques Bouchard, the advertising man who started at Steinberg and later ran BCP, one of Quebec's most successful francophone ad agencies, tried to convince her to do television commercials for the company, claiming that he could have made her a star. Mitzi seemed interested in the offer and sounded out a few executives about the idea. Ultimately she backed off.

Nevertheless she put a lot of stock in public relations. She made a large sale of winter coats to the federal government to help clothe the Vietnamese "boat people" who were arriving in Canada in the 1970s. On another occasion she donated $150,000 to sponsor a Quebec sailboat in a transatlantic race. The boat, *Le Mascaret-Steinberg*, eventually burned and sank, leaving its eight female crew members bobbing in a dinghy in the north Atlantic, where they were eventually rescued.

Part of her campaign at Miracle Mart was to upgrade the chain's fashion image, with a new accent on ready-to-wear clothing at an affordable price. As a publicity stunt, she once mounted a "magic lantern" fashion show, employing live models stepping in and out of film sequences. She sent models, photographers, and clothes to Mexico for six days to shoot against backgrounds such as the Mayan Ruins. Cost, it seemed, was no object.

She brought a flamboyant style to Miracle Mart, where her office was a definite eye-catcher. There was blue carpeting on the floor and walls, all the way up to the orange ceiling, which matched the color of the armchairs. On those walls hung a fortune in Canadian art. Later, when she became a corporate vice-president, her office was decorated in a striking combination of pink and beige with white lacquered furniture.

Even with her legendary drive, though, Mitzi was no match for the persistent problems at Miracle Mart. Although she still retained responsibility for it, Mitzi began to step away from a day-to-day role at the chain after her father died in 1978. She used her position as a Steinberg director and group vice-president to get involved in a wider range of Steinberg activities. Miracle Mart began to slide once again. Soon it was losing money and suffering from the same neglect that Mitzi had found when she first took it over. There would be no turnaround in the department stores.

When Michael Kershaw, who later transformed Miracle Mart into the M Store concept, took over, the situation was bleak. Every last nickel had been squeezed out of the stores. The place was slowly disappearing, like a melting ice cube. There was just one telephone in each store, rather than a line for each cashier to use when phoning for verification on a credit card. The company had changed to black telephones because they were cheaper. The stores were empty of customers, revenue was declining, and the only thing they knew how to do was cut expenses.

And Mitzi had bigger things to worry about. She and Mel were clearly calling the shots at Steinberg after Sam's death. Mitzi was fighting battles with Jack Levine and later with Peter McGoldrick, the two presidents who succeeded Sam. In 1983 she informed McGoldrick that she would be moving into the head office as executive vice-president, responsible for corporate and legal affairs. She was making the key decisions in the company, acting as president in everything but name.

She still wielded her power in a way that her employees found insensitive. Once she was planning to reorganize the company bakery and decided the best way to communicate with the employees would be through a video. When Frank DiMauro, a member of the communications department, went into her office with a video camera to tape her, he found Mitzi dressed in a flashy outfit and wearing what looked like several pounds of expensive gold jewelry. DiMauro explained that she couldn't dress like that, that her flamboyant look would detract from the presentation. He finally convinced her to take the jewelry off.

When he had finished taping Mitzi's speech, he thought it went well. But Mitzi had heard a couple of secretaries talking in the hallway outside her office during the taping and was furious. She insisted on doing it again. DiMauro waited uncomfortably while she went outside and tore into the employees, swearing loudly at them. You could have heard a pin drop after that.

She continued to treat the company as her personal fiefdom. In 1980 she decided that Steinberg should open a giftware and china shop to compete with Caplan's, a highly successful Montreal store that had become an institution in the city because of its low prices on quality crystal and china. Mitzi shopped there and knew the owner, a shrewd businesswoman by the name of Frances Isenberg. She invited Isenberg for coffee one day at Montreal's Ben Ash delicatessen and mentioned that she wanted to start a similar kind of store, asking whether Isenberg was interested in becoming a partner. When she was rebuffed, Mitzi decided to go ahead on her own.

What a store it was. She took a money-losing Miracle Mart outlet in west-end Montreal and completely gutted the interior, putting in the best of everything: oak floors, silk flower arrangements, brass fittings. She dreamed up a fancy sounding name for the store, calling it Lupton-Duvall, and stocked it with top quality merchandise. She even hired away an employee of Caplan's to manage the place.

The venture flopped. Caplan's fought back with an aggressive ad campaign, and Lupton-Duvall lost $3 million. Steinberg executives were terrified to say anything about it because Mitzi ran the store as if it were her own. But after two years of losses, she was forced to give it up. She made a deal with Caplan's in 1982 to merge the two stores, turning exclusive management of the operation over to Frances Isenberg, who quickly doubled the sales.

But Mitzi could also use her power effectively. Anyone who doubted that was convinced by the decisive way she settled a strike in November 1983. Steinberg food stores had been closed for a week with no hope of a settlement. During the strike, Mitzi had been so determined to keep a couple of stores open that she confronted some of the picketers blocking entrances to the stores and ordered them to go home. Once she scrambled into her Mercedes and followed one of the "rabble-rousers" who'd been picketing the warehouse.

A merry chase ensued, during which the elegantly dressed Steinberg heiress drove her Mercedes over a concrete median in her haste to catch her prey. When she finally caught up to him in a shopping-center parking lot, she leapt out of the car and screamed, "You better go home and park your car and if I see you around again I will personally fire you."

As that strike wore on, union leader Tom Kukovica had complained bitterly that the company negotiators did not seem to have much authority to reach an agreement. It was hard to know who to deal with. Finally, he called Mitzi and asked for a meeting. In a marathon bargaining session that lasted twenty-four hours, the two hammered out an agreement. Each gave a little but it was clear that Mitzi was not going to be the pushover her father had been with the unions. "She was very tough. For her, money was more important than anything else," Kukovica recalled. "It's funny, her father never worried too much about the money, he just asked someone to do the calculation. But Mitzi would say, 'What do you mean, a penny an hour? That's a lot of money.' "

Mitzi also proved her mettle with the unions that same year with the closure of the company's big east-end bakery. The workers were paid thirty percent more than at other union shops and the bakery was losing money. Mitzi proposed wage concessions to the workers; they refused, so she closed the place. She was a dramatic contrast to her father, who would have done anything to avert labor trouble, even if it hurt the company.

After the 1983 supermarket strike was settled, Mitzi spoke bravely about making Steinberg number one again. Even Kukovica, the union leader, seemed fired by her words and exhorted his members to help Steinberg reclaim the top spot in the market. But it wasn't to be. The company was in so much trouble that there was even talk of suspending the dividend to shareholders. Mitzi's hand-picked president, Peter McGoldrick, had been a disaster, the scheme to provide customers with 5-percent rebates on their grocery purchases had flopped.

Yet as bad as things were, no one believed Mitzi might relinquish her power over management. Even when McGoldrick, in whom so much hope had been invested, had quit, and Irving Ludmer was brought over from Ivanhoe to become the new president of Steinberg, she retained effective control of the company. Steinberg executives still streamed down the hall and into Mitzi's office, seeking her blessing for their projects and currying favor with her. She could still make or break an executive's career. And her new responsibilities at head office gave her the freedom to roam the place, getting involved in everybody else's business. It wasn't long before Ludmer's frustrations boiled over. The president made it clear he would quit if his authority continued to be undercut.

On September 6, 1985, Mitzi Dobrin abruptly resigned from Steinberg, quitting her job as executive vice-president of legal and corporate affairs, but retaining her position as a director of the company. There was no public confirmation of her departure for almost three weeks, when the company released her letter of resignation. Her letter stated that she wanted to devote more time to personal interests and that her willingness to withdraw from active management was an "expression of the highest confidence in the management team that now leads Steinberg".

The circumstances surrounding her departure remained a mystery for some time. It wasn't like her to quit, especially to leave the company that had been her lifeblood. Something serious had happened within the executive suite at Steinberg and the participants weren't saying much. Irving Ludmer tried to downplay the whole affair, saying that Mitzi had decided to go off on her own and start an investment company.

In fact, there had been an out-and-out confrontation between the two, and Ludmer had won. Arnold Steinberg recalled the events quite vividly. "Essentially, Irving said, 'It's either you or me, I'm not going to stay on as president.' Mitzi had realized, at last, that for the good of the company she would have to go. It put her husband, chairman Mel Dobrin, in a very awkward position, because the board of directors backed Ludmer. They really had no choice, given the turnaround Ludmer had already engineered at Steinberg. "It was very difficult for her. It was a real personal defeat," said one close associate of Mitzi's. "I think she met her master and backed off."

Ludmer remained diplomatic about it all, insisting that he had no personal differences with Mitzi. "The difference was, I was calling the shots." He acknowledged how painful the decision was for her, giving her credit for the decision. Yet the coolness between the two lingered, clearly visible at board meetings, according to Marc Lalonde, the former federal finance minister who served on the Steinberg board for five years. Mitzi just sat there, in stony silence.

The Mitzi era was over, and she left with mixed reviews. She had shaken up Miracle Mart temporarily. She had used her position in the family and on the board to confront Steinberg employees directly, demanding their personal loyalty to her, and in the process she had undermined the authority of many executives. The company had lurched around in disarray.

People who know Mitzi are struck by the contradictions within her. She and Mel are active in many charitable causes and they are great patrons of Canadian art. She has served with distinction on many boards and agencies. Socially, she is engaging and a lot of fun to be around, "a real ball of fire", according to friends. They admire this tiny woman who pushes herself so hard and is so determined to achieve.

But Mitzi was not fun to be around at the office, where employees found her abrasive and demanding. Sam had been tough with his people when he had to be, but always for a reason. Mitzi was tough because she didn't seem to know any other way. She was driven by hair-trigger emotions that would set her off in one direction, then another, as if the stress of living up to her father's name was just a little too much for her. "I think she tried her best, but I don't think her best was really good enough," observed Montreal money manager Stephen Jarislowsky, a longtime friend and adviser to the family. "It's obvious she's a bright girl with a good deal of competence and lots of get-up-and-go. I like her as a human being, I find her interesting. . . . But having that kind of father is a heavy cross to bear. It's not easy. It would have been more difficult for a boy, but it's very tough for a girl too."

Sitting in judgement of Mitzi Dobrin is not easy. Who could blame her for trying to save the company that her father built, the company that had been so completely intertwined with the family's interests for decades? Who could blame her for the many problems she inherited at both Miracle Mart and Steinberg, problems that Sam Steinberg himself had never been able to deal with successfully? To some people, she had acted like a spoiled rich girl, demanding that employees jump through hoops for her. At the same time she was equally hard on herself. "What I found was, she really wanted to do good for the company," said Diane Laurin, a former Steinberg lawyer who worked closely with Mitzi. "It was her company, but not only hers. She thought she had a duty."

Some of the Steinberg family members were unhappy at what she'd done, resentful of her star status and concerned that she had a negative impact on the company. Even Mitzi herself would have some regrets about her career, doubts that she later expressed to her uncle Morris Steinberg. "The way she sees it now, if she had the chance to do it over, she would not do it, she would have put somebody else in there," Morris said. Mitzi had wanted to emulate her father, had believed that she could succeed. But her uncle Morris had some gentle advice for her: "The real secret in life is to emulate yourself."

# 10

# *Daughters of the Empire*

Furnished with priceless antiques, vases, and Oriental rugs in rich burgundies and royal blues, the Dobrins' penthouse condominium in the exclusive Port Royal building on Sherbrooke Street looks more like a museum than a home. The two-story apartment with its spacious ceilings and private elevator boasts one of the finest art collections in Canada.

The Dobrins started purchasing art in the early 1950s, when you could still buy a painting by A. Y. Jackson for $250. They had to sell part of their enormous collection when they moved into the condominium — there simply wasn't enough space on the walls for all the Tommy Thomsons and Cornelius Kreighoffs and Group of Seven masterpieces. In 1986, some 128 oil paintings, watercolors, and sketches were auctioned off, fetching more than $4-million.

The Port Royal is just down the street from the Montreal Museum of Fine Arts, the Holt Renfrew store, and the Ritz-Carlton Hotel and faces some of the finest shops and art galleries in Montreal. But if the Dobrins' stunningly beautiful apartment reminds some people of a wing in the Guggenheim Museum, it also lacks the kind of warm, lived-in feeling one expects in a home. On entering the foyer with its huge gilt mirror, a visitor might wonder whether this is a corporate head office as well. Some big business is indeed transacted here.

This is where Mitzi Dobrin retreated following her resignation from Steinberg. She insisted she was relieved to be out of the company, away from the stresses and strains of a management job, but others who knew her felt she was bruised and embittered from her confrontation with Irving Ludmer. "Leaving Steinberg killed her," claimed her sister Marilyn.

Mitzi tried to compensate by throwing herself into new business ventures. An investment company she formed with son Ronny, DBRN Holdings Ltd., became the focus of her attention. The vowels were missing from the Dobrin name but there was something else missing as well: a sense of purpose, the kind of excitement Mitzi had thrived on while running the family business at Steinberg. She purchased ten percent of a ski resort, Mont Saint-Sauveur International Inc., located near her luxurious country home in the Laurentians, north of Montreal. But this was a passive investment, not the sort of thing that required her daily attention. She entered a couple of real estate deals on the recommendation of Harvey Wolfe and Ralph Berman, two Montreal businessmen who acted as advisers. But DBRN was a low-key affair and while it made some sound investments, it didn't exactly set the world on fire.

Anyone who knew Mitzi realized she would have trouble adjusting to life in the slow lane. What would she do with all that drive and energy? And how would she deal with her sense of loss at leaving Steinberg? She could not accept that loss peacefully. Her sister Marilyn sensed that Mitzi was bored and embittered. Her personal frustrations soon collided with those of her sisters, and a family that had once been a model of closeness was shattered by jealousy, rancor, and suspicion, which quickly boiled over into a lawsuit. Mitzi, who had once spent herself working so hard to preserve her father's corporate empire, would instead begin the process of dissolving it.

Searching later for the root cause of the dispute, friends and relatives still wonder how it could have happened. The Steinbergs were such a dream family that in the 1950s they had been the subject of a special photo essay in the New York magazine *McCall's*. The publication had named the Steinbergs "togetherness family of the month". On the cover of the special supplement was a photograph of Sam, seated squarely in the middle of a semicircular couch in his Westmount home, surrounded by Helen, five adoring young grandchildren, his daughters, and their husbands. "Posed for a family portrait," wrote *McCall's*, "the Steinbergs are a vibrant, appealing group. Informally . . . they radiate warmth and friendliness." In one photograph Helen was putting the finishing touches on a strawberry shortcake while spooning dinner into the mouths of her grandchildren Billy and Eileen. Another photograph showed Sam and the husbands playing cards, with Helen peeking over Sam's shoulder to look at his hand. "For relaxation," said *McCall's*, "Sam Steinberg finds nothing can beat a game of bridge with his sons-in-law."

The family looked the very picture of happiness, but reality is never quite captured in a photograph. Like any other family, the Steinbergs had internal problems that the public never glimpsed. The sisters' rivalries bubbled below the surface while their father was alive but once Sam died, they burst into view, propelling the girls into a bitter power struggle.

The four girls bore an astonishing resemblance to one another: they were all short, with similar hairstyles, constant tans, and those distinctive Steinberg eyes. Their personalities didn't mesh easily. While Mitzi was aggressive and driven, the second daughter, Rita, was warmer and more like Helen. She was quiet and personable, content to remain a housewife and mother while her entrepreneurial husband Leo Goldfarb ran the real estate side of Steinberg. There was always tremendous competition between Mitzi and Rita, which intensified when the girls married and their husbands came into the company. The rivalry then hinged on whether Mel or Leo would take over. It was an unusual kind of competition because Mel and Leo were best friends: the rivalry existed more in the minds of the girls.

Evelyn, the youngest, was the pampered child, doted on by her father, and emotionally and physically frail. She is doll-like, probably the tiniest of the sisters. Her slight frame, platinum-blond hair and penchant for funky fashions give her the air of a vulnerable young teenager, not a grandmother in her fifties. While not half as strong-willed as Mitzi and Marilyn, she was anguished by their torn relations and would emerge later as a family peacemaker.

Rita's death in 1970 devastated Evie, who was thirty-two at the time. The two sisters had been especially close; they had lived nearby in the suburb of Hampstead. After Rita's death Evelyn turned more toward her other sisters but her relations with them were always tenuous, especially with Mitzi. The two had "lots of ups and downs", as she put it. Their relationship worsened when Evelyn's husband William Alexander joined the company. Evelyn blamed Mitzi for the fact that her husband was going nowhere at Steinberg. Mitzi had made him feel completely unwelcome, she complained. There were many times when the two women wouldn't speak to each other.

Marilyn Steinberg, four years younger than Mitzi, grew up in the shadow of the older sister who always seemed to stand out from the others. Marilyn was a cute, chubby little redhead, who was content to stay in the kitchen with her mother while Mitzi was out in the street playing with the boys. Yet she later emerged as a powerful figure in the family, the sister most willing to challenge Mitzi's ascendancy.

Marilyn, like her sisters, is a tiny wisp of a woman, although what she lacks in height she makes up for in flamboyant personal style. When she walks into a room, you notice. She has a great sweep of copper-colored hair and a preference for heavy makeup, chunky jewelry, and stiletto heels. Beneath the flash she is down-to-earth and likeable, more easygoing and less intense than Mitzi. She has an extremely stubborn streak, however, that makes her a formidable adversary. Despite her lack of a university education, Marilyn has a native shrewdness that serves her well. Less impetuous than Mitzi, she likes to take her time and think things through.

In her childhood, Marilyn identified extremely closely with the business Sam had built. She accompanied her mother to the head office on Saturdays and would sit behind the switchboard, playing telephone operator. When they went to the stores, Marilyn would get behind the checkout counter and pretend she was a cashier. The stores were her playground. Like Mitzi, she frequently accompanied her father in search of choice real estate. "We were just children but the company was like part of our family."

Marilyn adored her father. She was always impressed by how carefully he listened to her and how he really seemed to care about her feelings for the company. "I remember when I was a kid, I went into a store and I saw a big fight or something. I phoned my father and said, 'Daddy, it was terrible, look what happened.' Before he went to the office he drove to that store. He went down and he phoned me back to tell me about it. I was just a kid but he listened. It made us feel we were a part of it." As a child, Marilyn said, her life was built around Steinberg activities. Whenever the company held one of its lavish length-of-service banquets at a downtown hotel for longtime Steinberg employees, she and her sisters always attended.

While Marilyn got along well with her father, she noticed an unusual relationship between her sister Mitzi and Sam. "Every one of us had a super relationship with him, except Mitzi," said Marilyn. "She thought she was really challenging him. He knew it, he laughed, and he didn't fight her about it." Mitzi was always so different. Even when the kids went to summer camp, three of the sisters would go to one camp, and Mitzi would go to another.

Marilyn's emotional identification with Steinberg was so strong that she never felt compelled to work in the business; Steinberg was already an integral part of her life. After graduating from Westmount High School, Marilyn was married at the age of eighteen to Len Pedvis, an ambitious young man who went into the company and hoped to take over Steinberg one day. They had three children, Billy, Penny, and Ricky, who were all nurtured on the Steinberg tradition and spent summers working in the stores. But Len Pedvis was a bit of a hothead. In the early 1960s, he squabbled with Sam when he was passed over for a promotion and quit in a huff. The marriage broke up a few years later, and Marilyn remarried, this time a millionaire Montreal clothing merchant named Simon Cobrin.

Although Mitzi and Marilyn have very different temperaments, they were close at an early age. Mitzi acted the part of the older sister, explaining things and showing the way. As adults they lived next to each other for many years in the Town of Mount Royal, one of Montreal's wealthiest suburbs. Their families shared a common backyard and they could wave to each other from the kitchen window. They golfed and shopped together, went to the same hairdresser and synagogue. Their kids lived in each other's houses and didn't think twice about borrowing a T-shirt or a pair of jeans from their cousins.

But even as back-to-back neighbors, there were tensions between the two. Mitzi was studying for her degree and she'd spend hours on end with her books. There were long periods when Marilyn would never see her older sister. "We lived different lives, even if we were back-to-back," Marilyn said. "She was lucky she lived there because I looked after her kids. They were accepted to eat in my house."

Whenever they did get together, signs of rivalry began to emerge. One summer the two were supposed to play against each other for the ladies' championship of their golf club. Mitzi had invested a lot of time and energy in her game and she hated to lose. On the day they were supposed to play, Sam called Marilyn at 7:00 o'clock in the morning and advised, "Let her win. She's older." Sam's old-world view of what was "right and proper" may not have accorded with a modern egalitarianism, but to his mind this was "fairness" toward his children.

While he spoiled them with cars, condos, and vacations, he was careful to treat the girls equally. And he brought that same sense of fair play into consideration in his will and estate-planning. He wanted the girls to share equally in the family fortune.

In 1952 Sam established four identical trusts designed to pass along his fortune to his daughters and grandchildren in equal measure. Drawn up by Sam's law firm, Phillips & Vineberg, the family trusts were typical devices used by wealthy Canadians to avoid tax. The Bronfman family had done exactly the same kind of thing.

The principle behind the trusts was a simple one. When someone dies, he is considered to have disposed of his capital. Suppose his assets had cost him $10-million to acquire and were worth $100-million at his death. The $90-million difference is taxable in the hands of the inheritor. By creating a trust for the spouse and children and putting the capital that accumulates over the years into it before death, the tax liability at death is deferred. If the inheritors in turn put the money into *their* children's trusts, the tax is deferred again.

In this case the principal asset of each trust was Steinberg common shares. The four trusts indirectly owned a holding company called Rockview Investments Inc., which controlled 2.4 million common shares of Steinberg, representing 40 percent of the voting stock in the company. These voting shares were not publicly traded on stock exchanges. Another 12 percent of Steinberg voting stock was held by Sam's estate, bequeathed on his death to his wife Helen. That gave Sam's immediate family 52 percent control of the company, not counting another 36 percent held by other branches of the Steinberg family. The four trusts also shared ownership of about 507,000 non-voting Class A Steinberg shares, which were listed and traded on the Montreal and Toronto Stock Exchanges.

Each of the four daughters' trusts provided that the capital would be held for her benefit until the eldest of her own children reached the age of twenty-five. At that point, 50 percent of the capital would be invested for the benefit of her children, in equal shares. The grandchildren would gain actual access to that invested capital later, as specified by the trusts: half of their share at the age of thirty, and the remaining half at forty. During her lifetime, the daughter would be paid the income on the other 50 percent of her original trust and would have rights to part of the capital.

When Sam Steinberg drew up those papers in 1952, they must have looked like a wonderful gift to his children and grandchildren. He tied the whole package together with a neat little bow, stipulating that the common shares held by Rockview and his estate be voted jointly under a voting-trust agreement. Sam exercised that vote until his death in 1978, when Helen became the sole voting trustee. When Helen took over she had the full confidence of her daughters, who believed she would vote the 52 percent block fairly and in everybody's best interests. Indeed, the whole idea of a voting trust agreement was to ensure that no child or group of children ganged up against the others for a personal reason.

The agreements called for the daughters to become trustees of their own funds after they reached the age of thirty-one. Initially, Sam asked family and friends to help teach the girls how to manage their money. His brother Nathan, along with physicians Sam Shuster and Michael Aronovitch, were the trustees in the early days, but the arrangement seemed to be fairly informal.

Sam Steinberg didn't want lawyers or professionals to manage the funds. He felt better having someone he knew in that position. "I was there because I knew the family," said Aronovitch. "If anything happened to him, I'd do for the children pretty much what he would have done. If they wanted to buy a yacht or a Rolls-Royce, I would have said no. If they wanted a Chevy or a Pontiac, okay."

Aronovitch didn't consider himself qualified to invest the money either, so he hired a stockbroker to start a portfolio and brought in a young newcomer to Montreal named Stephen Jarislowsky as money manager. Jarislowsky is a sophisticated European with a background in art history who has become one of Canada's most successful portfolio managers. He had befriended Sam Steinberg in the early 1950s, providing him with a link to the world of high finance. He was a natural choice to tutor the girls. Jarislowsky patiently explained why he selected certain investments and what benchmarks he used. The girls would then participate in the investment decisions at monthly dinner meetings.

The sisters voiced their opinions and it became apparent after a while that they wanted to do things on their own, especially Marilyn and Mitzi. They were uncomfortable with Jarislowsky's patient, long-term view of investing. Mitzi complained that Jarislowsky knew when to buy stocks but not when to sell them. By then, she had begun to invest heavily in art, especially Group of Seven paintings, and this became a source of friction for Marilyn, who thought the dividend money that Mitzi took to buy art should have gone back into the portfolios.

Any large sum of money attracts a lot of attention and a number of professionals started offering their services to the sisters, including people from Wall Street, causing a certain amount of confusion among the girls, who were still naive about the ways of the investment world. At the age of thirty-one, Marilyn went to New York to meet with the investment staff at the blue-chip firm of Morgan Guaranty. There she was thoroughly bewildered and intimidated by the starched-collar demeanor of the old patriarchs. Marilyn didn't like the sales pitch she was hearing, so she tried another Wall Street firm, the Lionel Edie Company. But when they recommended that she invest in Montana bulls and other more exotic commodities, she was again put off.

The sisters finally decided to make decisions themselves, but Marilyn wasn't completely happy with that arrangement either. Aronovitch had already noticed some dissension creeping into those monthly meetings. Basically each wanted to get hold of her percentage and run it her own way. But since each sister was one of the trustees for the others' trust, they seemed to be getting in one another's way.

Aronovitch believed the fault lay with Sam, for not having trained his daughters to live up to their responsibilities. They had grown up with little commitment to the community; they had too much money, too much time on their hands, and too little to keep themselves occupied, he believed. He grew tired of mediating their disputes and resigned as a trustee in the early 1970s.

Marilyn took a much more active role in managing the trusts after Aronovitch's departure. She started to learn about investing and she loved it. When Mitzi went off to join Miracle Mart in 1973, it was informally agreed that Marilyn would take over day-to-day responsibility for the trusts, Rockview, and the various other holding companies the sisters had established.

The trusts performed well. Steinberg made millions in profit, the dividends rolled in, and the money was invested for the benefit of the four sisters, each of whom had three children. As the twelve grandchildren grew up in the 1950s and 1960s, becoming wealthier on paper, the next generation of Steinbergs never considered their parents might one day disagree violently over how their money was managed and let the empire slip away.

By the time Sam died in 1978, there were seven trustees in place: Mitzi and Mel Dobrin, Marilyn and her second husband Simon Cobrin, Evelyn and William Alexander, and Morris Steinberg, Sam's youngest brother. According to the trust deeds, the seven were trustees of each fund, giving each sister a voice in the financial affairs of the others. That might have seemed like a good idea back when the Steinbergs were the *McCall's* magazine "togetherness family of the month", but years later it proved to be the family's undoing. When Mitzi filed her lawsuit against the other two sisters and their husbands in 1988, she had one goal in mind: to kick them out as administrators of her own trust.


The first hint of real trouble came in the winter of 1985, when Mitzi dropped a small bombshell. In late January she told Marilyn that a secret meeting had been arranged in New York with someone interested in buying Steinberg. In fact, that person represented two Vancouver businessmen — Jimmy Pattison and Sam Belzberg. Mitzi asked Marilyn to swear not to tell their sister Evelyn about it, because she couldn't trust her younger sister to keep a secret. Marilyn agreed, but later regretted the deception.

Marilyn wasn't interested in selling, but she accompanied her older sister to New York because she wanted to see what she was up

to. The meeting went badly. Marilyn was shocked to hear how her
sister put the company down. Mitzi's disenchantment with Steinberg was obvious. With Irving Ludmer in charge, she no longer had
a role to play. Now that she had lost her power at Steinberg, she
seemed bent on getting rid of the company at any price.

The New York meeting seriously damaged the family relationship. When Evelyn found out about it she was furious. She had
never been actively interested in the family business, but had,
nevertheless, always considered it part of her inheritance too. She
resolved to pay much closer attention; her trust in Mitzi was
severely diminished.

After the discussions in New York proved fruitless, Mitzi continued to seek out potential buyers. She acted as if the decision to sell
the business was hers alone. Twice she approached her wealthy
cousin and company vice-president Arnold Steinberg, first offering
him a chance to buy the business at $40 a share, with six weeks to
raise the money. Arnold was keenly interested; he felt the price was
cheap. The company was intending to split both classes of its stock
on a two-for-one basis, a common practice to attract buyers to
overpriced stock. So the $40 asking price was really $20. Arnold
raised the money through a U.S. investment banker, hoping to put
together a management buyout that would include Ludmer and
other senior executives. But when he went back to her, Mitzi said
she had reconsidered: the price was now $50. Arnold subsequently
discovered she'd never discussed the offer with her sisters, so he
didn't pursue it.

Indeed, Mitzi's secretive actions began to arouse the suspicions
of her sisters. Marilyn recalled several times that Mitzi would take
phone calls in another room with the door closed. For her part,
Marilyn still had faith in the company and believed it was the best
place for the family money to be invested. She also had confidence
that Ludmer was moving the company in the right direction. She
and Evelyn agreed to unite to oppose Mitzi's moves.

Mitzi continued to shop Steinberg around to prospective buyers.
She argued that the family trusts were weighted heavily in Steinberg
shares, which made up ninety percent of the trust assets. The family
had far too many eggs in the same basket and Mitzi was nervous
about what might happen if the company went down the tubes. It
was frightening when one's whole investment was riding on the

whim of a union that could strike at any time, slicing $6-million a day off the bottom line. She wasn't the only one in the family who felt that way. There had recently been a big gathering of all the branches of the Steinberg clan at the Dobrin home. Arnold and Mitzi had spoken, painting a fairly gloomy picture of the company, and some family members had decided that night to unload their shares.

Mitzi believed it was her duty as a trustee to consider any purchase offer that came along — and even to assist the process a little by inviting bids. In December 1985, the Caisse de dépôt et placement, Quebec's pension fund manager, made its first overture to Steinberg, offering privately to buy 50 percent of the shares held by the Helen Steinberg family. Jean Campeau, then the powerful chairman of the Caisse, knew Mitzi well and chatted regularly with her about Steinberg's problems. The Caisse was already a minor shareholder in Steinberg and was ready to help.

However, Marilyn wasn't interested in the Caisse offer and Mitzi felt it was impossible even to broach the subject with her. By the spring of 1986, Steinberg stock had recovered and was trading near $49. The market value of the company stock in the four trusts exceeded $150-million. The sisters stood to earn a nice payoff by selling some of their holdings.

Mitzi tried unsuccessfully to convince her sisters to profit from the stock market upsurge by unloading some of the family's non-voting stock held by Rockview. She also felt that other family holding companies (111762 Canada Inc., with $8.8-million in capital, and Four Stone Investments, with about $1.6-million in cash and marketable securities) weren't being properly looked after. The money was sitting in term deposits when it could have been invested in the market.

Whether or not Mitzi was right, her advice was not heeded, partly because her sisters felt she had again just barged in, without thinking, into someone else's territory. In Simon Cobrin's words, "One day Mitzi left Steinberg; the next day she moved into the [family] office and started taking over." Mitzi proposed that she run her own trust and the other sisters run theirs. But Marilyn felt she was being pushed out of her longtime role as trust administrator and she refused, claiming that the financial yield she had obtained on the family money — an average annual return of 13.4 percent to the end of 1987 — was more than competitive. Mitzi decided to pull her money out of Four Stone Investments Ltd.

However, that didn't solve the problem of who should manage the trusts, where most of the family money resided. Mitzi tried to set up a meeting with a money manager in New York. Marilyn didn't attend. She was clearly insulted and suspected that the only reason Mitzi was complaining about the administration of the family money was because she was trying to sell the company, just to get back at Irving Ludmer for having kicked her out. The more Mitzi pushed, the more Marilyn pushed back. An irresistible force had met an immovable object, and administration of the trusts became impossible.

Some family members tried to mediate the dispute, including Leo Goldfarb, Sam's estranged son-in-law. But the girls seemed intractable. Goldfarb came away unable to pronounce strongly in favor of one or the other. Mitzi had more business experience, but Marilyn had studied investing and finance on her own and had done "a pretty good job" of investing the inheritance conservatively, protecting it in the long term. Moreover, the trusts were the grandchildren's legacy as well, and she had to protect that. Goldfarb estimated that the funds earned what general certificates of deposit would have earned.

In May 1986, the Steinberg sisters attended a tribute dinner for their late father at the Ritz-Carlton, the elegant old hotel that caters to Montreal's elite. It was quite an occasion. The Weizmann Institute of Science, based in Rehovot, Israel, had received a large donation from the Steinberg family and was establishing the Helen and Sam Steinberg Plaza, a new home for scientific research into energy. The guest speaker at the black-tie affair was Quebec Premier Robert Bourassa.

Cocktails were served in the Gold and Grey Room and Helen Steinberg stood at the front, receiving guests. She had issued a statement in the dinner booklet, which read, "Throughout his life, my husband was a devoted admirer of those, who through the pursuit of research, seek the betterment of life for their fellow men." The sisters — Mitzi in white silk and satin, Marilyn wearing a black and silver sequined gown, Evie in pale pink — chatted with the invited guests, who included steel magnate Paul Ivanier and Quebec Chief Justice Alan Gold.

Later, each sister had a word to say at the podium about their father. It was a terribly difficult occasion for a family torn by dissension. The brave public face they displayed kept their feud well concealed and only those closest to the family had any idea of what was really happening. But the fact that each daughter had insisted on speaking publicly that night was a sign of change in the family. Before then, Mitzi had always been the one to step forward into the spotlight. Now, each sister felt compelled to establish a public persona. Mitzi no longer dominated the family.

While Sam was alive, they would never have become embroiled in a dispute like this. But without his autocratic authority to keep them in line, their mother was powerless to stop the quarrel. Suspicion and spitefulness had begun to corrode the sisters' relationship. They squabbled about money, but the real fight was about power. And, as the battle dragged on, allegations and accusations began to fly.

Mitzi charged that her sisters were guilty of a serious conflict of interest. Marilyn and Evelyn refused to allow any of the Steinberg Class A (non-voting) stock held by the trusts to be sold, yet they were personally selling Class A shares of their own. In the spring of 1986, Marilyn and Evelyn each sold 28,650 Class A shares. Furthermore, Marilyn had attempted to sell another large quantity of A shares she personally owned at $50. Marilyn and Evelyn "were preferring their own private interests to those of the trusts," Mitzi alleged, "but were totally unconcerned about any conflict of interest."

The other two sisters scoffed at Mitzi's charges. Outside the trusts they could all do what they wanted with their shares. At one time or other, almost everybody in the family had sold stock. When the price approached $50, Marilyn and Evelyn saw no harm in taking some profits by selling some of their personal holdings. The Dobrin family believed the two sisters were refusing to sell stock in the trusts so as not to depress the value of the personal holdings they were selling.

By this time the Dobrin children — lawyers Terry and Lewis and portfolio manager Ronny — were concerned at what they were hearing from their mother and they proposed a reorganization of the family holdings: they wanted the A shares moved out of Rock-view and into holding companies established by each trust. That way each could freely buy or sell independently of the others. Revenue Canada was asked for a draft ruling on the tax consequences of such a transfer. In the meantime, the Dobrin children also began to press Marilyn to provide them with the income and dividends from their share of capital in the trusts, which in 1986 alone amounted to more than $1.6-million.

Marilyn resisted on both counts. Frustrated by Mitzi's repeated demands, Marilyn told family members she would no longer have anything to do with the Dobrins or their children. She felt the whole issue was trumped up. The only reason they were criticizing her handling of the trusts was because they wanted to sell the company and she didn't.

The influence of Marilyn's husband Simon Cobrin was crucial in convincing her to fight back. Simon, energetic and outspoken, was a self-made millionaire. Some members of the Steinberg family accused him of sowing the seeds of dissension in his wife's mind whereas Simon believed he was helping Marilyn learn for the first time to stand up to her older sister.

Mitzi also made a personal attack on Evelyn, who had decided to back Marilyn in resisting the Dobrins' demands for a bigger payout of dividends. By claiming that Evelyn's decision was based solely on her desire to run her children's lives, Mitzi said that withholding the money was the only way Evelyn could "control them".

Like so many issues in this family dispute, the question of whether the children were receiving proper income from the trusts became obscured by emotion. The Cobrins claimed there was no reason to make a fuss about it. The sisters had always been in agreement about the disbursement of funds to their kids, they had all taken money out of the trusts on occasion to buy homes and cars for them. To them, the children were being used as pawns in the fight.

Marilyn and Evelyn counterattacked. They wanted to transfer all legal control of the trusts and holding companies from Phillips & Vineberg, the family attorneys for more than thirty years, to the firm of McKenzie, Gervais. Mitzi's son-in-law, Sam Mintzberg, was a partner at Phillips & Vineberg at the time and was providing advice to his mother-in-law. Marilyn felt she could no longer trust Phillips & Vineberg to act in her best interests.

Dumping the family's law firm was a dramatic move. The founder of the firm, the late Senator Lazarus Phillips, had devised and created the corporate framework of Steinberg. He had been deeply involved in a lot of the early financing ventures, enabling the family to turn their capital rapidly into stores. He had set up Ivanhoe and had taken Steinberg public. And he and Phil Vineberg had established the family trusts. The Steinbergs owed much of what they had to the firm of Phillips & Vineberg.

When she got wind of this, Helen Steinberg could no longer remain above the dispute. Even though she was silently grieving at the way her children were fighting, she hadn't wanted to get involved. This request was finally too much and Helen told Marilyn that she had no desire to transfer her legal affairs from the loyal firm that had served the family so well. An argument broke out and an incensed Marilyn ceased speaking to her mother.

This added a cruel twist to the dispute. Marilyn was convinced that her mother had fallen completely under Mitzi's sway and would do anything she asked. It was a bitter pill for Marilyn to swallow, say family acquaintances, because for many years Marilyn had actually been closer to her mother than Mitzi, always much more cheerful and easier to get along with than her older sister. Marilyn's personality was very like Helen's when the latter was young. This new intergenerational fracture made the family feud that much more distressing. Marilyn's resentment and anger over her mother's role in the dispute would grow so intense that when Helen celebrated her eightieth birthday with a lavish family party, Marilyn and her children refused to attend, spoiling the party for an aging and grieving grandmother.

"All my life I looked after my mother. . . . I sort of took it upon myself because Mitzi was never around," Marilyn said. At one time Helen had opposed Mitzi's plans to sell the company and backed Marilyn. But in the Steinberg family, alliances were constantly shifting and your friend today could be your enemy tomorrow. "I guess Mitzi hadn't spoken to my mother for a whole year because she didn't want to sell the business," Marilyn recalled. "Then one day, [Mitzi] came back to my mother, crying, and my mother came to me and said, 'Look, I have to go to Mitzi' and she walked out on me."

Helen suffered terribly and friends said she aged visibly during the dispute. She closed herself in her home and wouldn't speak to anyone, mourning the absence of her strong-willed husband, who would have put his foot down and solved the strife. Putting Helen in this position seemed so unfair, because she had always been the glue that kept the family together. Business may have been everything to Sam, but family was everything to Helen. Friends had continually remarked at what a perfect couple they made, strolling hand-in-hand through Westmount. In happier days they would take summer vacations, surrounded by their grandchildren. Helen had lived for her family, and "anyone who was friends with one was friends with all." Near the age of eighty, Helen lived to see a fourth generation of children and frequently babysat for the new-born great-grandchildren.

But settling the differences between the sisters was beyond a great-grandmother. Marilyn and Evelyn were determined to fight this out to the finish. In the fall of 1986 they asked Steinberg president Irving Ludmer for seats on the company's board of directors. This was an affront to Mitzi and her husband Mel, who had long represented the family's interests on the board. The Dobrins had both worked at Steinberg for years and they couldn't accept that Marilyn and Evelyn, neither of whom had worked a day in the business, could become directors of one of Canada's largest companies.

This convinced Mitzi that, to her sisters, Steinberg had become "a toy to be played with and manipulated" and that their goal was to humiliate her and Mel while placing themselves in the limelight. Mitzi suspected that Marilyn and Evelyn were not only seeking seats on the board; they were trying to have her removed as a director.

The other two believed they had a legitimate right to have a say in Steinberg's affairs. Although they were major shareholders, they were denied access to the board. They never really knew what was going on at Steinberg. To them it was unfair and highly irregular that the Dobrins should have two seats and they have none. Maybe if they had been named directors earlier, they felt, none of this would have happened.

Their initial request was turned down by Steinberg's management committee. As a result of that rejection, Mitzi later alleged, the two embarked on a secret plan "to acquire for themselves absolute control of Steinberg, so they could force themselves on the Steinberg board." In December 1986 Marilyn and Evelyn each purchased 10,000 common shares from a cousin. The shares hadn't been offered to the trusts and their purchase was "a clear breach" of the sisters' duties as trustees, Mitzi charged. Two months later, the two sisters acquired an additional 56,000 common shares each of Steinberg and bought a further 9,000 each in June 1987. They spent a total of $6-million on the buying spree, raising Mitzi's suspicions that they were planning a power grab. In fact, Marilyn and Evelyn were trying to protect the family against a possible sale of the company by buying as many shares as they could from other branches of the large Steinberg family.

If Marilyn and Evelyn ever came close to controlling Steinberg, it was because of a serious strategic error committed by the Dobrins. In October 1986, in an effort to end the family's civil war, the couple had agreed to allow the husbands of the other two to become directors of the holding company for Steinberg stock, Rockview Inc., and its parent, Hermms Investments Ltd. The dissident sisters and their husbands were then in a position to outvote Mitzi and Mel on every item of business. They did so regularly. One of the first votes was to finally effect the change of legal counsel from Phillips & Vineberg to McKenzie, Gervais.

Meanwhile lawyers for the two sides were trying to work out a solution to the problem of how dividends should be distributed from the trusts. Proposals went back and forth without success, each side suspecting the other's intentions. A directors' meeting of Hermms and Rockview was finally held in July 1987 to discuss the issue. Helen Steinberg planned to attend, to explain to her daughters what Sam's real intentions had been when he set up the trusts and to argue that it was wrong to withhold the income from the trusts and their share of the vested capital from the seven grandchildren who were over thirty.

When Helen arrived at the meeting, Marilyn immediately told her that she was not invited, that it was a business meeting, and that she was to leave immediately. If that was an unpleasant surprise for Helen, what came next was even more stunning.

The dissident sisters and their husbands had laid an ambush for Mitzi and Helen. Using their newfound control over the family holding company, they passed a resolution to break up the family's voting trust. The resolution authorized Rockview to remove its 40 percent of Steinberg common shares from the larger block of stock voted by Helen. This meant that the family holdings would no longer be voted as one. Combined with the other share purchases they had made, Marilyn and Evelyn together now controlled by far the largest single block of Steinberg shares.

This was an enormous step for the two sisters to take. The Steinberg family had voted their shares together ever since Sam had driven a horse and cart on St. Lawrence Boulevard. Evelyn had real reservations about the move, knowing the effect it would have on Helen, but the two sisters felt there was no other way to break Mitzi's control.

The Dobrins never believed the other two would go through with it. For years Marilyn and Evelyn had been pushovers, willing to go along with whatever the Dobrins wanted. Suddenly the quiet little sisters had been transformed into corporate streetfighters. The hard, cold confirmation that the voting trust would be broken up came a few weeks later when bailiffs arrived at Helen's home in Westmount, delivering legal notice that the agreement would be dissolved by the end of November 1987. The decision had to be disclosed to the press because it represented a material change in the affairs of Steinberg. Helen had in fact voted a total of 4.4 million common shares, almost 74 percent of the company's voting stock, once other family holdings were factored in. To outsiders, the obvious question now was, who controlled Steinberg?

For the first time since the dispute had begun to simmer two years before, the public heard of internal dissension in the family, although Steinberg officials tried hard to play it down. "This is a matter among the shareholders," executive vice-president Arnold Steinberg told the Montreal *Gazette* at the time. Rumors of family infighting were "grossly exaggerated", he maintained.

The stock market analysts weren't fooled. They saw the breakup of the voting trust as a sign of future instability in the company. Indeed, the decision sent a signal to the investment world that Steinberg, always considered a tightly controlled family enterprise, was now fair game for a takeover. This was just what the stock market jackals and corporate raiders looked for in a takeover target. When the owners could no longer agree on anything, then selling the company was usually the preferred solution. What's more, dissension among major shareholders was usually reflected in a declining share price, making the target company cheaper to acquire on the stock market.

That is just what had happened. Steinberg stock had fallen from the lofty height of $49 it had reached during the spring of 1986. Irving Ludmer's turnaround scheme at Steinberg had run into a few roadblocks, including a three-week strike at Miracle Mart, and a day and a half strike in the supermarkets. The company's financial results for fiscal 1986 were profoundly disappointing. Profit was sliced almost in half — to $39-million from $74-million the year before — reflecting the shutdown of eleven Miracle Mart stores and other restructuring moves. Steinberg looked like the classic corporate underachiever: rich in assets, poor in profits. It wasn't long before offers began to land in the family's lap. It began to look as if Marilyn and Evelyn's strategy could backfire; they who had earlier fought Mitzi's attempts to sell the company might bring about that very event by their attempt to gain greater control of the company's stock.

# 11

# *Family Feuds*

The Steinberg conflict attracted considerable public attention. This was one of Canada's wealthiest families, owning one of the country's largest corporate empires.

To people familiar with the intensely emotional world of family-owned businesses there was nothing particularly surprising about the daughters' messy feud. The accountants and tax lawyers who provide professional advice to family-owned enterprises see these kinds of conflicts almost daily. They are the first ones to admit that blood and money don't mix easily. Paul Marchand, a Montreal tax lawyer specializing in family practice, acknowledged that the Steinberg case was dramatic and interesting because there were prominent people and a lot of money involved, but he estimated that there are hundreds of such cases every year in North America.

The usual emotional tensions and rivalries that exist in every family are magnified tremendously when money is at stake. Unfortunately, family members often identify completely with the business they own. Many have no sense of personal worth or identity outside the corporation. When a dispute arises and they can't get their way, their very being seems threatened and they often lash out in irrational ways.

With other people the ego seems to take over. Once they have more than enough money they start looking for recognition. They feel jealous when a brother or sister gets a name in the newspaper and suspect that the other sibling is using the family capital to enhance his or her reputation.

The most common problem starts with an owner, like Sam Steinberg, who is not only unwilling to face his own mortality but cannot recognize the shortcomings of his heirs. He thinks his children are special and will be able to work it out between themselves. Sometimes it works out. The children carry on where their parents left off and build very successful businesses. But such stories are the exception. By one estimate, 80 percent of family-owned businesses in North America fail to remain in family hands beyond the second generation.

Part of the problem is that wealthy founders of family businesses want to make life easy for their kids, much easier than the life they had, and protect them from the stresses of working. As a result the second generation is less qualified to run the business than the first. Or the children express no real interest in the business and the father is suddenly confronted with a terrible dilemma: putting incompetent children in charge keeps the business in the family but at the risk of failure; bringing in outsiders ensures success but takes operating control away from the family. This was precisely the dilemma Sam Steinberg faced and never resolved.

The best solution may not be to divide the business equally among the heirs but rather to hand it over to the child who shows the greatest interest in it. In the case of Steinberg that would have been Mitzi. Sam could have bequeathed her the common shares in the company and compensated the other sisters with preferred (or fixed-income) shares and money from the family trusts. She may not have made a perfect chief executive but at least she could have run the company without interference.

The secret to avoiding family conflict is communication and long-term planning. One wealthy family that Paul Marchand represents has regular meetings at which all family members are expected to account for and explain their investment activities. When one member wanted to start a company with a loan from the family, he had to submit a business plan to the others for approval. That family is very close. They delegate responsibilities. They take it seriously. They don't have any drinks until the business part of the meeting is over.

Too many industrialists have failed to learn those lessons, though. The pages of Canadian newspapers have been filled with stories of tensions and feuding within prominent family-owned companies. Real estate developer and failed takeover artist Robert Campeau has taken two of his children, Jacques and Rachelle, to court in a battle over the family shareholdings. The late owner of the Toronto Maple Leafs, Harold Ballard, had well-publicized scraps with his children Harold, Jr., and Bill over control of Maple Leaf Gardens. The Billes family, who own Canadian Tire Corp., was torn apart when brothers Alfred and David wanted to sell the company but were later blocked by their sister Martha.

When family disputes wind up in court the dirty linen is aired publicly. Gene and Bernard Kruger, the reclusive Montreal brothers behind Kruger Inc., spent years fighting a legal battle over control of dividends from the huge pulp and paper company. Members of Montreal's Birks family waged a particularly nasty court fight for control of their jewelry empire. At one point, criminal charges were laid against Drummond Birks by his cousin Robert for allegedly defrauding the Birks Family Foundation, although the case was never pursued by the Quebec justice department.

Ironically, the manner in which the Drummond Birks family handled an internal struggle for company control offers a lesson for other family businesses. Until recently Drummond Birks's three sons controlled the company. One of them, Thomas, wished to buy the shares of his two brothers, Jonathan and Barrie, and in late 1989 he made them an offer. In so doing he triggered a "shotgun agreement" that forced them to either sell to him, or in turn make an offer for *his* shares. They chose the latter and Thomas had to accept. (Jonathan later bought out Barrie's stake too.) The shotgun prevented things from becoming ugly and protracted. Unlike the Steinberg situation there was no bitter fighting among siblings over whether to buy or sell. It was neat and tidy and the company stayed intact.

One of the most difficult truths to accept is that a family business may have to be run by professional management if it's going to survive in an ever more complex and competitive economic environment. Should one reasonably expect a son or daughter to run an enormous, family-owned business empire the way Dad did? That tough question is now being faced by prominent Canadian industrialists such as Paul Desmarais of Power Corp. of Canada and Pierre Péladeau of Quebecor Inc. Both men have built huge corporate conglomerates and both are getting on in years. Each has two sons working in the business who haven't yet demonstrated that they're ready to take over.

In many cases family members have to learn to take a back seat and let the paid employees do the job. That's easier said than done. The classic example of a family-owned company managed by professionals is the giant Ford Motor Company in the U.S. There hasn't been a family member running the auto company since 1979, when Henry Ford II retired as chief executive. Since that time Ford enjoyed great success under the direction of chief executive Donald Petersen. But by 1989 a new generation of Fords was determined to secure a more active role for the family, which controls 40 percent of the voting stock. Henry II's son Edsel Ford II and his cousin William Clay Ford, Jr., have been pressing for more family representation on the board and a greater say in decision-making. Many of the younger Fords complain they feel alienated from the company that bears their name. It's an open question whether their greater participation will be an asset to the company.


The same feeling of alienation spread through the Steinberg family like a stain in the years following Sam's death. By 1989 there were only three family members still employed there — a far cry from the days when Sam had filled the place with relatives. He had turned nepotism into a fine art, giving jobs to his brothers, cousins, nephews, and grandchildren, to anyone in the family who wanted one. The place was almost like a day-care center, with Sam watching proudly over his clan and giving them each an allowance in the form of a Steinberg salary. But over the years, and especially after Sam's death, family members fell by the wayside. For one reason or another they were no longer able to sustain their interest or emotional attachment in the company.

Murray Steinberg was one of the first to leave. His father Nathan was the brother closest to Sam, and Murray had wanted to go into the business ever since he was a toddler. During the war Murray rode his tricycle to the neighborhood Steinberg store to help out his brother Arnold in the bottle-return booth. In elementary school he sold Red Cross calendars for a dime each from a table in the

Steinberg supermarket on Queen Mary Road. His father Nathan, who was in charge of buying produce for many years, often took Murray with him on Sunday visits to the farms just north of Montreal.

Nathan expected his three sons, Lewis, Arnold, and Murray, to all go into the family business, and they didn't disappoint him. Murray studied at Sir George Williams University in Montreal, worked for a few months as a produce buyer; then after a year of travel abroad he returned in 1960 to become a Steinberg store manager.

Murray never entertained the kind of ambitions that his brother Arnold had of becoming Steinberg's chief executive officer. But he thought he would advance further in the company than he did. His career peaked when he eventually became manager of meat purchasing in Quebec, responsible for a $125-million business that bought millions of pounds of meat every year.

The job was dumped right in his lap. There had been some scandal involving management (part of the meat industry in Quebec at that time was under the control of organized crime) and Murray was asked to take over. It was a typical Sam Steinberg move. "Because I was family, they trusted me," Murray said. The job proved to be extremely demanding. He decided "there was more to life than dreaming of meat and worrying if there'd be a breakdown," so he eventually left the company — much to his father's disappointment — after twelve years there. He became an independent food broker, a job that allowed him much more time with his family, though he remained a substantial shareholder after he left.

Another of Sam's nephews, Brahm Steinberg, also reached the conclusion that a career at Steinberg was not for him. Brahm was the son of Max, the quiet and studious brother who kept the financial and real estate records in the company. Brahm grew up feeling that he was part of some larger entity. His dad looked up to Sam almost as a father figure. As a youngster Brahm would climb into a cardboard box at a Steinberg store and Max would push him along the metal rails that carried grocery orders. This was Brahm's world and it was assumed he would take his place in it when he finished his studies at Sir George Williams University.

Unfortunately, Brahm had an inauspicious start at Steinberg. After graduating with a commerce degree, he spent seven months learning to be a produce manager — not the most interesting work in the world. He left to obtain an MBA at the University of Western Ontario, then returned, to the Miracle Mart division, in 1965. On his first day back, his father died of a heart attack and Brahm was suddenly on his own. Mel Dobrin, the general manager, paid little attention to him after that.

He also discovered it was a curse having the Steinberg name. Fellow employees did not easily accept a member of the controlling family in their midst. Most of them figured he would go behind their backs to Sam with reports about them. It wasn't an easy time for him.

Eventually he rose to the position of vice-president and general merchandise manager at Miracle Mart, working under Mitzi Dobrin. He had a good relationship with her but turning Miracle Mart around proved to be an impossible challenge. Depressed by the poor financial results, and after eighteen years with the company, he finally left to start his own clothing business. He felt relieved to be gone.

One executive who saw absolutely no advantages in employing members of the Steinberg family was Irving Ludmer. That was abundantly clear from Ludmer's triumphant showdown with Mitzi in 1985. He believed strongly that nepotism had dragged Steinberg down and that if the practice were allowed to continue unchecked, the company would never be able to recruit the talent it needed. When he took the president's job he was determined to get rid of those family employees he felt weren't carrying their weight. "That was a test of me. It was a test to see whether I meant this was going to be a professionally run corporation or not," he said. As the company pruned its management staff, several more prominent family members left, including Sam's nephews Lewis and David and his grandson Billy. After the purge was over Ludmer admitted that he wasn't exactly loved by the family.

Ludmer's strategy was backed by a key Steinberg executive, Bill Cleman, who ran Ivanhoe Inc. He was being groomed to take over the top job at Steinberg once Ludmer retired. Cleman spent considerable time talking with the family employees, especially the young ones like Billy and Ricky Pedvis, Marilyn's kids, who were among the beneficiaries of the family trusts. He pleaded with them not to stay. "You don't need the company," he told them. "You have your millions of dollars." If they wanted to learn about business, they should go elsewhere, he said, someplace where they wouldn't get in the way. As shareholders, they would always have the option of coming back later. They ignored his advice.

Nor was the family very popular among members of middle management, who felt resentment every time a Steinberg heir took a job. Jimmy Alexander, Evelyn's son, believed some people in middle management were campaigning to get the family out, spreading malicious gossip about the competence of certain family members and using "subterfuge".

"The brightest ones in the family had the brains not to come here," Bill Cleman concluded. He particularly admired Morris Steinberg's daughter, Ivy, a bright young woman with entrepreneurial instincts who had spent two years at Steinberg as a financial analyst before deciding that the place just wasn't for her: there was too much family politicking. She opened a sporting-goods store and was much happier running her own show. Mitzi's son-in-law Sam Mintzberg was another case in point. He was a very bright tax lawyer, a prize-winning student at McGill University, and he always declined offers to join Steinberg.

As for those family members in the company, dismissing them became a delicate matter. In some cases they were major share-holders, such as Lewis Steinberg, Nathan's son, who owned 17 percent of the company in concert with his brothers Murray and Arnold. Lewis had been running the restaurant division, making virtually every important decision in that operation, when he was pushed out in 1988. Lewis was devastated, his whole status bound up in being a Steinberg vice-president. He was so bitter that he considered legal action against the company. David Steinberg, the son of Sam's older brother Jack, had worked closely with Lewis in the restaurant division and also became a casualty of the Ludmer purge, leaving in 1987 after he was passed over for a promotion.

Perhaps the most difficult and fateful decision Ludmer made was in sacking Billy Pedvis, Marilyn's son. Terminating one of Sam's grandchildren was a delicate matter because Billy was one of the beneficiaries of the Steinberg trusts. He and the 11 other grandchildren stood to inherit the company. By firing Billy, Ludmer alienated Marilyn, until then his staunchest supporter.

As a youngster, Billy had often told his grandfather that he wanted to become president of Steinberg one day, a dream his mother had encouraged. Billy had been very close to Sam. As a teenager he often drove his grandfather to his regular golf game, stopping frequently on the way to visit Steinberg stores. Billy remembered Sam as a very emotional man. "There was a Danny Kaye movie he loved, and he always cried at the same spot every time he saw it."

Billy studied economics at McGill and was brought into the company following a personal request by his father Len Pedvis. He rose to the position of director of real estate for Steinberg and felt he had earned his position through hard work, not family name. Being a Steinberg was actually a handicap, he believed, and forced one to work harder than other executives. For example, there was the time he was assigned to work in a supermarket and none of the employees would talk to him for the first couple of days. Word had spread quickly that a Steinberg heir was working there. "They didn't know why I was there, if I was going to spy on them, or what."

Billy spent more than ten years at Steinberg, and in the eyes of some employees he would have been a natural choice to run the company some day. "He was a good-looking, well-spoken young man who seemed quick to learn," recalled one former Steinberg executive, Frank DiMauro. "A lot of people expected he would eventually take over since he was a major shareholder and just about the only one of the younger generation still in the business."

But in 1988 Billy was dismissed at the age of thirty-four in one of Ludmer's executive shakeups. A few months, before he had been interviewed by a community newspaper and had made the mistake of publicly declaring his ambition to run Steinberg. Irving Ludmer was livid at this and Billy's fate was sealed. On the day he was fired, Billy asked if there wasn't another spot available for him in the company. Ludmer told him, "Nobody wanted you;" Billy, he said, hadn't embraced the gung-ho work ethic espoused by Ludmer. Billy figured he was simply a scapegoat. Steinberg was cutting staff and he was a family member they could point to as proof they were being evenhanded in their layoffs.

Almost everyone in the family was furious at what happened to
him. Even the Dobrin children, who by then were embroiled in
their own conflict with Marilyn, were appalled at the firing of her
son and said so to Ludmer. When Ludmer attended Helen Steinberg's eightieth birthday party at the Ritz-Carlton, several of the
grandchildren gathered around him at the bar and told him off.
Jimmy Alexander told him "another thirty-, forty-, fifty-, or sixty-
thousand dollar salary isn't going to change the bottom line. You
could have kept Billy around." Billy insisted he wasn't bitter, but in
the end his firing may have been Ludmer's crucial mistake because
it began to reunite the sisters — against Steinberg's chief executive.

From their position on the sidelines, other members of the family
viewed the squabble between Sam's daughters with a mixture of
fascination and mounting worry. Many of them still had stock in
the company and they were naturally concerned about the rumors
of discord they were hearing. No one was sure who represented the
controlling block anymore; they were unsure whether to buy more
shares, sell, or stay put.
    One thing was clear. The hairline cracks in the sisters' rela-
tionship had widened to gigantic fissures by 1987. Mitzi was no
longer speaking with Marilyn and Evelyn and all communication
between them was through their lawyers. The sisters all owned
condominiums in the same apartment building in Bal Harbor,
Florida, which made winter vacations decidedly uncomfortable.
They would often bump into each other on the elevator, riding
together in icy silence.
    Their dispute was not only causing concern in the family; it
alarmed Irving Ludmer. The Steinberg chief executive tried unsuccessfully to set up a meeting to reconcile the two camps. He
recognized that mediation was urgent because word of the dispute
had already leaked out to the investment community. Rumors of
takeover offers were starting to fly and it was important to keep the
control block together.
    Before Steinberg's annual meeting in the fall of 1987, the vice-
president of communications, Doug Long, tried to warn the company's top executives that they might be asked embarrassing questions about the family dispute by journalists or shareholders. Of

course the feud was such a sensitive subject in the management suite that nobody was anxious to discuss it publicly. Nevertheless Long conducted a briefing session with chairman Mel Dobrin and chief executive Irving Ludmer, during which he tried to prep them on possible questions.

Playing the role of an inquiring reporter, Long turned to Mel Dobrin and asked: "Sir, is there any truth to the rumor that your wife is in a dispute with her sisters?" Long still remembers the look of horror that spread across Dobrin's face. Turning to Irving Ludmer, Mel sputtered, "Is that a real question?" Ludmer turned back to Long and asked, "Is that a real question?" Assured that it was, Mel Dobrin threw his hands up in the air, turned to Ludmer, and implored, "Then you answer it."

Management survived the annual meeting, but by then Irving Ludmer had bigger things to worry about. By mid August 1987, a $1-billion offer to purchase the company had come from the Weston group, owners of the Loblaws supermarket chain. It was more than just a passing interest on Weston's part. Their executives came to Montreal to meet Ludmer, accompanied by their investment bankers, Burns Fry Ltd. Ludmer and Arnold Steinberg met separately with each sister and her husband to inform them of the details. Ludmer told them this wouldn't be the last offer for the company and that a potential purchaser might be willing to pay more than $1-billion.

The sale of the company might be the best way for them to resolve the family dispute, Ludmer suggested. It would allow the family to diversify its holdings, which were heavily weighted in Steinberg shares. Ludmer also advised them that if they wanted to sell, they should act quickly because the tax on capital gains would increase after 1987. In addition Steinberg's lawyers had advised that the family could receive a substantial premium on their voting stock, as opposed to what the non-voting shareholders would collect. A stock with a vote was always worth a lot more than a stock without one, perhaps 25 to 50 percent more.

The Dobrins wanted to explore the offer, but the Cobrins and Alexanders had no interest. This refusal by her sisters to consider the matter was too much for Mitzi. The Dobrins wanted to unload the business because they saw that they weren't actively involved in it and they saw no assurance they would be able to turn it around.

The company was getting no response from the union in its efforts to lower labor costs and the Quebec supermarkets were in trouble. If the food stores continued to bleed red ink, they could conceivably bring down the whole company.

Marilyn and Evelyn didn't share Mitzi's alarm. They were more interested in exercising their newly acquired control over Steinberg and once again they pressed Ludmer to appoint them to the board. Mitzi alleged that the two dissident sisters, who now controlled the largest block of Steinberg voting shares, were planning to call a special shareholders' meeting to remove Mitzi and Mel as directors.

Marilyn denied that intention, saying only that she had raised the valid question: "If Mitzi wants to sell and we don't, why is she sitting [on the board] and we're not? Don't you think we have an equal right to be there?"

Mitzi's little sisters were gaining more gumption every day, looking for every tactical edge they could find. They had already managed to place their husbands on the board of directors of 111762 Canada Inc., the holding company Helen had set up to distribute income to her children. To Mitzi this was another blatant move by her sisters to win control of the empire. There were 92,000 Steinberg common shares in 111762 and if the two sisters could gain voting control of them, they would have even more leverage in the power struggle.

Helen, who had put up the initial capital in 111762 by issuing preferred shares, was equally alarmed at the move by Marilyn and Evelyn. Her preferreds were refundable to her on 30 days' notice and in July 1987, she filed a formal request with 111762 to redeem the shares. No immediate action was taken. There was more than enough money in term deposits to meet Helen's redemption request but her sisters were stalling on approving it, Mitzi claimed.

Tempers boiled over on September 29, 1987, when the directors of 111762 convened. Helen chaired the meeting, and all three daughters attended. There was plenty of business on the table — the financial statements of the holding company hadn't been approved for over a year because of the ongoing feud. There was also some dispute over the accuracy of the financial statements. Mitzi claimed that the auditors, the Montreal firm of Sorkin & Richer, had sided with Marilyn and Evelyn. Indeed, Sorkin & Richer had already resigned as auditors for the Dobrin family. Mitzi believed that Marilyn used her privileged position with them to manage the family holding companies to her own advantage. Helen promptly removed Sorkin & Richer as auditors of her personal affairs.

But the really contentious issue at the meeting was Helen's request to redeem her preferred shares. Mitzi and Helen were threatening a lawsuit to force the redemption, but Marilyn and Evelyn weren't budging. The two sides had reached an impasse. Suddenly, on that September morning, the Steinberg sisters turned the boardroom meeting into a tragi-comic farce. They were up on their feet, yelling and finger-pointing and getting red in the face. The meeting disintegrated into a screaming match in which all the seething resentment that had been pent up inside for so long boiled over. There was no point in continuing. Marilyn and Evelyn walked out of the room and later advised their sister and mother they would not be attending a meeting of the trusts scheduled for 11:30 that morning.

On the following day, September 30, Marilyn and Evelyn moved out of the Ste. Catherine Street office they shared with Mitzi. Mitzi claimed that her sisters removed every single piece of furniture, including her personal effects. They also carted off the records and files of 111762 Canada Inc. to their new office in the Alexis Nihon Plaza building, where Mitzi was now persona non grata.

This was not the way Steinberg girls were supposed to behave. Sam had raised them to be little ladies: what would he have said now? The dispute was now so all-encompassing that even his grandchildren were being drawn in. Before the squabble began they had never really been aware of the precise terms of the trusts. But on September 14, 1987 the Dobrin children Terry, Lewis, and Ronny wrote a letter requesting that the seven trustees provide them with their share of capital in the trusts. "Each of us, as you know, is over the age of 30 and the Trust expressly provides in Clause 12 that we are entitled to delivery of one-half of our respective vested share of capital," they wrote. Three of the trustees — Mitzi, Mel, and Morris Steinberg — agreed to disburse the capital but the other four trustees — the dissident sisters and their husbands — did not respond to the letter because they suspected the motives of its authors.

The three children of the late Rita Steinberg and Leo Goldfarb — Eileen, Gail, and Robert — also wrote a letter expressing their

concern about the trusts. The Goldfarb children had lived a difficult life, suffering through the divorce of their parents and then the
death of their mother a year later. They were considered interested
sellers of Steinberg stock but their trust was managed by the other
three families. The trustees agreed on December 3 to distribute part
of the capital in the trust to the Goldfarb children, resolving at least
part of the impasse.

The logical way to end the fight would have been for one side to
buy out the other. Indeed, rumors were spreading within the family
that Marilyn and Evelyn wanted to buy out Mitzi's stake in Steinberg. A price of $30 was mentioned, an amount well below what the
company stock was worth. Marilyn and Evelyn probably couldn't
have afforded to pay market value for Mitzi's holdings anyway,
since most of their personal wealth was tied up in Steinberg shares.

There was another potential solution. Marilyn attempted to
convince Irving Ludmer, Arnold Steinberg, and his two brothers to
form a voting trust with her and Evelyn. Such an arrangement
would have created an effective control block of almost 40 percent
of the common stock. Ludmer and Arnold, however, turned down
her offer. As senior executives within the company, they couldn't
be seen to take sides.

By this time Mitzi had had enough. "They were squeezing me on
everything, just to harass me," she complained. "I had lost control
of my own trust." After talking the situation over with her children
and their spouses, Mitzi made her most dramatic move. She told
her family to brace themselves. "I told them, fasten your seat belts,
it's going to be a rough ride." The turbulence was more than she
could ever have imagined.


Marilyn and Simon were spending the holiday at their condominium in Bal Harbor, Florida, when the phone rang on December 30, 1987. On the line was a family lawyer, telling them the
Dobrins had just filed a lawsuit in Quebec Superior Court seeking
to remove them and the Alexanders as trustees and charging them
with "gross negligence and reprehensible disregard" in their management of the Dobrin and Goldfarb trusts. The Cobrins were
caught off guard and deeply shocked.

A copy of the lawsuit was sent to the Cobrins by courier in
Florida. It contained a few well-aimed barbs and putdowns: "Mar-

ilyn Steinberg, while doing the best she was capable of, had no experience in business matters, had never been involved in the administration of any active business, had little education," the document alleged. It also described Simon Cobrin and William Alexander as little more than putty in their wives' hands, men who "deferred on every matter to their wives and refused to exercise independent judgement or intervene in any way to influence or moderate the views of their wives". The claim contained enough details of the family fight to titillate the press, who made it front-page news.

Simon Cobrin was furious at the allegations. What particularly galled him was "all the dirt in there, all the personal things about the conflict with the mother and the children." He couldn't understand why the Dobrins would go to such lengths and he was simply itching to take them to court. Other family members were equally shocked and incredulous that Mitzi, despite all the bickering, would actually take her sisters to court.

Mitzi knew full well what she was doing. She had been blocked at every turn and had exhausted every other avenue. She was being outvoted by her sisters and had lost control of her own destiny. She had been thinking about legal action for almost a year but one of the senior lawyers at her son's legal firm initially talked her out of it. A year later the same lawyer had completely changed his mind, telling her, "You've got to sue. You have no other choice."

Some family members felt the lawsuit was a carefully calculated strategy, not an impulsive reaction. "There was no intention of going ahead" with it, said Morris Steinberg, the trustee who had usually sided with the Dobrins at family meetings. "This was just a way of shaking them up, a tactical move."

No doubt about it, the Cobrins were shaken, but they weren't about to give up the fight. Their lawyer, Jack Greenstein of the firm McKenzie & Gervais, prepared a point-by-point statement of defence to Mitzi's charges. Marilyn was "outraged"; she wanted to be vindicated. Whatever Mitzi's original intent, Marilyn's reaction made an out-of-court settlement seem impossible. As Mitzi's son Ronny observed, it was no longer a fight about money. The sisters all had enough of that. It was more about emotion and power and all the politics that go along with them.

The emotions got out of control and spilled over into the press. On February 16, 1988, *The Globe and Mail* published interviews with the Steinberg sisters that only threw oil on the fire. Like squabbling adolescents, the sisters traded more jabs. Marilyn bristled at Mitzi's comments about her lack of education and business experience, complaining that her older sister was making her look "dumb" and like "another rich broad". Marilyn complained about Mitzi's desire to hog the spotlight. Mitzi responded that Marilyn was simply jealous of her achievements.

Marilyn defended her management of the trusts and claimed that Mitzi had been prepared to sell the company to Arnold three years earlier for the ridiculously low price of $20 a share. She deflected the allegations that she had been in conflict of interest with the family by selling non-voting shares, revealing that Mitzi had sold some Class A shares at the very same time. "There seem to be two sets of rules, one for her and another for the rest of us."

The spectacle of a public brawl between the sisters was just too delicious for the press to ignore. There were stories about how much the sisters weighed and where they got their hair done. *The Gazette*'s famed cartoonist, Aislin, depicted the sisters as a trio of spattered mud wrestlers. Some of the coverage incensed the family.

Yet despite the public and private sniping among the sisters, peacemaking efforts continued behind the scenes. Leo Goldfarb was the key player in trying to bring them together. The sisters met individually with him at his apartment in Florida. He traveled and golfed with both couples and was a keen judge of their moods. At one point in that winter of 1988, he believed he had made a breakthrough. A peace agreement was worked out on New Year's Eve under which the three sisters would agree to share two seats on the Steinberg board, rotated on a regular basis.

In return the Cobrins wanted Mitzi to drop her lawsuit and to issue a public apology for her allegations. At the last minute the deal fell through. The Cobrins were told by their lawyer that there had been "a deal-breaker". The Dobrins wouldn't issue the kind of apology that Simon and Marilyn demanded.

While Marilyn remained intransigent, her sister Evelyn was coming under growing pressure from family members to end the hostilities. Her uncle and fellow trustee Morris Steinberg had been trying to convince her to stop the fighting. Of the three sisters,

Evelyn was perhaps the most objective about the dispute. She hadn't approved of Mitzi's tactics, but she was able to control her emotions and act as a kind of balance between the other two. Her overriding desire was to restore peace to the family, especially to her mother Helen. Evelyn knew she didn't want to go through a public courtroom battle. A little more than two months after the lawsuit was filed, she and Mitzi made peace. Three of the four trusts — the Dobrins', the Alexanders', and the Goldfarbs' — agreed they would act in concert. That left Marilyn out in the cold, angered at her abandonment by Evelyn.

On March 9 Mitzi and Evelyn agreed that for a period of at least one year, the trusts would vote their Steinberg shares unanimously. They also agreed that, subject to the approval of Steinberg's directors, Marilyn and Evelyn would stand for election to the board and Mitzi would resign her director's seat. The Dobrin family would continue to be represented on the board by Mel, the chairman. A management circular later stated that the three sisters would share two board seats on a specified rotation basis. Although Marilyn eventually took a seat on the board she never actually signed the agreement.

Shortly before the parties were to appear in court Mitzi withdrew her lawsuit on March 22. It was more a ceasefire than a peace treaty. While the worst of the fighting was over, the bitterness lingered. The sisters began to talk with each other at business meetings, but the relationship between Mitzi and Marilyn remained cold and tense. They could never again be as close as they once were. Nor could Marilyn and Helen, although they too began talking again.

The affair had become a classic example of everything that can go wrong in estate planning. Sam Steinberg had wanted to divide his inheritance equally among four daughters, but hadn't specified what would happen if they disagreed. Sam's primary motivation in establishing the trusts in 1952 was to minimize taxes; financial considerations had taken precedence over commonsense judgement. It seemed so intelligent not to pay estate taxes when you could pass the family fortune down to your children and grandchildren. But Sam had never even considered that the children might have different degrees of interest and competency as owners of the company.

After the battle was over Simon Cobrin still wondered why it had happened in the first place. The lawyers' fees were probably a million dollars for all the trusts, he figured. Mitzi wanted to remove them as trustees, but they were still there, in exactly the same position as before, except that there had been a lot of dirt and every major newspaper had picked it up.

While the lawsuit had been withdrawn, it was naive to suggest that nothing had changed. Like a stone tossed into a pool of water, Mitzi's legal action created ever-widening ripples of reaction that spread through the family, the management, the employees, and the investment community. The family had been wrenched apart the way a civil war divides a nation. Senior management had been distracted by the dispute and important decisions had been postponed. The unionized employees realized for the first time that members of the Steinberg family wanted to sell the company and that their jobs might be threatened.

Steinberg directors were alarmed too. They met on January 18, 1988, about seven weeks before the truce agreement, and made a fateful decision: they invited bids for all the stock as one way of ending the ownership dispute. "Clearly, whatever would come out of the dispute would be messy and would probably require a lot of cash," said Marc Lalonde, the former federal finance minister, who sat on the board along with six other independent directors. He felt the decision to invite bids was unavoidable. "You can't run a company like this when the controlling shareholders are at each other's throats. This was not the kind of environment where you could recruit and keep senior staff. People wouldn't risk their careers." One way or another the problem had to be resolved, even if it meant that Steinberg would have to offer itself to outside buyers.

Analysts and big institutional shareholders such as pension funds were also concerned by the revelations at Steinberg. The lawsuit seemed to suggest that potentially lucrative takeover offers for Steinberg stock, such as the August 1987 offer by Weston, hadn't been given proper consideration. These investors owned non-voting Class A shares in the company, which accounted for 71 percent of the equity. There was no "coat-tail" provision protecting them in the event of a takeover; that is, it was legally possible, according to Steinberg's corporate bylaws, for somebody to acquire control of the company by buying only the voting shares from the family, without making any offer for the Class A shares.

It wasn't clear what the fate of the minority shareholders would be. Nobody really expected they would be ignored in a takeover bid, but the real question was: how much more would the sisters get for their stock than the non-voting shareholders? Stephen Jarislowsky had been saying that if control of a company changed, the non-voting shareholders deserved the same deal as the others.

Steinberg management recognized the problem. They knew that some family members wanted to sell, but the existence of two classes of stock complicated matters enormously. Because the voting shares weren't publicly traded, there was no market for them. If you were a family member with voting shares, you couldn't just wake up one morning, call your broker, and place an order to sell some. You were stuck with them, for better or worse.

And even if you were able to find someone to buy your voting shares, what would you do with the money? Most Steinberg family members had no idea how to go about investing in the stock market or in real estate. Ludmer believed those tough decisions would have been much easier for the family to make with a change in the capital structure of the company: if the voting shares were listed on the stock exchange, family members who wanted to cash in some of their shares could find a ready market for them, yet still keep control of the company if they wanted to.

Ludmer and Arnold Steinberg came up with a plan. They would list the voting shares on the stock exchange, and give non-voting shareholders a "coat-tail", guaranteeing that they would be included in a takeover. There was a problem, however. The family knew that if the voting shares could be publicly traded, the "takeover premium" — their excess value over the non-voting stock — would shrink. The common shares would trade on the market at just about the same price as the Class A shares. This might cost the family some money in the event of a takeover.

One solution proposed by Ludmer was to issue preferred shares, paying a regular, fixed dividend, to the family as compensation. At a meeting in the Steinberg boardroom in early 1988 attended by Irving Ludmer, Arnold Steinberg, and two representatives from each side of the family, management made its case for the plan, with Ludmer, who stood to gain nothing either way, pushing for the restructuring.

But he could never convince the family to go along with the idea. They were suspicious of his motives, figuring he was trying to somehow steal the company out from under them. They told him he was "dreaming in technicolor" and that he'd never get share-holder approval for such a move.

The family felt that if they kept the control block together, they would get a much higher price in the event of a takeover bid — and they were proven right in the end. But despite the family's rejection of the plan, it was clear that a bidder for the company would have to pay a decent price to take out the Class A shareholders. There would be too much of a fuss if it didn't. Not long after Mitzi Dobrin had filed her lawsuit, the first such bid arrived and the lengthy, lusty takeover battle for Steinberg began.

# 12

# *Raiders*

Irving Ludmer got a nasty surprise when he read the newspapers on the morning of January 25, 1988. He was used to seeing Steinberg make the headlines, but he didn't expect the scoop on the front page of *The Financial Post*. It made his stomach churn. A high-powered trio of Bay Street investors had formed a partnership called Oxdon Investments Inc., and were going to make a $980-million bid for all the shares of Steinberg.

They had put together $90-million in equity and were prepared to borrow more than $1-billion to complete the purchase. Financing had already been lined up through Citibank Canada and the National Bank. Oxdon was proposing a two-stage offer: $50 a share for the voting stock and up to $40 for the non-voting Class As, depending on how many voting shares were tendered.

The three partners in Oxdon were well-known corporate names: Unicorp Canada Corp., a Toronto-based holding company; Gordon Capital Corp., a prominent investment dealer; and Oxford Development Group, an aggressive real estate developer. They had never once called Ludmer about their plans. He read on, becoming even more uneasy.

One look at the roster of players made it clear that if Oxdon were successful in acquiring Steinberg, it would dismantle the company. None of the three partners had any experience in the grocery business and it was a safe bet that they would sell off the food stores after the takeover. Ludmer figured they would try to sell other parts of the Steinberg empire too, including the department stores, the restaurants, the sugar refineries, the wholesaling operation, and the Smitty's supermarket chain in Arizona.

It was obvious this was an "asset strip", as the investment world called it. Oxdon's scheme was to buy the company; then, in order to pay off the enormous debt racked up in doing so, sell off the assets in bits and pieces, making a big profit along the way. To Ludmer, these weren't corporate raiders: they were corporate wreckers. They were prepared to bust up a company with 37,000 employees and $4.5-billion in sales because they figured the parts were worth more than the whole. Indeed, a banker familiar with their plans had predicted that each of the Oxdon partners could pocket as much as $200-million in profit from the sale of Steinberg assets. Not a bad return on a cash investment of less than $100-million.

The biggest attraction for Oxdon was Steinberg's real estate, the crown jewel in the company. Through its subsidiary, Ivanhoe Inc., Steinberg owned 5.8-million square feet of choice commercial space in thirty-six shopping centers in Quebec and Ontario, making it the sixth largest real estate company in Canada. The Ivanhoe properties had been appraised at almost $600-million in 1985 and their value had substantially risen since then.

Later that day, when Oxdon executives delivered the offer to Steinberg, they were given a cool but polite reception. After all, it was the Steinberg board that had invited bids for the company. It was the sisters' feud that had pushed matters this far. Nevertheless, privately, Ludmer was appalled at the prospect of Oxdon busting up the company he had so painstakingly tried to turn around. It was his company now, now that he had transformed it completely. He wouldn't give it up without a fight.

Ludmer knew that a breakup would be difficult to accomplish because so many parts of the Steinberg empire were intertwined. It would not be easy to pry apart the grocery stores from the wholesaling operation or the department stores from the real estate. There would be a lot of internal bleeding in the company and senior management would flee. Moreover, if Steinberg shareholders wanted the assets sold, the company could do the job itself. That way the shareholders could pocket the profits instead of a trio of Toronto financiers.

Steinberg issued a terse, one-sentence statement that it would review the offer. But if management wasn't excited about Oxdon's bid, the stock market definitely was. There had been feverish speculation in Steinberg shares for days. On January 19, one day after the Steinberg board had invited bids for the company, the publicly traded Class A shares soared $6.62 on the Toronto Stock Exchange, closing at $37.75. On January 26, following Oxdon's announcement, the A shares gained $2.37 after a brief trading halt on the TSE, closing at $42.12. The fact that investors had driven the price of the A shares above Oxdon's proposed bid of $40 indicated that Bay Street anticipated a bidding war. Investment analysts, however, weren't impressed by Oxdon's offer, calling it a low-ball bid.

The three partners in Oxdon were used to this kind of heat. They were brawlers in the Wall Street mold, experienced in the rough-and-tumble takeover game, and they would not be easily deflected from their goal. Their bid was the first of three attempts to acquire Steinberg that would span more than a year and a half.

The impetus for the Oxdon bid came from Oxford Develop-ment, the big Toronto-based development firm controlled by a reclusive millionaire, Donald Love. A Westerner who grew up in Calgary, Love had made a fortune in real estate through shrewd dealmaking. He had studied engineering at Montreal's McGill University, worked as a stockbroker for a while and returned to Alberta in the late 1950s, opening an office for Dominion Securities in Edmonton. As Alberta's oil-fired economy heated up, Love had assembled real estate deals for himself and various partners.

Backed by a group of insurance companies, including Great-West Life Assurance of Winnipeg, Love eventually pushed ag-gressively into the United States market. By the late 1970s he had developed or bought major properties in Denver, Minneapolis, and the U.S. Sunbelt. In 1981, Oxford became partners with the Toronto Dominion Bank in a deal that made the bank a major player in Canadian real estate. The bank financed a deal that allowed Love to save his company from a potential takeover. He was able to buy back Oxford's shares on the stock market and take the company private in the nick of time. As Love turned his attention to Steinberg, he knew what it felt like to be the prey.

In the fall of 1987, when word of the sisters' dispute first leaked out, Oxford Development began looking at ways to make a bid for Steinberg. Love wanted the real estate in Ivanhoe. This was a rare chance to buy a big package of prime shopping malls in Quebec and Ontario. Oxford's executives did their homework, visiting every Ivanhoe mall, interviewing tenants and estimating what the leases contained. They put together a stack of financial information on Ivanhoe about two feet high.

But Oxford alone didn't have the experience to pull off a $1-billion takeover. Love had given the Steinberg project to his son Jon, a young man who was clearly out of his depth with an acquisition deal of this size. For help in arranging the transaction, Oxford turned to Bay Street's most aggressive securities dealer, Gordon Capital Corp.

An outfit that operates as secretively as Oxford does, Gordon is the most ambitious brokerage firm in the country, with a reputation as the best pure trader in the stock market. Run by the wily broker Jimmy Connacher, Gordon Capital specializes in moving large blocks of stock for clients. It operates discreetly and doesn't tip its hand when one of its clients begins to accumulate stock in a takeover target.

Gordon's involvement in the offer raised a red flag in the eyes of some Steinberg watchers. It was Gordon that had choreographed a highly controversial scheme at Canadian Tire Corp. Ltd., another company where family members controlled the voting stock. Gordon had recommended that the voting shareholders receive a huge premium for their stock over what the non-voting shareholders could get. Once again, Gordon was proposing a split-bid, although the spread wasn't as large. The leopard had curbed his appetite but hadn't changed his spots.

Once Oxford Development and Gordon Capital had developed a game plan for Steinberg, they needed another partner to kick in more equity and share the risk. Who better to approach than George Mann, Canada's quintessential paper entrepreneur? The chairman of Unicorp Canada is an opportunistic bargain hunter who can't resist the lure of an undervalued asset. Steinberg was just the sort of company to spark his interest.

A high-school dropout, Mann developed his business smarts while working for his father's real estate company in Toronto. He shook up the business by becoming one of the first to sell both homes and mortgages. His holding company, Unicorp Canada, grew on the strength of real estate investment in Canada and the U.S. Mann dreamed up the deals and his administrative sidekick, Jim Leech, set the wheels in motion.

Gordon Capital and Unicorp had done business together before. In a stormy 1985 takeover battle Unicorp had swallowed Union Enterprises Ltd. of Toronto, an energy company four times its size. Union's minority shareholders felt they got a raw deal and were outraged at some of the tactics used in the takeover fight. They were vindicated by the Ontario Securities Commission. Gordon Capital, which had been acting on behalf of Unicorp, was slapped with a temporary trading ban for its role in the affair and Unicorp was ordered to pay $7.1-million in compensation to Union's minority shareholders.

These guys loved a bare-knuckle fight. They didn't operate in the civilized and genteel style that had long characterized business dealings in the Canadian establishment. When they made their bid for Steinberg, they didn't bother to court the family and management, nor did they stroke any egos. It was a crucial error on Oxdon's part. The sisters still controlled the company's voting shares and without their assent there could be no deal.

After the bid was made, Oxdon finally arranged a meeting with the family and their financial advisors, Prudential Bache Securities and Dominion Securities. One participant at that meeting sensed that the sisters came within an eyelash of accepting the offer. But they were reluctant to sell to an Ontario group whom they didn't really know. A little stroking might have helped.

In fact, there were connections between Oxdon and Steinberg that the Toronto team might have put to use to warm up to the family. George Mann's wife Saundra is related to the Steinberg family; she and Arnold Steinberg have an aunt in common through marriage. And one of the principal partners in Gordon Capital, Gordon Eberts, is a longtime friend of Arnold's, who shares his interest in art collecting.

The Oxdon offer put added pressure on the Steinberg board to resolve the family fight. The directors met on February 2 and decided it was their legal responsibility to invite other bids. The board did not have an evaluation of the worth of Steinberg shares and there was no indication of what a floor price for the company might be in a bidding war. In the absence of an evaluation, the only way to determine what the stock was worth was to invite other offers to see what people were willing to pay.

To the deal hounds in the investment community, the invitation for more bids was like the starter's gun at a racetrack. The investment bankers of the world raced to the phone and called the company. The Steinberg story had been getting regular play in international business publications like *The Wall Street Journal* and management soon found itself deluged with calls from investment bankers in the U.S., Canada, and Europe. The dealmakers figured that since Steinberg was for sale, the most logical candidates to buy it were its top executives: Irving Ludmer and Arnold Steinberg.

Management buyouts had become the favorite parlor game of corporations in the United States during the 1980s. The game is played with other people's money, allowing management to purchase a company from its shareholders in highly leveraged transactions financed by high-interest, or junk, bonds. To pay off the acquisition debt, the new owners usually have to sell off a portion of the assets they acquire.

Ludmer and Arnold Steinberg were inundated with inquiries — 50 to 100 offers between the two of them. Among the suitors was Kohlberg, Kravis, Roberts & Co., America's leading leveraged buyout firm. KKR had financed the mammoth $25-billion buyout of RJR Nabisco Inc., the largest-ever transaction on Wall Street. KKR's principal partner, Henry Kravis, spent a half-hour on the phone trying to convince Arnold to do a management buyout. Donald Trump, the brash New York real estate whiz who later bought a portion of Eastern Airlines, also made an inquiry. So did the prestigious Wall Street broker Goldman Sachs and the Montreal branch of the Bronfman family, through its holding company, Claridge Investments Ltd. Arnold figured that by the time it was all over, every leading bank and investment house had called at least once, motivated by the possibility of fat fees for arranging the transaction.

Ludmer and Arnold had grave concerns about a management buyout. Sure, they would have liked to purchase Steinberg, but not at the expense of breaking it up. Without an asset sale, there was no way the cash generated by the business could support the enormous debt they would have to assume. They had spent a great deal of time and effort fixing the place up and bringing in new executive talent, so why would they want to undo all that? Besides, a management buyout would have placed Ludmer and Arnold in a serious conflict of interest, Ludmer believed. "We would have had to ally ourselves with a third party that wanted to make a quick buck really, against the existing shareholders. There's no way we would be party to anything like that."

While management answered their phones, the Steinberg sisters met with their financial advisers to consider their own options. By this time Evelyn was talking with Mitzi again and was prepared to settle her sister's lawsuit out of court. But there were many people's interests to consider. Sam's daughters had children who were now married and raising families of their own. As many as twenty-five family members attended meetings and Ludmer had noted the wide spectrum of opinion throughout the family. Some felt they were better off keeping their money in Steinberg than in selling and paying capital-gains taxes. Others, especially Mitzi, were unhappy at the chronically low dividends Steinberg had been paying, which amounted to little more than a 1 percent return on their investment, and wanted to sell — the sooner the better.

Although Mitzi remained deeply interested in selling the company, the Oxdon offer was not good enough for her, or for the other two. Notwithstanding their personal differences, the sisters were all against the prospect that Oxdon might break up the company. When they finally met with Ludmer, they had prepared a sharp rebuff for Oxdon. They asked him to say they wouldn't sell at $50 a share but were prepared to sell at $100. It was a none-too-subtle message to Oxdon to get lost. Ludmer, delighted at their decision, issued a short press release stating that the family had turned down the offer and that Steinberg management was looking at other ways of "maximizing shareholder values".

The decision didn't sit well with Oxdon. The meter was running on its financing and it had to pay several million dollars in fees to the banks just to line up the money for the bid. Unicorp's Jim Leech complained that despite the Steinberg board's invitation for bids, the family didn't seem interested in selling. Steinberg was starting to look like a big tease — all talk and no action — and the stock began to retreat on the market.

Irving Ludmer has a good poker face and he needed it now. He was playing three hands simultaneously, dealing cards to the family, to the takeover artists, and to the union. His next move was to convince the board of directors to put the company's 115 Quebec grocery stores up for sale. Since Oxdon would have sold off the stores anyway, Ludmer believed it made sense for Steinberg to try and find out what they were worth. If they could fetch a good price, then the money could go to Steinberg shareholders rather than to a bunch of breakup artists. And if the supermarkets were sold, then Steinberg would be out of the unprofitable food business, which the investment community regarded as a cancer. The company could then concentrate its efforts on real estate.

Ironically the supermarkets, which employed the most people and had the most capital, produced the worst financial results. They had become totally uncompetitive because of the huge differential in the cost of doing business, mainly due to the high wages they paid. For every dollar Steinberg received from its customers, it passed along 13 cents to its employees in wages while its competitors passed along an average of just 9 cents. That four-percent gap was an enormous handicap in a very competitive business. Even at the best of times, food retailing is a business with low profit margins: a typical supermarket company makes less than 2 cents of profit on each sales dollar. If Steinberg had equivalent wage rates to its competitors, it could have increased its profit before tax by $60-million a year.

And wages weren't the only problem. The union contract bound Steinberg hand and foot, giving it no flexibility to control its costs. For example, there was a clause in the labor agreement that effectively guaranteed lifetime job security to any employees hired before September 1978. They had the right to transfer to another store whenever Steinberg shut down a money-losing outlet. In doing so, they would "bump" workers with less seniority. Steinberg was rapidly approaching the point where all the full-time employees had such seniority rights.

It was an expensive problem, because full-time workers cost more than part-timers. With each store closing, more of the full-time workers would move into the profitable stores, upsetting the balance between full- and part-time workers on which each store's profitability depends.

Arnold was nothing short of fatalistic about the food stores. He believed they would continue to lose money, eventually dragging down the whole company. Steinberg had just come out of a lengthy strike in the warehouse that had wiped $10-million off the bottom line. The remaining labor contracts in the food stores were up for renegotiation in September 1988, and there were indications the union wanted more money and improved working conditions, which the company would not be able to provide. For that reason, management supported the idea of selling the grocery division, even if that meant selling Mr. Sam's greatest legacy. If the money-losing food operation was gone, earnings per share to Steinberg stockholders would increase dramatically.

But privately, some analysts wondered whether the For Sale sign placed on the supermarkets wasn't an enormous bluff. It seemed like the perfect way to scare the unions into accepting wage concessions that would make the stores more competitive. The union hadn't been very sympathetic to Steinberg's plight. Talk to them about wage rollbacks and they would laugh you right out of the room. They had always felt that if the stores were losing money, Steinberg would survive anyway because the real estate was profitable. But if the stores were sold to new owners, the supermarkets would almost certainly be franchised and the union would lose the job guarantees and bargaining power it enjoyed in the corporate-owned network of Steinberg stores.

If the threat to sell was a bluff, it had an immediate impact. The union responded to Steinberg's announcement the same day with a promise not to strike for five years if the company kept the stores. It offered to extend the existing labor agreement for five years, with salaries indexed each year to the cost-of-living.

At the same time Irving Ludmer wanted much more than labor peace. He wanted major concessions on wages and staffing, plus the right to franchise. The union was uncertain how to respond. They had been aware of the family feud for some time and knew there was a risk the whole company might be sold. Now that Mitzi had suddenly withdrawn from the operation, Tom Kukovica, the union's top negotiator, feared that she would just say to hell with it and sell. Mitzi's lawsuit confirmed that fear and gave management new credibility when it asked for wage rollbacks.

In late February and early March Steinberg management approached the union and outlined the company's problems. They presented figures that showed a dramatic decline in sales and asked for relief in several areas of the collective agreement. "They said, 'If we leave it like this, we'll be down the tubes in no time at all,' " Kukovica recalled. Steinberg asked for a $1-an-hour reduction in wages for everybody; no transfers between stores (so that if they closed a store, employees were laid off, with no bumping rights); new wage rates that were 25 percent lower than the current starting rates; and a three-hour increase in the work week, to 40 hours. Kukovica figured the concessions were worth $100-million over three years. There was no way he would make that kind of deal.

Just when it appeared that talks with the union would go nowhere, the stakes suddenly increased dramatically. On March 30, Steinberg's two main competitors in the Quebec grocery business announced a joint offer for the Steinberg supermarkets. Métro-Richelieu Inc. and Provigo Inc. said that if their bid was successful, they would franchise the 100-plus supermarkets in Quebec to independent owners.

The joint bid by Provigo and Métro-Richelieu was a clever piece of strategy that surprised everybody, even if it raised serious concerns about competition. When Steinberg executives heard about it they were crestfallen. By putting their rivalry aside the two companies managed to avoid what Steinberg had hoped for: a bidding war that would drive up the price. Their offer — $20-million for the 100-odd stores — was well below what Steinberg had hoped to get. A Steinberg representative called the then-president of Métro-Richelieu, Jacques Maltais, and asked to talk business with him alone. Maltais refused to break his deal with Provigo.

The Provigo-Métro bid had been carefully orchestrated in secrecy. When it came to choosing the stores that each company wanted, the process was like a hockey draft. First Provigo picked a store it wanted to buy and relayed the decision to Métro-Richelieu.

Then Métro would choose, and so it went, back and forth. On a map, each side marked with a pin the location of the stores its rival had chosen before making its next move.

Before carving up the Steinberg carcass, Provigo and Métro tried to appeal to Quebec's nationalist sentiment. The acquisition would be good for the province, they said, because it would keep the supermarkets under Quebec ownership and would ensure that Quebec food producers still had access to a major distribution network. Pierre Lortie, then chief executive of Provigo, argued that consumers would benefit because prices at Provigo were lower than at Steinberg. He also implied that federal officials would allow the deal to go through, even if it seemed to reduce competition.

The unions were outraged at the prospect of Provigo and Métro getting together, and they enlisted the help of Louis Laberge, the powerful president of the Quebec Federation of Labour. The stocky, five foot-five inch Laberge, who has all the subtlety of a battering ram, predicted the deal would be "disastrous for all Quebecers". The two chains would have 80 percent of the market in Quebec, a near monopoly, he said. "If Provigo and Métro are in cahoots, imagine what they can do to prices."

Laberge asked the Quebec government to block the bid. Steinberg, he said, was the most "Québécois" of all the chains — "more Québécois than Métro-Richelieu with its two fleurs-de-lis and Provigo". Steinberg spent $800-million a year on purchases from Quebec-based farmers and food manufacturers, far more than the other chains, he argued.

While the Provigo-Métro bid made the headlines, several other major Canadian grocery chains submitted bids for the Steinberg food stores, including George Weston Ltd. and Oshawa Group Inc., suppliers of the IGA stores. The serious interest from potential buyers specifically in the grocery stores had created the predictable effect in union circles — panic. "Quite clearly, the unions were damn scared of us selling to Provigo and Métro," said Marc Lalonde, the former federal Cabinet minister who was one of the Steinberg directors at the time. "They could see franchising coming in. For them it was the end of the game." With the advent of franchising, each store owner would be able to negotiate his own contract with employees, leaving the union powerless to strike the whole chain.

Union local president Jacques Toupin went to Steinberg management in desperation and began to negotiate a secret deal. Toupin was willing to make major concessions to keep Steinberg alive, and management grabbed at the opportunity to lower the company's labor costs. But just when it appeared that an agreement would be signed, the deal collapsed. Toupin had been acting on his own, behind the backs of the union executive, and was willing to go much further than his members were to meet Steinberg's demands. When they found out what he had done, they were outraged and asked for his head. "His deal would have meant the end of the union," said one union official. Toupin abruptly resigned on April 14 and the company was back to square one.

At the same time the prospective buyers of the Steinberg stores, which now included the owners of the A & P chain as well, were all trying to cut their own sweet deals with the union before committing themselves to a purchase, even though it was forbidden and they had signed confidentiality agreements to the contrary. If a buyer could get the union into the deal as a partner in return for wage concessions, so much the better. The promises being made to the union behind Steinberg's back made the company's own dealings with union officials all the more difficult. The whole thing was becoming a circus.

Even Oxdon, the rejected suitor, had come back to the union with a proposal for an employee buyout. Oxdon offered to make the union a partner in a $100-million deal to buy Steinberg's Quebec supermarkets and distribution center. There were several other parties to the deal, including former federal Liberal cabinet minister Jean Chrétien, who was ready to take a piece of the action himself. He talked with union negotiator Tom Kukovica's office repeatedly through the spring of 1988 to gauge the union's interest. But Kukovica's response was, "You buy the company and then come and see me." The union was reluctant to commit itself to an equity contribution because 60 percent of its members were part-timers, who couldn't afford the investment.

The chauffeur-driven limousine of Quebec cabinet minister John Ciaccia sped down Highway 20 from Quebec City to Montreal on the evening of May 12, 1988. It's a long and tedious stretch of road, and government drivers aren't known for respecting the speed limit. As the pine trees rushed by at 130 kilometers an hour, Ciaccia sat in the back seat, working the crackly car phone. When the signal was cut a few times near Trois-Rivières, the cabinet minister persisted. He had an urgent message to deliver.

The night before, Ciaccia had met Jean Campeau, chairman of the Caisse de dépôt et placement, at a dinner in Quebec City given by the National Bank of Canada. Campeau had been looking at ways to keep Steinberg intact, under Quebec ownership. Ciaccia, who had started at Steinberg as a young real estate lawyer and had worked with Irving Ludmer, remarked that it would be a shame if the stores were sold and the company broken up.

Campeau reminded Ciaccia that there would be a Steinberg board meeting on Friday, May 13, and asked the cabinet minister if he could use his influence to delay a decision on the sale of the stores. On Thursday, as Ciaccia sped down Highway 20, he called his old friend Irving Ludmer and the two spent two hours on the phone. The board was set to meet the following day to consider three offers — from George Weston Ltd., Oshawa Group Inc., and Provigo-Métro — and Ludmer said they would have to accept one. Ciaccia pleaded with him for a delay and hinted for the first time that the government might get involved to save the stores. "You've got to postpone it," Ciaccia said. "You've got to give us a chance."

Ludmer wasn't convinced. How could he justify a further delay? The bidders might walk away and meanwhile the stores were going to lose $20- to $40-million because of the union contracts. Ciaccia tugged at Ludmer's heartstrings. "Irving," he said, "Sam's going to roll over in his grave if you sell these properties. . . . I think you owe it to Quebec, to the government, to your company, for one last stand."

Ludmer knew the board would need some convincing that the premier's office would step in. But Ciaccia assured him that Mario Bertrand, Bourassa's powerful top aide, was already working on the case and was ready to mediate the talks. Based on that information, the board announced it would postpone a decision on selling the stores and offer a new package of concessions to its unionized workers.

The decision simply increased public confusion about Steinberg's real intentions. There was no announcement that the government was willing to get involved in the bargaining process, and investors were tiring of the waiting game. The following trading day, Steinberg Class A stock fell $5.50 on the Toronto Stock Exchange and $5.75 on the Montreal Exchange.

Provigo and Métro were also disappointed at the postponement and pulled the plug on their joint $20-million bid, thereby committing a major strategic error. Steinberg had much better store locations than they did, and once it lowered its labor costs and franchised its operations it could have been a real winner. Provigo and Métro had the opportunity not only to put a competitor out of business but to grab some of the choicest locations in Quebec. Arnold compared the situation to what happened in Ontario when A & P bought Dominion Stores. Everyone had predicted the Dominion acquisition would bleed A & P to death. Yet after an initial period of heavy losses, A & P found itself owning a jewel in the lucrative Ontario retailing market. It had acquired ninety stores at rock-bottom prices, stores that it probably never could have bought any other way.

Ludmer now returned to the union, asking for only $20-million worth of labor concessions over three years instead of a total of $100-million. But François Lauzon, the new president of the Steinberg union local, turned him down again. Lauzon had been a longtime Steinberg employee, working twelve years in the Cavendish Mall store where he had often chatted with Helen Steinberg on her shopping trips. Lauzon felt some loyalty to the company. He liked and trusted Irving Ludmer and accepted the fact the Steinberg stores were hurting. But he couldn't recommend this deal to his members.

The monetary concessions weren't so bad. They would have cost each member a $1 an hour in wages, an extra hour of work per week, and a 2.5-percent reduction in salary for part-time employees. What really bothered Lauzon was the loss of job guarantees and Steinberg's absolute insistence on six years of labor peace. The union would have had to surrender its right to strike. The Steinberg offer was voted down by over 80 percent of the membership at a meeting on May 29 at the Place Bonaventure in downtown Montreal.

Arnold Steinberg remembered how bitterly the news of the rejection was greeted at head office. Several people wept. It looked like the end of the game for the food stores: Steinberg would surely have to sell them to somebody or shut them down. Indeed, the company announced the imminent closing of six stores and the dismissal of 341 workers.

Few people realized the Quebec government was waiting to step in. Ludmer and Bourassa had kept their little secret right up until May 28, when a newspaper story revealed to a surprised union that the two men had been in regular contact. In fact the wheels had already been set in motion for a marathon bargaining session in Quebec City between Steinberg, Quebec's third-largest employer, and the union, under the watchful eye of the premier's staff. Kukovica confirmed Bourassa's keen interest in seeing the two sides get together himself. Once more there was hope.

Across the street from the stately architecture of Quebec City's parliament buildings is a squat, windowless structure called the Bunker. It has the look of a concrete fortress with gun slits in the walls. It's an appropriate location for the office of Premier Robert Bourassa, a man who's been frequently under siege during his years in power. At times like the FLQ crisis, the strikes by public service workers, and the emotional battles over language rights, the Bunker has provided welcome refuge for the embattled premier and his coterie of advisers. An elaborate system of electric locks controls access to the premier's inner sanctum. The complex boasts its own War Room, a sort of high-tech command center where the premier can monitor developments during a crisis.

It was in the Bunker that delegations from Steinberg and the United Food and Commercial Workers met on June 14 to begin 70 hours of almost round-the-clock bargaining. On one side of the table sat the union group headed by Tom Kukovica and François Lauzon. On the other was the Steinberg team, led by Jean-Roch Vachon, then president of Steinberg's supermarket group, and Alain Bilodeau, its vice-president of labor relations. A government-appointed mediator, Marc Cantin, kept order. Bourassa himself did not sit in on the face-to-face talks but stayed well briefed and met separately with both sides.

Before the proceedings began, Bourassa's top aide, Mario Bertrand gave both sides a sharp pep talk and he didn't mince his words. Bertrand's tough, no-nonsense way of operating had earned him the nickname *l'abrasif* — the abrasive one. Today was no time for niceties. The negotiations must succeed, he told the group. There was too much at stake for Quebec and its food industry. Bertrand didn't have to mention the considerable political risk that Bourassa had undertaken in sponsoring the talks. This was the first time the premier's office had ever become directly involved in a private sector labor dispute. To have the talks fail would have been deeply embarrassing to him.

Steinberg's opening position proposed a six-year labor agreement with a no-strike clause. But Quebec labor law limits collective agreements to three years, and a change would have required passage of a private bill in the National Assembly. The union categorically refused to establish such a precedent, insisting that the membership must have the right to a strike vote every three years.

When Steinberg refused to budge from its demand, Bourassa called the company's representatives into his office and gave them hell. There was no way they would get a private bill, he told them, so give up the whole idea. Steinberg backed off.

An elaborate compromise was worked out. The union gave its word that there would be labor peace for six years, expiring in 1994. There would be a three-year collective agreement, renewable for another three years in 1991. If for any reason the union balked at renewing, the membership would have the right to vote on whether to send the contract dispute to binding arbitration. It was a way for the union to save face, but in return they had to guarantee labor peace publicly and to Bourassa. "It was based on trust," Ludmer said of the compromise. Given the adversarial relationship that existed, it was tough for the company to accept the union's promise. But there was no other way.

The rest of the talks were equally arduous and negotiators on both sides got little more than 15 hours of sleep all week. Steinberg wanted the right to franchise its operations while the union asked the company to keep at least 50 corporate-owned stores in the Montreal area. Both sides were convinced they got what they wanted, although after the company was sold in 1989 there would be a major dispute over the exact terms of the settlement. "Maintaining a corporate network was important for our bargaining power," said union local president François Lauzon. "Steinberg was always the leader in wages. What Steinberg gave, you could then negotiate from the independents."

Steinberg also promised to halt its efforts to sell the food stores. In the event of a sale of the food division, the Quebec City agreement would be abrogated and the old labor contract would immediately take effect. In return, the union accepted wage and benefit cuts totaling at least $11-million a year.

On Saturday, June 18, Ludmer flew to Quebec City to assist with an urgent issue demanding his attention and involving a very substantial amount of money. The issue was the company's offer to buy out longtime employees for $1,000 per year of service.

This was probably the most significant development in Steinberg labor relations since Mr. Sam first started to give away the candy store to his workers. The buyout program offered the company a way out of the trap it had fallen into over worker seniority. The more unprofitable stores that were closed, the more full-time people would go into the remaining stores, bumping out the lower-paid part-timers. The problem was to find a means to take away job security from the people who had negotiated it.

The financial incentive of a buyout was clearly the best way. A cashier with 15 years' experience at Steinberg could then walk out the door with $15,000, opening the way for a part-timer. This would prove to be an expensive program for Steinberg, costing $15-million in the first year, but it changed the balance of power. Steinberg stipulated in the agreement that any newly hired employees be limited to 24 hours a week of employment, ending the grip that full-timers had on the company.

Once the deal was signed Steinberg management crossed its fingers and prayed the union executive could get it ratified by the rank and file. It was never easy to convince workers to accept rollbacks but Lauzon sensed good will on the part of the membership. "People still believed in the company and wanted to help it. The company would probably have been sold and dismantled without an agreement. What we accepted was in order to save the business."

When close to 2,000 Montreal-area workers gathered at Place Bonaventure on June 27 to vote on the deal, there was a strong undercurrent of resentment from part-time workers, whose wage rates were to be cut by $1 an hour. The union wasn't used to rolling over and playing dead. Speaker after speaker rose to angrily denounce the deal. But by this point Steinberg now had the upper hand, and the workers knew it. When the vote was over, the deal was narrowly accepted by a margin of 53 percent. Workers in some other parts of Quebec rejected the deal but most of the 8,000 members in Quebec and Ontario approved it. The battle was over and the sale of Steinberg stores appeared to have been averted.

Once the smoke had cleared there were many questions for Irving Ludmer to answer. He had played a dazzling game of brinksmanship with the unions, extracting a deal that would never have been possible a year before. Even so, there had been tremendous confusion among investors, shareholders, and workers over Steinberg's real intentions, aggravated by the total dearth of public announcements during the first six months of 1988.

This behavior raised the ire of institutional investors who had bought the stock expecting the price to rise during a takeover battle — only to see it slide steadily back down.

Stung by repeated criticism, Irving Ludmer and Arnold Steinberg began a campaign to woo back those investors. Now that the company was off the auction block, Steinberg promised to enhance values for the shareholders by selling assets and restructuring. Trust us, they said, and we'll deliver the goods. It was a message of particular interest to one shareholder — Oxdon Investments Inc.

By this time, Oxdon had acquired several blocks of Steinberg stock. It had purchased 400,000 common shares from the Ontario Municipal Employees Retirement Service at $50 a share and another 119,976 common shares from the CBC pension fund, at a price of $45. These voting shares had originally been held by cousins of the Steinberg sisters. In addition, Oxdon arranged for the purchase of 558,625 Class A non-voting shares. That gave Oxdon a toehold of 1,078,601 shares in Steinberg — 8.7 percent of the common and 3.7 percent of the Class A. The partners paid $42-million for their stake, plus financing costs.

It wasn't a huge stake in Steinberg but it was a subtle reminder to management that Oxdon wasn't going away, despite being rebuffed the first time. Sooner or later, it was clear that Oxdon would take another run at Steinberg — that is, if somebody else didn't get there first.

# 13

# *The Three-Ring Circus*

The turbulence that had rocked Steinberg during 1988 died down as a new year dawned. All seemed strangely quiet. Oxdon was no longer stalking the company, a union settlement had been reached with Steinberg employees, and the sisters, while certainly not bosom buddies, had agreed to take turns as members of the board. It seemed that Steinberg could finally get back to business without being sidetracked by talk of a sale.

In fact this was merely the calm before the storm. Below the surface, the story read quite differently. Mitzi Dobrin had retained corporate matchmaker Maurice Sauvé, a former federal cabinet minister and the husband of then governor general Jeanne Sauvé, to continue searching for potential buyers. In early 1989 he got a nibble from a Toronto mergers-and-acquisitions firm called Westbourne Management Group that was willing to finance a bid. The three Steinberg sisters met with two Westbourne executives, Bill Young and Guy Cogan. Westbourne was already talking with Morgan Stanley, one of Wall Street's hottest leveraged-buyout firms, about ways of structuring the deal. However, Westbourne stipulated it was not interested in a hostile takeover, and would act only with the participation of the company president, Irving Ludmer.

After Westbourne declared its interest, the sisters and Ludmer gathered in Suite 1810 of the Alexis Nihon Plaza, several floors down from the head offices of Steinberg Inc. This was the bright, spacious office where Evelyn and Marilyn ran Bi-Lyn, the company formed to invest their millions. They called the meeting to inform Ludmer of Westbourne's plans and to determine if he wished to take part.

At that stage there was nothing he wanted less. Ludmer had sweated to turn Steinberg around and he wished to keep it intact, not participate in a deal that would surely see it broken up into bits and pieces. While he had once advised the sisters to sell, things had changed. The Steinberg turnaround was well under way and he was too involved in it to give up the company now. His patience was wearing thin. How could he continue steering the company toward recovery while its controlling shareholders were forever looking for buyers? Irritated, he told the sisters icily they were dreamers to think they could ever get $75 a share. The comment was a dig at Marilyn in particular, who had set that price based on an evaluation of the company done for Steinberg's board of directors. The shares had been valued at between $72 and $78 and Marilyn had picked what Mitzi described as "the nice, comfortable number of $75".

At the time of the meeting, Marilyn's relationship with Ludmer was precarious at best. Although she and her husband had once felt a close rapport with the chief executive and although she had supported him through the company's trying times, her feelings of bitterness and betrayal for having abruptly fired her son Billy without her knowledge still burned sharply. She could not forgive him.

"What was Billy? How could Billy have affected the business in any way?" she asked angrily. "Maybe if he had come to me and said, 'Look, Marilyn, I'm doing a cleanup. . . .' But what he really was saying was, 'We don't need any family.' And if he didn't need family, what the hell were we holding on for?" Marilyn believed Irving was telling her something: that it was time for the family to get out.

Ludmer's comportment galled her. He was so condescending, toying with her emotions, goading her. He asked what she would do with all the money from a $75-a-share offer, how she would cope with seeing her father's name stripped from the stores if a new owner came in and broke up the company. His manner merely reinforced Marilyn and Evie's perception that the company they supposedly controlled wasn't theirs; it was his.

While her sisters seethed, Mitzi secretly brimmed with delight. She of course had long been ready to sell, ever since her own showdown with Ludmer in 1985. It had just been a question of getting her sisters on side. Now, with both so enraged at the boss, solidarity with them seemed tantalizingly close. After the meeting Mitzi reiterated her view of the situation. "Look," she told her sisters. "You have no decision-making power whatsoever and Steinberg is the most ridiculous investment we have, the returns are so low." The only option, she told them, was to sell.

It was remarkable. After months of deep rifts, Marilyn and Evie were seeing things her way — they were incensed by Ludmer and alienated from their father's company. If someone met their price, then yes, they would sell. It was a classic family enterprise scenario: a major business decision, the biggest decision in the history of this company, was being made on emotion. Anger had put Steinberg on the auction block, not financial considerations or visions of the future; anger over the firing of a son and anger over a manager whose self-interest seemed to eclipse the interests of the company owners.

There was an ironic edge to Irving Ludmer's role. If his strategy had been to ward off a sale by dividing the family and presenting a picture of dissension to would-be buyers, it was backfiring. In fact he was doing what no lawyer, court action, or family mediator had been able to do: unite the sisters in their wish to sell. Ludmer himself had sensed this might happen. Months before, at the height of the family tensions, he'd spoken with Helen Steinberg. Deeply anguished over the discord that was dividing her daughters, Helen asked him, "What would it take to get these girls back together?" He replied matter-of- factly, "The only thing that would unite them would be their common hatred of me."

On Friday afternoon, March 17, 1989, the phone rang in Irving Ludmer's office. On the line were two of Oxdon Investments Inc.'s top players, Don Love and Earl Rotman. They had flown in to Montreal from Toronto and wanted to see Ludmer immediately. Although Oxdon had kept a low profile since its failed $988-

million bid for Steinberg a year earlier, Ludmer figured the group was still interested in buying the company.

Love and Rotman arrived at Steinberg's head office in the Alexis Nihon Plaza with a stack of documents describing a new offer for the company. They were ushered into Ludmer's twenty-fourth-floor office overlooking Westmount Mountain.

Just after 4:00 p.m., a reporter from the Dow Jones news service called Steinberg seeking the company's reaction to the new take-over offer by Oxdon. It was the last thing Doug Long, then vice-president of communications, needed to hear. All week he'd been up to his elbows in grapes. A crisis had erupted after the discovery in the U.S. of some cyanide-laced grapes from Chile. The Canadian government had slapped a ban on the fruit and Long had been fielding reporters' calls on how Steinberg was coping. But the Oxdon story soon eclipsed the grapes, even ones laced with toxins. Long told the reporter he had not been advised of a new bid, then rushed upstairs to ask Ludmer about it. The chief executive had just received the Oxdon proposal. Arnold Steinberg was there too, looking red-faced and as furious as Long had ever seen him.

Oxdon had just issued a press release outlining its plan to change Steinberg's share structure, sell the food stores, and transform the firm into a real estate company. The statement was issued over the strong objections of Ludmer and Arnold, who had pleaded that the proposal remain confidential. They were concerned about the effect the latest Oxdon bombshell would have on Steinberg em-ployees. Every time a takeover offer was made, management was raided by the competition.

It was a deliberate attempt to blindside Steinberg, to take the company by surprise and cause panic. To control the potential damage, Steinberg issued its own statement within 45 minutes, calling Oxdon's scheme "completely unsolicited" and vowing to respond in due course.

Ludmer and Arnold Steinberg immediately canceled plans for a vacation and rolled up their sleeves to do battle yet again. Their wrath was palpable. They had gone through six months of anguish in 1988 trying to keep the company intact, fending off Oxdon's previous offer, and with a new union agreement in place they were trying to get on with their business plan. They hardly needed another disruption like this.

Worse, this so-called offer was as hostile as they came. Since Oxdon had previously been rebuffed by the Steinberg sisters, the Toronto group believed an aggressive approach was its only recourse. But once again, the Oxdon partners had failed to size up the family situation. The very fact that the sisters now loathed Ludmer and were ready to negotiate a sale had escaped them. Lobbing a hand grenade into the family's lap, Oxdon devised an explosive scheme to strip the family of the control it had held all these years. Oxdon wanted to eliminate the distinction between the 6-million voting shares, held mostly by the family, and the 15.2-million non-voting shares traded on the stock exchanges. It wanted the shareholders of both classes to vote as one group on a proposal to amalgamate Steinberg with Oxdon.

Following the amalgamation, Steinberg shareholders would be given three options: they could sell their shares for $50 cash, exchange them for a voting common share in the new company that Oxdon would control, or exchange them for $35 in cash and one-third of a voting share in the new company. The offer was worth about $1.16-billion. If successful, Oxdon then planned to spin off the food stores to Loblaw Companies Ltd., and sell everything else except the valuable real estate. The inspiration for the whole proposal was a little-known section of the Quebec Companies Act, refined by Oxdon's securities lawyer Earl Rotman.

But the entire proposal rested on a flimsy legal reed — that non-voting shareholders could have an equal voice with common shareholders on an amalgamation plan. Oxdon argued that under Quebec law, all of a company's shares, regardless of class, are entitled to vote on an amalgamation. With a condition of two-thirds approval from all shareholders, the 15.2-million non-voting shares could carry the day over the 6-million common shares.

The proposal contained an ominous warning. If Steinberg's board refused to accept, Oxdon said it would go to court and ask a judge to order that a vote be held. Oxdon suggested that the rights of common shareholders would not be affected by the proposal but it was patently obvious to the family shareholders that they would be forced out. Even if the sisters were now united in their desire to sell, the offer had no appeal for them because they would not collect a higher price for their common shares than for the A stock.

If management and the family were both outraged, the stock market loved the idea. Investors became excited about Steinberg again. The non-voting shares shot up $4.37 to $39.87 on the first day of trading, even though analysts had their doubts that Oxdon could succeed in court. Its legal scheme had never been tried before in Canada and most legal experts still believed each class of shares would have the right to vote separately. Moreover, the notion that a judge could impose his own authority over a board of directors and order an amalgamation vote stretched the limits of credulity.

Oxdon's tactic was known in the trade as "a bear hug", and for good reason: somebody comes along with a plan to recapitalize your company, squeezes you, and doesn't let go until you give in. But Irving Ludmer was not one to be squeezed. On Monday, March 20, he sent a letter to Steinberg employees to reassure them. He noted that Oxdon's proposal was completely unfinanced and made no mention of the price Loblaws would pay for Steinberg's grocery stores.

The board met on April 7 to hear legal opinions about the Oxdon proposal. Twenty minutes before the close of trading on stock exchanges, Steinberg delivered the verdict: the 12 board members, including seven outside directors, voted unanimously to reject it. They said the plan was full of holes, unfinanced, and lacking such details as interest rates, terms, and conditions. For Irving Ludmer it was no offer at all. In effect Oxdon was asking for the chance to hold a vote before it even raised a penny to buy the Steinberg shares. At any point Oxdon could walk away from the takeover bid, leaving Ludmer to repair whatever damage might be inflicted on Steinberg.

If Oxdon had hoped to scare Steinberg into action, it had failed. Ludmer had some big institutions on his side and had every confidence that if the issue went to court, a judge would throw out Oxdon's petition in a second. He heaped scorn on the Oxdon maneuver in a series of public statements to the press. The Steinberg chief executive was anything but happy about the latest turn of events. It was now clear to him that sooner or later, the company that he'd labored to turn around would be sold. Offers would keep coming until somebody met the sisters' price of $75. In the meantime Steinberg would become next to impossible to manage.

He saw only one option left to keep the company intact. He needed partners with deep pockets and patient money, people who could help him buy the company from the sisters and keep it together. He needed to convince some wealthy investors that if they put their money into Steinberg and waited a few years, they wouldn't be sorry. His strategy would pay handsome dividends in the end, he believed, justifying any investment they could make.

But Ludmer didn't have much time, and there weren't many financial institutions around with the kind of money he was looking for. The first and most obvious potential partner was the Caisse de dépôt et placement du Québec, the $35-billion government agency that invests the Quebec Pension Plan and auto insurance premiums. In April Ludmer approached the Caisse and began to talk. He didn't want a leveraged buyout of Steinberg — that is, one involving massive amounts of borrowed money to be repaid later by selling company assets. Rather, he wanted long-term investment from the Caisse and a few other big financial institutions in Quebec. He wanted to buy out all the Steinberg shareholders and take the company private. Once the company was restored to health, he would take it back out on the stock market again. The real estate portfolio would be kept and only lesser assets such as Steinberg's 50 percent stake in Lantic Sugar might be sold (Cartier Sugar had merged with Lantic in 1981).

The Caisse was intrigued by the idea. Ludmer was a logical partner since he knew the business like the back of his hand. After the plan had piqued the Caisse's interest, Arnold Steinberg also became involved in the discussions, although he thought Ludmer's estimate of how much the Caisse might be prepared to invest — around $300-million — was ridiculously high. "You're dreaming," he told Ludmer. As it turned out, the Caisse had much deeper pockets than the two ever thought possible.

Arnold Steinberg and Irving Ludmer were both prepared to put their own money where their mouths were. Arnold and his two brothers, Murray and Lewis, had agreed that in the event of a deal with the Caisse, they would leave all their shares in the company as equity, including their 17 percent block of common stock, worth about $100-million. Irving Ludmer had said he would leave in his stock options, worth about $20-million.

But while they toiled to make a deal with the Caisse, Irving Ludmer and Arnold Steinberg did not know that another suitor was quietly stalking the company. His name was Michel Gaucher, the young, bright, and highly ambitious chairman of a Montreal shipping company called Socanav, a fraction of Steinberg's size.

Michel Gaucher learned in February 1989 of the family's willingness to sell through Maurice Sauvé, the corporate matchmaker who had earlier tried to pair Westbourne with Steinberg. The Sauvés and Gauchers were good friends. In fact, that winter, Jeanne and Maurice Sauvé had invited Michel and Nancy Orr-Gaucher on a state visit to South America. During that trip Gaucher told Sauvé of his previous efforts to purchase Texaco Canada and the First Republic Bank of Texas. The latter was surprised and not unimpressed by the size of Gaucher's ambitions.

During the South American trip, Maurice Sauvé returned inexplicably and abruptly to Montreal. Two weeks later Gaucher discovered why. The Westbourne deal had more or less collapsed and Sauvé needed to find another buyer for Steinberg. To Gaucher's complete surprise, Sauvé then asked him if he were interested in bidding for the company. No thanks, said Gaucher. He'd read the papers. Steinberg wasn't just another acquisition target, it was a complicated nest of torn family and management relationships. It didn't seem worth the trouble.

Sauvé continued to work on Gaucher anyway. He told him not to worry about the sisters: they all wanted to sell and he knew their price. Gaucher mulled it over. Then he asked himself, what did he really have to lose by giving it a try? Finally he agreed to see the family, and in March 1989 the Dobrins came to his Westmount home for a meeting Sauvé had organized. Sauvé was pleased by Gaucher's interest, which would ultimately translate into a fat "finder's fee" for the corporate matchmaker.

Mitzi was pleased that Sauvé had found a Quebec buyer interested in Steinberg because she wanted her father's company to remain under Quebec ownership. She confirmed that all three sisters did want to sell, but for no less than $75 for the common shares and between $45 and $50 for the A stock.

On March 28 Gaucher made his interest official, sending a letter to each sister expressing his desire to buy Steinberg at their specified price. He hadn't raised any money yet, but he described his June 1988 attempt to buy the troubled First Republic Bank in Texas. Though he'd been beaten out by a North Carolina bank, at least his effort would show the Dobrins that he knew how to finance a major acquisition deal.

While Gaucher picked up the scent, Oxdon was suddenly back in the hunt as well. They wouldn't take no for an answer. Their merger proposal had gone nowhere, but they were ready to talk again about a better offer. Oxdon's clumsy handling of the two previous bids had cost them dearly, but now they were willing to do a little stroking. They sought out Leo Goldfarb, the ex-son-in-law of Sam Steinberg and former company executive, who was acting as an adviser to the family during the takeover affair.

Goldfarb had learned through the grapevine that Neil Baker of Oxdon's Gordon Capital arm wanted to meet him. Goldfarb had known him when Baker worked at Edper Enterprises Ltd., the Toronto corporate empire controlled by Peter and Edward Bronfman. Goldfarb grudgingly agreed to meet with him, still remembering Oxdon's attempt to wrest voting control of the company away from the family with its cockamamy merger proposal. "What kind of fast one are you guys trying to pull?" he asked when Baker arrived at his downtown office. Then again, being a consummate dealmaker, Goldfarb wasn't so angry that he wouldn't hear Baker out.

Baker, a smooth and unflappable man, got right to the point. "Is there any chance this company might be sold?" he asked. "Yes," Goldfarb replied, "there's a big possibility if you guys make a realistic offer." Baker asked him to please define "realistic". "For the voting shares," he answered firmly, "if you're talking less than $75 a share, forget it." Privately Leo thought the company wasn't worth that much, but he didn't voice his opinion, knowing full well Marilyn's rigid position on price. Baker did not offer his thoughts but was clearly interested.

Steinberg was the belle of the ball now, courted by Irving Ludmer and Arnold Steinberg, Michel Gaucher, and Oxdon. Each suitor had a different reason for wanting the company so badly. Ludmer and Arnold wished to keep the enterprise whole, Oxdon wanted the real estate, and Gaucher — who knew? Perhaps he wanted the sheer ego rush of proving he could pull it off. For Leo Goldfarb, who would have contact with all three groups, it was a bit like watching a three-ring circus. Except in this case, only one act would get the final applause.

The quest for Steinberg was starting to take on a life of its own. The three acquisitors danced around the company like flies circling a light, each hungry for information about the family's wishes and about the possible existence of other bids.

Irving Ludmer and Arnold Steinberg knew they weren't the only ones in the race. They had discovered that Leo Goldarb, the family representative, had been in contact with Oxdon and Gaucher, and they didn't like it. On Friday, April 28, Goldfarb got a call from an agitated Irving Ludmer. "I know you're dealing with both parties," Ludmer said indignantly, "and I just want to tell you our top management is very disturbed about what's going on." Goldfarb, who knew Ludmer well enough by now to realize this was bluster, probed gently for details, and heard Ludmer confirm his own attempt to buy the company with the Caisse's help. Goldfarb then offered to set up a meeting with the family so Ludmer and Arnold could make their pitch directly.

No such meeting ever took place. By now the complex web of relationships between family and management was breaking down under the weight of suspicion and mistrust. Everybody seemed to be going behind each other's back, cutting secret deals or trying to twist each other's arms. Arnold Steinberg, desperate to save the company from breaking up, had paid a Sunday visit to Evie Alexander's home, where he tried to convince her to let go of her shares from her two sisters and side with Ludmer and Arnold.

When Marilyn heard about this, she was incredulous and called Leo Goldfarb immediately to report on it. In her next breath she revealed that Irving Ludmer had been after her too, and wanted to meet her within the next few days. Goldfarb was furious that such pressure tactics from the Ludmer-Steinberg team were taking place behind his back. He wanted it clearly understood that he was the family's emissary, and that any approach from an interested party must go through him.

As the infighting between the family and Steinberg management grew worse, Oxdon's Neil Baker began to visit Leo Goldfarb more frequently. His opening bid for the family's shares was $60 apiece. He was perhaps willing to offer a little more, but nowhere near the family's demand of $75. Indeed, Baker felt confident enough of success that he told Oxdon's bankers in April: "We think we can get them for $65."

Leo Goldfarb was tiring of Oxdon's antics. He told Baker for the umpteenth time that nothing less than $75 would be entertained. Goldfarb also told Baker that another suitor was waiting in the wings, quite prepared to pay $75. Baker did not believe him. "Leo," he said calmly, as if trying to call his bluff, "if you guys are able to get $75 you go right ahead. It'll be the greatest thing to happen because we have a lot of Steinberg shares and we'll make a pile of money."

Goldfarb asked Baker if that was his final message for the family. Baker said yes, that $60 to $65 was their best offer. Baker ended the conversation and Leo Goldfarb concluded that Oxdon's designs on Steinberg were finished for good.

But he had misread Oxdon's intentions. It wasn't out of the game; it was recouping for yet another charge. The Oxdon partners met again and concluded that if the only way to win the company was to dangle $75 a share in front of the family, then so be it. Easier said than done. The Toronto trio was still having trouble lining up bankers to finance their offer and adding another $10 to the share price would push up the cost of the bid dramatically. It would take time to get such a bid ready.

Oxdon was confident there were no other serious bidders for Steinberg, but it was wrong. On May 10 Michel Gaucher came to meet Goldfarb for breakfast at the top of the Place Bonaventure, upstairs from Leo's office. Gaucher knew the sisters wanted $50 for the non-voting stock and $75 for the voting stock and he was willing to pay — provided he could raise the financing. He also knew the only way he could succeed was to sell off part of the company. It would have to be the most lucrative part — the Steinberg real estate subsidiary, Ivanhoe.

Gaucher had been quietly trying to convince some major Canadian banks, including the Toronto Dominion and the Bank of Montreal, to back his effort, but everyone he contacted told him the same thing. He needed to find a buyer for the real estate, otherwise he wouldn't be able to raise enough money to swallow the whole company himself. Frankly, the bankers were skeptical. They just didn't believe he could pull it off. Who was he? Who was Socanav? Gaucher knew that to get the support of the banks he needed a committed buyer for the Ivanhoe real estate.

So, over breakfast with Goldfarb, he hoped Leo would provide him with an accurate appraisal of Ivanhoe's value. Goldfarb was the perfect source for Gaucher to tap because he had spent years in Steinberg's real estate division, buying many of the properties that Ivanhoe now owned. "Very conservatively," Goldfarb told him, "Ivanhoe is worth at least $600-million." Gaucher seemed relieved. "That's fine," he said, "that's great." It was a number he could take to the bank.

While Gaucher consulted his bankers, Oxdon turned up the heat a notch, dispatching three of its top guns to Montreal. On May 19, Neil Baker, Tom Allen, and Earl Rotman met with Mitzi Dobrin's son-in-law Sam Mintzberg. Marilyn's husband Simon Cobrin and Evelyn's husband William Alexander were also there, but at Leo's insistence none of the sisters attended. Not that Leo feared a renewed outbreak of civil war between them. What he was really worried about was "cross-talk", the sisters' bizarre habit of straying completely off topic during business meetings, just when the stakes were really high. It was embarrassing and disconcerting.

The meeting went well. Oxdon hadn't named its price, but it also hadn't turned down $75. Its executives started to get very specific about their offer. The bid would be conditional on getting 90 percent of each class of shares in the offer, both the family's common shares and the publicly traded A shares, subject to financing. This was a routine condition in takeover offers, since by law the bidder could force the remaining 10 percent to tender their shares. These details signaled to Leo that Oxdon was ready to bid. But if they were ready in spirit, in reality they were still hamstrung by their bankers. It would take a few more weeks for Oxdon's banking syndicate — which included the National Bank of Canada and Citibank — to tie up the loose ends. Oxdon's three partners were getting increasingly edgy. At one meeting, Chris Jamieson, a Unicorp executive, lost his cool and blasted the bankers. "You guys are screwing us around," he exploded. "There are three other offers going to be made and if we don't get this thing rolling it will be too late."

While Oxdon's bankers dithered, Michel Gaucher was making significant progress on his own bid for Steinberg. May 15 was a particularly lucky day. That's when Gaucher pitched his plans to Pierre Laurin, the senior vice-president and Quebec manager of the investment dealer Merrill Lynch Canada Inc. The two were strolling along a downtown Montreal street, headed for a 2:15 meeting. They were scheduled to discuss the construction of a new building for a Quebec drug-addiction treatment center called Le Portage. Along the way Gaucher revealed that he wanted to buy Steinberg, and Laurin jumped at the chance to get involved.

Behind Laurin's small, slight frame and quiet-spoken manner lurked a sharp financier with an eye for a lucrative deal. He knew the Steinberg situation well. Before Gaucher came along, Laurin had tried unsuccessfully to convince Irving Ludmer to do a management buyout of Steinberg, financed by Merrill. Now Laurin had another fish on the hook.

Laurin is the brother of former Parti Québécois cabinet minister Camille Laurin, although parents are about the only thing the two have in common. Camille is a strong separatist and is considered the architect of Bill 101, the law that banned English on Quebec's commercial signs. Pierre, who made his mark as head of the prestigious Montreal business school École des hautes études commerciales, is fiercely pro-business, to the point that he once suggested Montreal companies be excluded from regulations requiring French as the language of work.

After the May 15 meeting Pierre Laurin had an idea. He knew Gaucher needed a real estate partner. Maybe Merrill Lynch could help find a buyer for Ivanhoe. Laurin and Gaucher traveled to New York to meet with Merrill's executives. The tall confident Gaucher was an instant hit. During his presentation of several hours, he impressed the Merrill people with his entrepreneurial edge and his résumé.

To be sure, Merrill had qualms about his ability to take over Steinberg, a company thirty times Socanav's size. This was the minnow swallowing the whale. But Merrill became convinced that if Gaucher could get a buyer for the real estate he could well pull off the deal. So confident was Merrill in Gaucher that it offered him a $1.5-billion line of credit — a bridge, or temporary loan — pledged against the real estate assets.

Merrill's offer gave Gaucher instant credibility on the street. His ambitions, once lofty and abstract, were now taking shape. He had a backer, and the erstwhile skepticism of financial groups was giving way to acceptance. Rumors of Gaucher's involvement with Merrill leaked out and Pierre Laurin soon got separate calls from Irving Ludmer and Caisse chairman Jean Campeau, each fishing for information.

Ludmer was curious to know what was happening, because his own talks with the Caisse about buying Steinberg were going badly. The Caisse kept insisting that the deal was too big. It wouldn't participate unless Ludmer and Arnold Steinberg agreed to sell off some assets, especially the real estate. What the Caisse really wanted to do was to buy the real estate for itself.

Campeau was anxious to dump Ludmer and Arnold and deal with Gaucher instead. There was some irony in this change of heart. The Caisse had already turned Gaucher down on the Steinberg deal. Two months earlier Gaucher had been at a dinner given by the National Bank of Canada and by chance he had sat at the same table as Campeau. Gaucher asked if the Caisse might consider backing him but Campeau replied he was committed to another interested bidder, which, of course, was the Ludmer-and-Arnold team.

Now, the Caisse was determined to get involved in a deal with Gaucher. His intentions fit those of the Caisse like a glove. For some time Campeau had wanted to boost the Caisse's real estate holdings and here was Gaucher, looking to sell one of Canada's most prized real estate portfolios. With Ivanhoe in its sole possession, the Caisse would double its real estate assets in one fell swoop. It was a lot better than the deal Ludmer and Arnold were offering, which would have given the Caisse only an indirect stake in Ivanhoe.

So Jean Campeau picked up the phone and called Merrill Lynch's Pierre Laurin. He asked for permission to speak with Laurin's client. Gaucher had several days to decide if he wanted to negotiate with the Caisse and he quickly concluded that a pre-sale of the real estate to the pension fund manager would make his life a lot easier. Sure, Merrill Lynch had offered him a big line of credit, but that was too risky. Gaucher would still have had to find a real estate buyer, with the clock ticking on his debt. He didn't have the stomach for that kind of gamble.

The Caisse's world was unfolding as it should. If it was once dubious, almost derisive, about Gaucher's ability to pull off the deal, now it had every confidence in him. "Why did we choose Michel Gaucher?" Jean Campeau would later ask, rhetorically. "Because he is a dynamic partner, he had money, he's a hard worker." And, most of all, because he was in a position to sell the Caisse a rich real estate portfolio.

At first Gaucher wanted to keep some of the real estate. But he soon realized the financial advantages of selling all of Ivanhoe to the Caisse. While the real estate was highly valuable, it did not bring in regular income as the supermarkets did. That was an important consideration for someone who would have to support a huge debt load.

With the Caisse on board, Gaucher continued to look for other partners to help finance his enormous deal. In mid June, he approached Galen Weston, the wealthy Toronto scion of the powerful grocery family which owned Loblaws. Gaucher was returning from a trip in Cameroon and stopped in England where he met Weston at the grocery king's sumptuous castle outside London. The two chatted for two or three hours about a possible joint venture in the Steinberg food stores. But Weston said he couldn't participate. Loblaws was still committed to an agreement it had reached in the spring of 1989 with none other than Oxdon. If Oxdon were successful in acquiring Steinberg, Loblaws had offered to buy most of Steinberg's retailing assets.

In the last week of June, Irving Ludmer, Arnold Steinberg, and other top executives flew to Chicago for a series of meetings with the management of Smitty's Super Valu, the Arizona-based grocery chain owned by Steinberg. While they were away, all hell broke loose. Early on Tuesday, June 27, trading was halted in Steinberg shares after heavy buying pushed the stock up to $46 — a rise of over $2 on the Montreal Exchange. The scuttlebutt was that a takeover was imminent, but analysts couldn't figure out who the buyer would be. The one suspect, Oxdon, flatly denied it was the bidder. The next day the trading halt continued.

On Thursday, June 29, the flurry of rumors ended with a press release from Oxdon. It was making a third attempt to buy Steinberg — this one much more serious. Oxdon was offering $75 for the common shares and $50 for the non-voting shares, just as the family had wanted. The total value of the bid was a cool $1.3-billion.

The Steinberg executives hurried back from Chicago. Irving Ludmer wasn't surprised at the Oxdon offer but he was bitter that the family hadn't told him about it first.

Michel Gaucher found out about the bid from Merrill Lynch. He too had known Oxdon was working on something and could bid at any time, but the news still left him distraught. He knew he was getting close, doing the financial analysis, working out agreements with his partner, the Caisse. Then all of a sudden Oxdon pulled the rug from under their feet.

As unsettling as the news was, it gave Gaucher a bit of leverage against the Caisse, which, as he was rapidly discovering, was a powerful creature. Negotiations between the two partners had been putting Gaucher at a decided disadvantage. "Every day they'd circle around and take this and that, they'd pay a little less and we'd pay a little more," Gaucher recalled. But Oxdon's offer lit a fire under the negotiators and got the Caisse to realize the sense of urgency. There was no more time to dicker; it was time to make a bid. To emphasize that point, Gaucher pulled a disappearing act for a few days, leaving the Caisse frantic to get in touch with him. He went underground, "just to make them think they wanted it more than I did". And the Caisse did want it, very badly. As Jean Campeau observed later, "The Oxdon bid shook us up."

If Campeau was edgy, so was his boss, Quebec Premier Robert Bourassa. The day after Oxdon's bid, Bourassa called Campeau and asked if he could "do something about Steinberg". Campeau replied that "it's been two years since we've been working on [Steinberg] and if I can I will." Although the premier's gesture smacked of political interference, Campeau could understand Bourassa's motivations. There were 18,000 Quebec jobs at stake and if a head office left Quebec, Bourassa could be defeated in an election, rumored to take place that fall.

The Caisse and Socanav gathered for several days of crucial negotiations. The talks almost collapsed four or five times over a

variety of points. How much would the Caisse pay for the real
estate? What would the terms of financing be? What would the
leasing arrangements in the stores be after the purchase? With the
Oxdon bid officially submitted, time was running out and the
pressure weighed heavily. At least the negotiators didn't have far to
travel each morning. The offices of the three groups — the Caisse,
Merrill Lynch, and Socanav — were at the same busy downtown
intersection in Montreal: McGill College Avenue and Boulevard
de Maisonneuve.

A little over a week later Arnold Steinberg and Irving Ludmer
learned for certain that their dealings with the Caisse were over.
They had tried everything to get the Caisse on their side. They had
been assured by Jean Campeau that he would not do a deal with
Gaucher, that they were still Campeau's first choice to take over
Steinberg. But somehow they couldn't get to first base with the
Caisse.

What really sank Ludmer and Arnold was their attempt to bring
the Belzberg family of Vancouver into the deal as investors. Irving
Ludmer had served briefly on the board of First City Financial
Corp., the Belzbergs' holding company. He knew First City's chairman Samuel Belzberg and Sam's nephew Brent, head of the company's merchant-banking operation. The Belzbergs had long been
anxious to invest in Steinberg. They were so enthused about participating that, on June 29 — hours before Oxdon made its bid —
Irving and Arnold took Brent Belzberg to meet Jean Campeau.

Belzberg told Campeau he was willing to put in several hundred
million dollars of long-term equity into Steinberg, but the meeting
went badly. The Caisse chairman was not a particular fan of the
Belzbergs, finding their business style altogether too slick for his
taste. Besides, although he didn't say so, Campeau was virtually
committed to the deal with Gaucher. Ludmer and Arnold may not
have known it then, but any hopes they'd had of wooing the Caisse
and buying Steinberg ended right there.

Of course, whether the sisters would have sold to them was
another question. Their mistrust was so great that Arnold and
Irving had serious doubts that the sisters would ever have agreed to
sell them the business.

On the morning of July 7, shortly before the Steinberg board was
to meet, Campeau called Ludmer and delivered the bad news. The

Caisse was going to finance Michel Gaucher's bid for Steinberg. Campeau asked Ludmer to keep the information confidential. As it turned out, his discretion was not necessary. Ludmer was the last to know. When Ludmer arrived at the Steinberg directors' meeting, believing he held exclusive information, he discovered the other board members had received the news the previous evening. It was not Ludmer, but another Steinberg director, Raymond Cyr, who had been designated to make the announcement at the board meeting. Cyr, the chief executive of powerful BCE Inc., carried an envelope containing a document that outlined the Caisse-Socanav intentions to buy Steinberg.

Irving Ludmer felt supremely offended. Here he was, the chief executive, and the last to be informed. If not for Campeau, who was unaware the directors had already been briefed by the Gaucher team, Ludmer would have found out from them at the board meeting. How insulting. "It was like a circus," he said. "The document had been delivered to Raymond Cyr and not to me because I guess there was a fear that Irving Ludmer might eat it," he recalled with a smile that tried to mask his bitterness.

The document said Socanav had lined up the financing to make its bid, the Caisse would buy the real estate, and Socanav would later put up for sale Steinberg's stake in Lantic Sugar and other assets. But the work of the Socanav-Caisse team was far from done. Before actually making a bid, the Quebec partners had one more hurdle to leap.

Gaucher and the Caisse had decided that they would not pursue Steinberg unless the sisters agreed to give them an exclusive option on the family's block of shares, which included 52 percent of the outstanding common shares and three percent of all the A shares. Such a "lockup" agreement would prevent another bidder from coming along and making a higher offer for the family's stock, including the all-important 52 percent control block. It was a contentious proposal, because it automatically ruled out an auction process for the company. No one else would bid for Steinberg if sale of the control block was already a fait accompli.

Mitzi was all for the lockup. She knew how capricious her sisters could be, especially Evie, who, Mitzi said, changed her mind the way people change their socks. Mitzi could just imagine what might happen without a lockup: the sisters would give the nod to Socanav-Caisse, then Oxdon would up the ante, then an even higher bid might come along. There were no guarantees in such a free-for-all. If a bidder walked away for any reason, the shares of Steinberg Inc. might plummet in value on the stock market and other bidders might be scared off. Then the sisters would be stuck with their blessed shares for eternity.

On the evening of July 7 a meeting was convened in the Sherbrooke Street offices of the family's lawyer, André Gervais. The three Steinberg daughters and their husbands were there, along with Leo Goldfarb, Michel Gaucher, and his partner Louis Rochette. Jean Campeau was out of town. The family was in one room, the Socanav and Caisse team was in another, and the tension filled the atmosphere. Gervais's role was to shuttle back and forth between the two camps, like a diplomat, relaying the latest message from each side.

Marilyn and Evelyn were still stewing over the deal. They doubted that Gaucher had lined up the financing and they didn't like the possibility of locking themselves out of a higher bid. Gervais relayed their hesitation to Gaucher. His response to the family lawyer had a ring of finality. Playing on the sisters' feelings for Quebec, he said, "You've got to convince them this is the one time they will see an option that will keep the company in Quebec." As for the lockup, Gaucher was adamant. A small company like Socanav could not afford to get into a bidding war and did not wish to risk so much financing without a firm commitment in place. Gaucher's message was that if Socanav and the Caisse met the family's price, the sisters had to decide: no lockup, no deal. And so it went, back and forth. By the end of the meeting the sisters were still not convinced. The group agreed to reconvene the next morning.

Gaucher could have walked away from the deal easily if the sisters refused him. He had told them that if they wanted to sell, his price was there; if they didn't, then he'd happily resume his life. The sisters weren't quite so cavalier. They went home that night and reflected for a long time about the ultimatum. Marilyn was starting to believe that without a lockup, odious as it might be, the company would never be sold. Evie shared those feelings. She recalled how Arnold Steinberg had approached her the week before, saying, "Whatever you do, don't lock up." But she feared that if they didn't sign a lockup, Arnold and Ludmer would find some way to prevent a sale.

As for Mitzi, she knew Gaucher's proposal needed more credibility if her reluctant sisters were to be convinced. That credibility could come from only one man — Jean Campeau himself. At 6:00 the next morning, Mitzi placed a call to Gaucher. "If you want to make a deal," she said, "you'd better get Campeau to the meeting." Two hours later Campeau arrived at the Merrill Lynch office from his cottage in the Laurentian hills north of Montreal. He met both groups, this time gathered together. Campeau liked the sisters right away. He felt relaxed and welcome and he spoke eloquently of their father. "Sam Steinberg could have become president of the Caisse de dépôt," he said, "because he knew how to make a profit and because the enrichment, the well-being of others was important to him." He continued, "At the Caisse, I have the welfare of Quebecers at heart. They're my depositors."

Campeau said a Socanav-Caisse purchase would ensure that Sam's company remained in Quebec where it began. "But if we pay $75, we're in it to win and we need a lockup in return." Whether Campeau's speech was a calculated ploy to win the sisters over or whether it came from the heart, it seemed to press the right emotional buttons. The sisters found him gracious, gentlemanly — and convincing. They agreed to sign a lockup.

There was one more piece of business left to conduct. A price for the publicly traded A shares had to be determined. The family was adamant that the minority shareholders would have to be treated fairly in the bid. The sisters still wanted to walk down the street with their heads held high — something they couldn't do if they gave the A stockholders a raw deal. The family was gunning for a figure higher than Oxdon's $50 a share. Anything less would smack of favoritism to the Caisse. Leo Goldfarb tried to nudge the price up to $53 a share. The bidders said $51. "Let's settle for $52 and call it a deal," persisted Goldfarb, but the Socanav-Caisse side wouldn't budge beyond $51.

At 1:51 p.m., the parties put their signatures to a four-page document. Socanav had until July 21 to make clear its intentions to make an offer for the company, during which time it would examine Steinberg's corporate information and complete its financing arrangements. It then had until July 31 to make a bid at $75 for the common shares and $51 for the non-voting shares. If it failed to meet these deadlines, the option agreement would expire.

Minutes later the premier called to say how pleased he was the sisters decided on the Quebec deal. The agreement committed the family to relinquishing their seventy-two-year-old company to a brash Quebec entrepeneur and a powerful government agency. What would Sam have made of it? A collective sigh of relief was almost audible from the family. But if they had known what tortuous twists and turns lay ahead, they might have held their breath a little longer.

# 14

# *The Minnow Swallows the Whale*

On Saturday, July 8, a front-page story in the Montreal daily newspaper *La Presse* proclaimed that Oxdon's offer for Steinberg was "in the bag". The Steinberg sisters and the others who signed the lockup agreement that same day read the article and chuckled. They knew what was in the bag and it wasn't a bid from Oxdon. Later that day the real story began to trickle out. By evening newscasts were reporting that the Caisse de dépôt had mounted a rival bid to keep Steinberg Quebec-owned and that the bid had the blessing of Premier Robert Bourassa.

Arnold Steinberg arrived home late Sunday afternoon July 9 and checked his answering machine for messages. One of the calls made him freeze in his tracks. Jean Campeau had telephoned to say the sisters had signed a lockup with Socanav and the Caisse. Arnold was furious. "How could they?" he fumed. He and Ludmer had warned the sisters not to tie up their shares that way. It was simply bad business for sellers to sign an exclusive option because it precluded a higher offer for the shares.

Irving Ludmer was at home when Campeau called around 7:00 p.m. After breaking the news, Campeau asked Ludmer not to do anything abrupt, like quit, before speaking to him. Ludmer had other ideas. The strong-minded Steinberg chief could never be the company's second-in-command. "Listen, Jean," he said firmly, "I don't want to stay. It's not for me. I ran that company as though I owned 100 percent of it for five years, so what am I going to do there now? Good luck to you guys, you made your choice, you wanted to go with Michel and that's fine." Campeau begged him once more to just hold on for a while. "Fine," sighed Ludmer finally. "I'm not running away." Campeau ended the conversation by telling the chief executive to tune in to the evening news for the details of the lockup.

Both Ludmer and Arnold were crushed by this turn of events. They had feared it might happen, but just as the death of someone after a terminal illness can still be a shock, there was something terribly final about the news of the lockup. Their spirited fight to keep the company together had all been in vain. The news was especially hard on Arnold. It was now highly likely that Steinberg Inc., the company that had been the biggest part of his life since childhood, would no longer belong to the Steinberg family.

The freshest wrinkle in the Steinberg plot was officially announced at 7:30 p.m., prompting Quebec's news media to dig through library files to find out just who Michel Gaucher really was. Symphony halls . . . ships . . . some involvement there. The guy wasn't exactly a household name. They also tried to figure out why the Caisse was buying the choicest part of Steinberg, the real estate, and leaving Gaucher the food operations. Although it was starting to turn around, the food business was still the most fragile part of the company's operations — what one financial analyst later termed the "scraps".

The news media called Oxdon for reaction to the stunning turnabout in the Steinberg story. A Montreal *Gazette* reporter telephoned Oxdon vice-president Earl Rotman at his Toronto home and asked if he had heard the latest news. "No," he said cautiously, a slightly nervous "now what?" tone to his voice. Upon being told that the sisters had signed an exclusive option with the Quebec bidders, Rotman gasped, "Oh my God. That's interesting." He hung up and scrambled to relay the news to his partners, trying to suppress the sick feeling in the pit of his stomach. Oxdon had been poised for victory, with its bid on the table at the right price. Suddenly it had been swept away by a fast-breaking tornado.

The Socanav-Caisse offer was the front-page story in all the Montreal papers the next day. Gaucher and the Caisse were painted as the white knights of Quebec economic nationalism who had moved in to rescue a provincial treasure from the claws of avaricious Toronto corporate raiders. The press reported that Gaucher would maintain Steinberg as a wholesale and retail company and keep the head office in Quebec. The improbability of a yuppie shipping magnate as a bidder for a supermarket chain captured the media's fancy too. What did Michel Gaucher know about groceries? they asked.

The news media reported that the deal was done with the eleventh-hour help of the premier, Robert Bourassa. It wasn't hard to figure out Bourassa's involvement: with hints of a fall provincial election in the air he couldn't afford to lose votes from all those Steinberg employees, farmers, and food industry workers. An Oxdon victory would have been a political disaster.

Bourassa got all the political mileage he could out of the story. Shortly after the bid was announced, he made himself uncharacteristically available to reporters, actually returning their phone calls. He made a point of defending the Caisse's involvement and he played down his own role in the deal, saying the Caisse acted independently.

At around 5:30 p.m. the day after the bid was announced, Gaucher the Grocer and Corporate Savior strode into the fast-food section of a downtown shopping mall, Place Montreal Trust, to meet with Jean-Roch Vachon, then president of Steinberg's Canada Food Group. The two were close friends, having met through the Young Presidents' Organization about eight years before. Amid the frozen yogurt stands and Chinese food takeout counters Gaucher disclosed that if he won, he planned to name himself Steinberg's chief executive officer and he wanted Vachon to stay on as president. The gesture seemed like a cocky, premature declaration of victory. The option deal had been signed but nothing was guaranteed; and here was Gaucher already fashioning Steinberg in his own image. Socanav and the Caisse hadn't even raised the money to make their bid. Vachon asked a few questions, for which Gaucher did not yet have answers, and he asked for Vachon's trust.

This was not the first time Vachon had discussed Steinberg with Gaucher. Early in 1988, when the family strife had prompted management to put Steinberg's grocery division up for sale, the two men had discussed making a bid for the food stores. Nothing had come of their talks, but their friendship became well known around Steinberg.

Before they ended their meeting that July day they agreed it was only right that Irving Ludmer be informed of the plan to make

Vachon president. Ever since the Socanav-Caisse deal was announced Ludmer had been pressuring Vachon about his future plans, especially given his friendship with Gaucher. So why not get everything out in the open right away? They decided that Vachon should call Ludmer, because as a senior Steinberg executive he had to clarify his position immediately.

Vachon left the Food Court and just before seven o'clock that evening he phoned Ludmer to tell him of the plan. Ludmer didn't have to be a genius to figure out where his own future was heading. The Steinberg chief promptly phoned Jean Campeau of the Caisse to complain about reneging on his implied promise to keep him in place. "I'm now calling you to tell you what I'm going to do," said Ludmer angrily. "I'm going to sell my stock and resign."

"Oh come on," said Campeau, alarmed. "Surely we can work something out in Ivanhoe. It's going to be ours."

"I have no interest, really," replied Ludmer. "I wasn't looking for a job when I came in. This whole thing was a passion, it was the alma mater. It was Sam Steinberg's," he said.

The news soon trickled out that Vachon, whom the media began to describe as "Gaucher's good friend", was also his president-in-waiting. Another perception of Vachon was building: that his position in the company and knowledge of its operations had helped Gaucher in his quest for Steinberg. Senior executives believed that information about some of the company's operations had leaked out and they suspected that Vachon had been the conduit. When Gaucher made his offer, he had intimate knowledge of many aspects of the business. The letter Gaucher sent to the board on July 7 dealt with highly specific areas of Steinberg's operations. "He couldn't possibly have known these things unless he had some inside information," Arnold Steinberg believed.

Jean-Roch Vachon denied the insinuations, insisting he had acted honorably and with integrity. "I can look at myself in the mirror," he said later. Nonetheless he knew his credibility was on the line.

If the Gaucher-Campeau team believed success was theirs from the outset, perceptions quickly changed after the first week. The jubilant reception their bid had received in Quebec became rather frosty, especially among organized labor. The union representing Steinberg workers had at first been relieved by news of the Socanav-

Caisse bid, believing that their jobs and company control would stay in Quebec. But now the workers were becoming fearful that the deal would be a disaster for them. The union was worried that Michel Gaucher was financially shaky and would have to sell off large parts of the business to survive.

Their worst fears were confirmed on Wednesday, July 12, just three days after the bid was announced. Executives of the United Food and Commercial Workers union met with Gaucher and his partner, Louis Rochette. During the three-hour meeting the So-canav team presented its long list of intentions. Gaucher planned to sell the restaurants, the M department stores, the Smitty's chain in Arizona, Steinberg's meat wholesaling business, Trillium Meats, and the 50 percent stake in Lantic Sugar. Most important, he planned to franchise Steinberg's nearly 200 supermarkets and transform the company into a wholesaler, in the fashion of Provigo and Métro-Richelieu.

It was cheaper for Steinberg to franchise supermarkets and shed the expensive overhead of corporate-owned stores. Naturally the union feared that separate contract negotiations in each franchised store would spell the end of its bargaining power, leading to lower wages and working conditions. The union also believed that fran-chising violated a commitment the company had made during the marathon negotiating session in Quebec City in 1988. The union had understood that a network of at least 50 corporate stores would be maintained.

But Gaucher provided no such assurances, leaving the labor leaders in a state of shock. As François Lauzon, the union ex-ecutive, left the meeting, he concluded the new owner was an arrogant, vain man and a fly-by-night operator who wanted to make his money and get out.

So what if Michel Gaucher was a Québécois? thought Lauzon. Given his intentions to tear Steinberg up, this francophone was no friend of the working man, just another capitalist riding on the backs of the workers for his quick millions. "What's the advantage in getting screwed by a Québécois?" asked Lauzon, who was presi-dent of Local 500 of the UFCW. Later the union took its cynicism public. "It is strongly possible that a dismemberment of Steinberg *à la québécoise* rather than *à l'ontarienne* is hiding behind a na-tionalist facade," it charged.

Through the week Gaucher had said nothing publicly about the anxieties and questions his bid had raised but on Friday he broke his silence at a tightly controlled news conference lasting only 20 minutes. Gaucher appeared on schedule at 11:00 a.m., tall, stylishly dressed, and slightly ill at ease, to confront the tangle of print, radio, and television people before him. He said he would not sell the company to interests outside Quebec for at least ten years. He said the food business would not be dismantled, that the plan was to make it grow. As for asset sales, he admitted he was interested in selling Lantic Sugar, but that he was committed only to selling Ivanhoe.

The union was not reassured by the entrepreneur's declarations. It did not trust his intentions and scrambled for a strategy to protect its workers from Gaucher's impending takeover. There was still time to act, since the Socanav-Caisse group hadn't yet mailed its purchase offer to shareholders.

Incredibly, the union turned to Ontario for salvation, throwing itself into the waiting arms of the Oxdon group and its ally, Loblaw Companies Ltd. On July 19, the union announced it was supporting Oxdon's takeover offer for Steinberg. By now, Loblaws had been confirmed as the chain that would buy Steinberg's supermarkets if Oxdon won its bid. Loblaws was known to be especially interested in acquiring Steinberg's valuable chain of Miracle Food Mart stores in Ontario.

The idea to forge ties with Loblaws had occurred to the union executives after their first uneasy meeting with Gaucher. They pondered their options. Then it struck them: a number of their members were employees of Loblaws stores across Canada, so why not gather Oxdon and Loblaws together and see if a deal could be worked out? The three parties met for a hurried round of talks at a hotel near Montreal's Dorval airport. François Lauzon admitted that meeting a group of financiers to talk dealmaking was a bit disconcerting for a union member. "It was the first time I had met financial whizzes like that," he said. "It was another world."

Loblaws gave the union leaders the guarantees they were seeking. It vowed to keep a minimum of 60 Quebec stores under corporate ownership until 1994, keep the head office and a distribution center in Quebec, continue to employ a largely francophone work force, and continue to buy Quebec agricultural goods. For its part, Oxdon promised to sell the grocery stores to Loblaws and keep the M Stores going until the union contracts expired in 1991.

Oxdon director Tom Allen told a Montreal press conference convened to announce this strange marriage that the Caisse de dépôt was welcome to join the group and share in the real estate. He drily expressed his gratitude to Gaucher in helping to make it possible to do business with the union. "The salutary effect of Mr. Gaucher's bid was that the union got quite excited about what it meant to them," he said. Then he signaled that Oxdon wasn't going to give up on Steinberg in a hurry. "I hate to go away without one last drink until they close the bar," he said.

Oxdon's strategy was obvious. It knew Michel Gaucher held the trump card in the takeover game, with his exclusive option on the Steinberg family shares. There was little it could do to stop Gaucher from going ahead with the deal — except to scare him off. The union was promising to make Gaucher's life a living hell if he took over Steinberg, and was quite capable of doing so. Perhaps that prospect would frighten him enough to make him walk away from the deal and allow Oxdon to slip through the back door.

But at that point union angst was not Gaucher's principal concern. According to the option agreement, he had to declare his intention to bid for Steinberg by midnight of July 21, a deadline that was fast approaching. There was a staggering amount of legal and accounting work still to be done, not to mention a grueling set of negotiations with the four banks and financial institutions who were lending him money. A battalion of 50 lawyers and dozens of accountants and representatives from the banks had been sequestered in a second-floor suite of Montreal's Ritz-Carlton Hotel, poring over Steinberg's books.

Friday, July 21 finally rolled around but there was no word from the Socanav-Caisse pair throughout the day. The only noise came from Louis Laberge, the rotund, gravelly voiced president of the Quebec Federation of Labor, who, it turned out, was a member of the Caisse board. He declared his support for the Oxdon bid.

The clock ticked on. Still no announcement. Would Gaucher bid or not? There was speculation he was having trouble obtaining the financing. Finally at 10:20 p.m. a communiqué was sent out: Gaucher was going to exercise his option on the control block of Steinberg's shares, and according to the lockup deal would make an offer to all shareholders within ten days. The delay in declaring his intentions was caused by haggling over a transfer price for the real estate as well as the sheer labor and organization involved in signing the flood of paperwork the bid had generated. The last documents were signed at 5:00 a.m. on July 22. With that news one more nail went into the coffin of Oxdon's offer.

Or so it seemed. For Oxdon was tenacious. Like a punch-drunk boxer that wouldn't quit, it dragged itself off the canvas one more time and came back swinging. On July 27, barely a week after Gaucher's declaration, Oxdon increased its bid for the A shares to $53 each — $2 more than the Quebec bid. Its $75 offer for the voting shares remained unchanged. Oxdon also sweetened the pot by making its offer all-cash rather than the choice of cash and securities contained in its June 29 bid.

Others found Oxdon's move puzzling. Why would it bother trying to woo the A shareholders? What good was the non-voting stock to Oxdon when it was clear the family's 52-percent control block was bound to go to Socanav?

The financial analysts following the story had several theories. Oxdon's attempt to attract the non-voting shareholders with a higher bid might have been a way to bully the Socanav-Caisse side into abandoning its own bid, which was conditional on receiving 90 percent of each class of shares. It was possible that the Quebec side wouldn't get that 90 percent with Oxdon's sweeter offer on the table.

Even if the Quebec team didn't get 90 percent, it still needed two-thirds of each class of shares to hold a vote on taking the company private. Oxdon could prevent that from taking place by buying up enough shares under its offer. It was crucial for Socanav to take Steinberg private and operate it as a wholly owned subsidiary, not only for tax reasons but because Socanav could then call all the shots. But if Oxdon won enough A stock to be a minority share-holder, it would be a constant thorn in Socanav's side, resting only until Socanav offered to buy out Oxdon's Steinberg shares at a handsome price.

Or Oxdon's move may have just been a ploy to pressure Socanav and the Caisse to increase their offer. Since Oxdon owned an 8.7-percent block of Steinberg voting shares and 3.7 percent of the A stock, it stood to collect more money if it tendered to a more generous offer from the Socanav-Caisse group.

Stock market analysts weren't the only ones who were confused by the byzantine situation. The competing offers placed Steinberg's board of directors in a very delicate quandary. An open split was developing between the family directors on one side — Mel Dobrin, Marilyn Cobrin, and Evelyn Alexander — and the outside directors on the other. The family directors had locked their shares up with Socanav but the outside directors felt a responsibility to the minority shareholders.

They took that responsibility seriously. They weren't light-weights. This was one of the more impressive corporate boards in the country, a blue-chip roster from Canada's corporate and political elite that included former Liberal cabinet minister Marc Lalonde; Raymond Cyr, chief executive of BCE Inc.; André Charron, chairman of the Montreal securities firm, Lévesque, Beaubien, Geoffrion Inc.; Dean Muncaster, the former head of Canadian Tire Corp.; Gerald Plourde, who ran a huge auto parts firm in Quebec; and Guylaine Saucier, a successful businesswoman in the forest products industry.

The outside directors were supposed to act in the interests of all shareholders, including those of the family. But the secret lockup agreement was particularly frustrating to them. They felt hamstrung in their responsibilities to all shareholders because the lockup ruled out higher bids. "We felt it was not very clever on the part of the family," said Marc Lalonde. "What could we do? It put us in an impossible situation in terms of enhancing the value of the Class A shares." The outside directors also felt the $24 gap between the A shares and the common shares in Socanav's offer was too wide and said so publicly.

The dilemma was this: as directors, their job was to decide on a course of action that would reap the most money for all Steinberg investors. Under normal conditions that would have meant giving the nod to a higher offer, which by late July, was clearly Oxdon's. But how could they recommend a bid which in all likelihood would fail because it had no hope of getting the control block? Oxdon's offer was still contingent on getting 90 percent of both classes of shares; otherwise it could walk away from the deal. The annoyance the directors felt toward the three family members came through clearly. Board meetings were tense. Whenever the three family directors were asked direct questions about their strategy, they would respond by reading carefully worded statements from their lawyers.

The board duly advised shareholders to accept Oxdon's $53-a-share bid. It had no other choice. All along it had stated that $51 for the non-voting shares wasn't enough, so it could hardly turn down Oxdon's bid. The three family directors did not join in the recommendation.

On July 28, three days before the day he had to make his bid, Michel Gaucher made his offer to shareholders through a thin offering circular that contained few details on his bid. Gaucher's company, Socanav, was contributing a relatively tiny amount of equity money into the deal — $50-million — and borrowing the rest. Even of that $50-million, only $20-million was coming directly from Socanav; the remainder was coming indirectly from the Caisse via a $30-million investment in Socanav. Gaucher himself was putting in only $16-million of his own money and his partner Louis Rochette put in another $4-million. Even at that late date, the financing arrangements weren't complete. Of the $1.3-billion required to buy Steinberg, at least $820-million would come from the sale of the real estate to the Caisse. But of the almost $500-million that remained, $330-million hadn't yet been secured. Socanav declared it was "confident" of borrowing that sum from its bankers, but if it wasn't able to line up the money right away the Caisse said it would bridge the gap, perhaps with a little help from another Quebec government agency, the Société de developpement industriel.

It was clear that without the Caisse de dépôt, Michel Gaucher could never have come within a stone's throw of Steinberg. The sources of financing revealed in the bid raised some interesting questions. Who was the real bidder for Steinberg — Socanav or the Caisse? Socanav was putting only $50-million into a $1.3-billion deal. It seemed Steinberg was on the verge of becoming a state-owned company. The Caisse's charter limited its investments in non-real estate companies to 30 percent, but with funds of the sort the Caisse was pouring in, a legal argument was building that the Caisse was violating its own charter.

Socanav's bid provided Oxdon with choice ammunition for a legal challenge. Late in the day on Friday, August 4, it reached into its inexhaustible bag of tricks and filed a court action seeking to stop the Socanav deal. The almost laughably small amounts of money Socanav was putting towards the acquisition of Steinberg made the Caisse de dépôt the real buyer, the court action alleged. And that, charged Oxdon, was illegal. And so the backdrop for the Steinberg drama moved from the corporate boardroom to Quebec Superior Court.

Proceedings got under way in court on Monday morning, August 7. Mr. Justice Pierre Tessier listened to arguments from Oxdon's lawyers seeking a ten-day emergency injunction to block the Quebec bid. Oxdon was trying to delay the bid and hoped eventually to obtain a permanent injunction.

After almost four hours of legal arguments Oxdon had failed to prove any urgency and withdrew the request. The case was adjourned until the following Friday, when Socanav and the Caisse would argue why the court should throw out Oxdon's injunction request altogether.

The Quebec bidders knew what Oxdon was up to. It wanted to stall the bid in the courts so the lockup would expire (the option ran out in November) and the sisters would be freed from their agreement with Socanav. Oxdon was betting that the family wouldn't renew the option once it expired. The sisters wanted out and they wanted their money. Maybe if matters dragged on long enough they would get so impatient that they might even sell to Oxdon.

Whether bluff or not, Oxdon's counteroffensive had the Quebec rivals spooked. An emergency meeting of the Caisse's board was convened at 6:00 p.m. on August 7 and the Quebec team decided it would waive the condition in its offer that at least 90 percent of each class of shares had to be tendered before any shares would be purchased. Clearly this was something of a gamble for the Quebec team since it would be stuck paying for any share tendered — no matter how few.

Arnold Steinberg played a role in the decision to lift the 90 percent condition. He, together with brothers Murray and Lewis, held a valuable 17-percent chunk of voting stock, a crucial catch for the Quebec bidders in their race to win enough shares to take the company private. If the brothers held back, Gaucher would not win enough shares to do so.

The Quebec team wanted the brothers' block so badly it tried to strike a deal with them. According to Gaucher, Arnold said twice he would tender the shares to Socanav-Caisse if the 90-percent condition were waived. So with an apparent guarantee from Arnold the Caisse and Socanav scrapped the condition. They hoped to send the message to Steinberg's non-voting stockholders that the bid was serious, and unlike Oxdon's offer any share received would be paid for. By comparison, Oxdon's condition that it needed 90 percent of both classes of shares meant it could abandon its bid at any point.

But a week after the condition was waived, there was a serious difference of interpretation between Gaucher and Arnold over just what the two had agreed upon. Arnold demanded $5 a share more for his common stock, and that made Gaucher livid. As Gaucher had understood it, Arnold had committed to the Socanav-Caisse offer. Now this further bartering made necessary by Arnold's holdout was causing big problems with his bankers.

Arnold saw things quite differently. He wasn't even going to think about the Quebec bid unless the 90-percent condition was waived. He wanted some assurance that the offer was serious and that the bidders wouldn't just walk away from it.

By now Socanav and the Caisse were more firmly committed to their bid than ever. They had to take up any shares tendered, unlike Oxdon, which could abandon its bid at any time. Most observers believed that Oxdon would ultimately do just that.

Yet at that point matters were so complicated that few shareholders knew what to do. This takeover battle had all the consistency of a bowl of Jell-O. It was always moving, never easy to get a grip on. To which side should a Steinberg investor tender his or her shares? Adding to the confusion was the report that three Steinberg executives — Irving Ludmer, Arnold Steinberg, and Bill Cleman — were selling large blocks of non-voting shares they owned on the open market, at prices almost $2 below Oxdon's $53 bid. They were doing the reverse of what the board of directors had recommended to shareholders — which was to accept Oxdon's offer. It was clear that Steinberg management believed Oxdon's bid would fail.

On Friday, August 11, it was back to court for everyone. The Quebec team argued that Oxdon's request for an injunction should be scrapped. "Oxdon wants to disqualify us, eliminate Socanav from the race to leave the road free for itself," charged Raynold Langlois, the lawyer for Socanav. Short, balding, and acid-tongued, he injected wit into proceedings that often plodded along. He was a charismatic counterpoint to the Oxdon team of lawyers, who seemed harried and ill-prepared.

While the legal arguments dragged on, the people who turned up to watch the show provided some conversational fodder. On that Friday, among the hodgepodge of journalists, shareholders, lawyers, and other interested spectators, Michel Gaucher himself appeared. He arrived impeccably dressed, as usual, in suit and trademark striped shirt topped by a white starched collar, so crisp-looking it seemed fresh out of its package. The *Gentleman's Quarterly* elegance was compromised a shade by his insistence on carrying around a thick neon yellow Hi-Liter in his breast pocket.

Gaucher, the aspiring corporate raider with the Westmount lifestyle, the dazzling résumé, and the requisite ego, looked tentative. Sometimes his eyebrows would furrow into a forlorn frown, like a lost puppy's. He was no stranger to the publicity this case was generating, yet he seemed discomfited by it all. When reporters chased him down the courthouse corridor to the drinking fountain that day, he brushed them aside, muttering in a harried voice, "Let the judge do his job."

From that day hence Gaucher was a regular spectator, prompting speculation about who was minding the Socanav store. His business partner watched the case too. Tall, thin, and silent, with glassy eyes and a wave of white hair, Louis Rochette had an enigmatic, almost imperious bearing. He contrasted with the elfin Pierre Laurin of Merrill Lynch, who had no qualms about gushing to reporters that Socanav-Caisse would win. Yes, Oxdon could prevent Socanav and the Caisse from getting two-thirds of each class of shares, Laurin explained, but that would mean hanging onto their stock for a long time. Would they really entertain such an expensive proposition?

That same day Oxdon's bid expired. And when the tally of shares was counted, the news was bad. While Oxdon didn't collect a single common share, it did receive 71 percent of the Class A shares. That was more than enough for Oxdon to block Socanav and the Caisse from getting the two-thirds of each class of share they needed to take Steinberg private.

The financial press began to speculate on the possibility of "a Mexican standoff" at Steinberg, with neither side able to gain control. The Caisse's immediate response was to haul out some more of its heavy financial artillery. The pension agency revised its offer, saying it would lend Socanav up to $1.25-billion, with interest payable only at the end of five years, in order to pay for the Steinberg shares Socanav needed. The message to Oxdon was clear: the Caisse was prepared to sit patiently for at least five years and wait for Oxdon to give up the fight.

Oxdon was getting edgy by now and it had few options left. But the tenacious group from Toronto had one more trick up its sleeve. On August 18 it announced yet another proposal to merge with Steinberg, distinct from its current bid: this one would pay $60 to the A shareholders and $80 to the common shareholders. Now this new proposal would have to be discussed with Steinberg's board, then eventually presented to shareholders for a vote.

When Arnold Steinberg heard about it, he felt nothing but contempt. It was a cheap trick, he believed, to boost the price of Steinberg stock so that Oxdon could later benefit as a company shareholder. He was certain that Oxdon had no intentions of going through with the plan.

Mitzi Dobrin and Helen Steinberg were upset by the news. They wondered if Campeau would fall for this trap and try to cut some kind of deal with Oxdon, perhaps tender the Caisse's Steinberg shares to receive $60 and $80 from the Toronto side. That morning Mitzi called Jean Campeau from her lawyer's office on McGill College Avenue. Gaucher happened to be in Campeau's office when the call came in. Mitzi said that she and her mother would like Gaucher and Campeau to hop across the street and meet with them. She sounded worried.

Campeau and Gaucher arrived within minutes and Mitzi got right to her point. First, she was concerned that the court case might succeed in blocking the Quebec offer. Then she told Campeau her other worry: "Jean," she said, "we think you're in the process of allying with Oxdon. Is it true?" A loophole in the lockup agreement was making her anxious. There was nothing in it to prevent

Gaucher's group from buying stock as it had planned, then turning around and selling to Oxdon at $60 and $80; there were no guarantees to prevent Gaucher from flipping the stock for a minimum period of time, say five years. That was why the lockup was never made public. Campeau tried to reassure the two women everything was on track, that no such resale was in mind.

Judgment Day was August 21, a day compelling enough to bring Oxdon vice-president Earl Rotman to Montreal. The former securities lawyer was short, clean-cut, and surprisingly boyish-looking, almost too young and unblemished for the shark-toothed world of billion-dollar takeovers. He brushed away the phalanx of reporters who tried to squeeze a comment out of him, took his place in the courtroom, and awaited the decision on Oxdon's injunction request.

Rotman likely wished he'd never got up that morning. As the day wore on, Oxdon was battered and humiliated on every front. The first blow came when Justice Tessier threw out the injunction request. Srike one. Sweat on their brows, Oxdon's lawyers quickly moved to appeal. They requested a restraining order to block the Quebec bid until their appeal could be heard, but were rejected. Strike two. Then the Steinberg board recommended that shareholders tender their shares to the Socanav-Caisse offer. Strike three. Oxdon may have had nine lives, but they were all used up by now.

At about 6:00 p.m. that day, Pierre Brunet, president of brokerage house Lévesque Beaubien Geoffrion, one of Oxdon's dealer-managers, placed a call to Jean Campeau. He had an urgent message. George Mann, the chairman of Unicorp and one of the key players in Oxdon, wanted a meeting with the Quebec team. "What the heck does he want?" Campeau grumbled suspiciously. "He just wants to meet with you," replied Brunet.

Oxdon was ready to concede defeat and because of the mighty power of the Caisse in Canada's financial markets, it wanted to make peace. Nobody could offend the Caisse and hope to do business in Quebec again. So when Campeau came to the meeting, accompanied by Gaucher and Louis Rochette, he found the Oxdon people all smiles. Neil Baker was there and so was George Mann. They were cordial and courteous, as if the acrimonious battle for Steinberg had never happened. They congratulated the Quebec team on its victory, agreeing to withdraw their offer and sell their shares to Socanav. The battle was over.

At 4:30 p.m. on August 22, Michel Gaucher, the newest beneficiary of the Caisse's largesse, joined Jean Campeau in a plush, carpeted Montreal office of Merrill Lynch Canada. The room was crammed with reporters eager to record the details of their win. The two men were exultant. "We Québécois," declared Campeau, considered the sale an "extraordinary transaction," adding that the day was a historic one for the Caisse as well.

The thrill of victory was tempered somewhat by questions about the excessive power of the Caisse, the treatment of the minority shareholders, the perception that the sale was rooted in politics and not business. This last suggestion particularly riled Jean Campeau, who prided himself on investing public money astutely. "The Caisse is there because it's going to make money," he said flatly. Pierre Laurin shared his view. "Anybody who says this was not a business transaction is dead wrong," he said later. "Toronto did not understand that it was a clear business transaction, very profitable for the Caisse and very convenient for Gaucher. There was no gift to anybody." Except maybe to Merrill Lynch: it earned $13.5-million in fees for putting the deal together.

Earlier, the Steinberg family had met in the offices of Merrill Lynch, and over a bottle of champagne handed over their shares to the new owners of the company. The three sisters were there, along with Sam Steinberg's 12 grandchildren. Pierre Laurin joked that the sisters should be entitled to free shopping at Steinberg for the rest of their lives.

Helen Steinberg was also present. Some of the family feared she would fall apart at this meeting, overcome by decades of memories of the company she was now selling. Would she be thinking about Sam, of that day many years ago when she had walked into his little grocery store and captured his heart? Or of the afternoons that she, Sam, and their four young daughters spent visiting the super-markets together? Would she be mourning the loss of the empire crafted out of his sweat and his genius?

Whatever montage of images might have been spinning through her mind that day, the family matriarch remained composed. Leo Goldfarb, also at the meeting, believed it was a relief for her, indeed for all the family to bid farewell to something that had been the source of such intense pain in recent years. Once everyone was paid and the thing was thoroughly, finally, finished, everybody seemed ready to breathe a sigh of relief and say, "Enough fighting. We got our money, everybody go your own way, do your own thing, and nobody can blame anybody else for any problems anymore."

But it wouldn't be so easy to forget the past. After the euphoria of the day had calmed and the glow of the celebratory champagne had worn off, emotional debris still lay everywhere. The sale of Steinberg was not an instant cure that would restore the family's torn relationships to health again, and it was simplistic to think it ever would be. Indeed, several months later Marilyn was still firm in her conviction that she and Mitzi would never bury the hatchet. The damage was irreparable, she said. Memories of that lawsuit still stung like a hard slap as if it had been launched yesterday. "I think it was the worst thing in the world," she said later, her voice dropping to an intense whisper. "I think it was cruel." Her strained relations with her mother, and the fact that she had sided with Mitzi, was also still a painful truth. "My mother had a preference for one child. I have to learn how to accept that."

Evie had not patched things up with Mitzi several months after the sale either. As she put it, "Mitzi and I have had our ups and downs and we're still down." But she relished the fact that while the family still did not know the close kinship of other days, there were no further lawsuits, no company to fight over anymore. The warfare would not be repeated. There was peace, blessed peace.

Mitzi maintained a convincing air of insouciance about Marilyn despite hints that the barrier between the two was still up. Her tendency to refer to Marilyn as "Cobrin" was a good clue the relationship wasn't particularly intimate. As for reconciling with her nemesis, Irving Ludmer, Mitzi claimed to be optimistic.

Her sisters didn't share those feelings. They acknowledged that, yes, Irving was fantastically bright, he had turned the company around and he had made the family bags of money, but he wasn't infallible. His fatal flaw was that he stopped listening to the owners, preferring instead to call all the shots himself. His dismissal of Billy Pedvis was the one move he couldn't get away with.

After the sale Irving Ludmer was characteristically philosophical. It was clear he'd been burned; his dream had been yanked away. Money was never the issue for him, already a wealthy man; he just wanted to see the company thrive, and preferably under his direction. He admitted a measure of ego was involved. "But to see this thing flourish after the efforts that were put in, why not? I believed it was important to hold the company together for many reasons, including maximizing shareholder values. I admit I was also concerned about the people here. It's not that simple to hire people, set up a plan, lead them through this thing and then see this thing get smashed apart. If it's a crime [to care about that], then I plead guilty."

In another way Ludmer wanted the company to survive for Sam Steinberg. He loved and admired Mr. Sam; that was evident every time he spoke about the man. Ludmer was trying to live up to Sam and he hated to see the company slip below the standards that had been in place when the founder was running the show.

As for his own reconciliation with the family, Ludmer felt it would take time, but that it would happen eventually. In November 1989, several months after the sale, he received an award at a B'nai Brith dinner. None of the sisters attended, though some of their children did. The implied message Ludmer got from the family was, "We don't like you, but we're not your enemy."

Arnold Steinberg felt the same bitterness and resentment after the sale as Ludmer. His relations with the sisters had never been great, especially with Mitzi, and he doubted they would improve now. He felt the sisters had somehow sullied the legacy of Steinberg. "The company was an important institution within the community here. A lot of people felt very proud to be associated with it. The irony is that the people who owned it didn't feel that way."

It's not that Arnold didn't understand the sisters' wish to sell. As with many family businesses, the Steinbergs were finding that with each successive generation, the connection to the company had grown less powerful. If you aren't involved, why not cash in your stock and sever the ties?

That was fine with Arnold and Ludmer. "We never wanted to tell the sisters, 'You can't sell your shares to other people,' " said Arnold. But as managers, the only thing they asked was to be kept informed and to have a chance to propose some alternatives. Arnold felt that kind of cooperation between family and management had never existed. Management became the enemy and it was distressing. "It's been that rivalry between them and us that has been most bothersome," he said. But life goes on. "I don't go home at night and put pins in their dolls."

There wasn't just the problem of repairing broken family relations. There was the very personal struggle of dealing with the reality that the stores that bore the Steinberg name weren't the family's property anymore. How would they ever get used to that? Marilyn was confused. Of course it wasn't her company anymore, but she felt as if it were. She still could not bring herself to shop in a Provigo store and give her business to the competition.

The public seemed to go through a sense of loss along with the family. Mitzi got letters — "all kinds of crazy, anonymous letters," she said — from people who viewed the sale as a travesty, a kind of betrayal. It was as if Quebec consumers had laid unofficial claim to the grocery chain as their very own.

Evie's son Jimmy had started working at Steinberg part-time when he was fifteen. It was always assumed that he would work for his grandpa's company. The day in 1989 that he got paid for his shares he drove home afterward, past the Westmount store at the corner of Sherbrooke and Victoria. It was a strange sensation. Technically the company didn't belong to the Steinbergs anymore; the fat cheques he and his family now clutched were evidence enough of that. But he didn't feel any different. It was as if that store there, Store Number Four, was still in the family. But then, how could a simple business deal wipe out something that had been woven so tightly into his life? The company that Sam Steinberg built had become a part of him, a part of every Steinberg, every worker, who had played any role in it over the past seven decades. Nothing could change that. Someone else was taking care of it now but it would always belong to the Steinbergs. So he didn't feel sad.

"I hope they take good care of it," he thought as he drove away. "I hope it will prosper."

# *Epilogue*

L ife as the new owner of Steinberg was no picnic for Michel
Gaucher. Even after the sale of Ivanhoe, he raced against the
clock to reduce the crushing $700-million in debt that was still on
Steinberg's books. He sold the company's 50 per cent interest in
Lantic Sugar to the owner of the other half, Jannock Ltd., early in
1990, netting $110 million. And by June he had sold three of
Steinberg's four restaurant chains, which as a group would bring in
another $25-million.

Gaucher also started an austerity kick. He launched plans to
merge Steinberg's well-appointed head office in the Alexis Nihon
Plaza with the company's Quebec Division on Hochelaga Street in
the east end of Montreal and move them both to another location.
The expensive corporate art collection, which contained hundreds
of works, was sold off. Several senior executives of the company
quit after the takeover and others were asked to leave. By March
1990, 75 head office employees had been given pink slips, and later
the company announced it would eliminate 150 positions in its
Quebec Division by the fall.

The state of Steinberg's business affairs was a far cry from the
glorious days 25 years earlier when it was one of the most successful
and renowned retailing companies in North America. Now it was
hobbled by debt and slowly being dismantled, a victim of the
"Greed is Good" ethic in the corporate world that has inspired so
many costly takeover deals. All you had to do was look at Socanav's
books to see that the company it had swallowed was causing it a lot
of pain. Socanav lost almost $5-million during the first three

months of 1990, in large part because of the crippling $100-million-a-year in interest payments it was forking out to pay off the Steinberg debt.

Caisse chairman Jean Campeau, who had overseen the buyout wouldn't be around to see how Gaucher handled his problems. Campeau, who had finished his 10-year mandate at the Caisse, moved over to head Domtar Inc., the big Montreal-based forest products company.

Irving Ludmer, Arnold Steinberg and Bill Cleman left to form an investment firm of their own, Cleman Ludmer Steinberg Inc., which specialized in retailing and real estate deals. Ironically, one of their first deals was to purchase the Pik-Nik restaurant chain from Steinberg.

When he looked at Gaucher's chances for success, Irving Ludmer was far from sanguine. "A lot is going to depend on the prices he gets for the assets he wants to sell," he said.

Gaucher wasn't going to have much to say about the prices he got. High interest rates were making it a buyer's market. He found that out with another of the assets he wanted to unload quickly, Smitty's Super Valu Inc., the big Phoenix-based food and general merchandise chain that boasted sales of more than $1-billion U.S. For a while, growth in Arizona had been phenomenal, but by 1989 the U.S. southwest had been hit hard by an economic downturn, competition had heated up and the value of Smitty's had declined. Gaucher had vowed to sell it by February 1990 but when the bids came in during the early part of the year they were far below the $250-million (U.S.) he had hoped for. One rumour had it that he hadn't even been able to get $140-million. In June he pulled Smitty's off the block and decided instead to pump $20-million into sprucing up the existing stores and expanding Smitty's throughout Arizona.

Gaucher then concentrated on an alternative plan: selling the lucrative Ontario grocery chain of Miracle Food Marts. Steinberg's share of the Ontario market was small but its potential growth in that booming province was enormous. The Ontario stores had become the most valuable remaining asset in Steinberg, with excellent locations in the hot Toronto market. Gaucher had been unofficially shopping it around in early 1990, and many thought a deal with the owners off the A&P grocery chain had been all but signed.

Then suddenly in early June, Steinberg announced it was officially seeking buyers. Richard Currie, the boss at another persistent Miracle Foods' suitor, Loblaws, had publicly declared that Gaucher's $275-million asking price was $100-million too high. Finally one day in July, A&P announced they would buy the chain after all, for a price of $235.5-million.

Another whopping headache was the M Store chain of department stores Gaucher had inherited as part of the Steinberg takeover. Despite Ludmer's strategic change to a new accent on quality fashion at affordable prices, the department stores lost $20-million between 1987 and 1989. The trouble was, no one would buy it because of its history of losses and because the stores were unionized, unlike competing chains. Mike Kershaw, who had played a big role in the turnaround, left as M's president in early 1990 and Gaucher installed a new boss, Mario Bertrand, the former right-hand man to Quebec Premier Robert Bourassa. His mandate was to work out a new ownership structure — and quickly. One scheme was to spin out a third of the equity to each of the Caisse and the Fonds de Solidarité du Québec, the venture capital fund of the Quebec Federation of Labor.

But the Caisse and the Fonds were slow to bite, and things at M were reaching a crisis point. In June, Bertrand sent a letter to the union pleading for them to turn down a 4 per cent pay raise coming to M workers to ease the pressure on the chain's bottom line. He called the situation at M "disastrous" and said that if new financial partners weren't found soon, the chain wouldn't make it to the end of the year. Then in June, M asked its suppliers to accept a 5 percent cut to the $18-million owed to them.

The hot rumor in retailing circles was that Steinberg was also prepared to sell its 50 percent interest in Price Club Canada, a chain of discount retailing warehouses that was really starting to catch fire with consumers. Again, in late July Gaucher sold to the owner of the other half, The Price Co., for some $55-million.

In the spring of 1990 Gaucher got some breathing space when the Bank of Montreal and the Toronto Dominion Bank agreed to refinance their loans. But some prominent institutional investors who owned preferred shares in Steinberg were becoming extremely impatient with him. At the time of the takeover, Gaucher had promised to redeem the preferred shares, worth close to $80-

million. Eight months later, at least 15 big-time investors, including the powerful Bronfman-controlled merchant bank, Hees International Bancorp, sent him a stiffly worded letter reminding him of that promise. They demanded to be paid in full for their shares before Gaucher used any more of the cash from the sale of Steinberg assets to pay off the company's debt. In July 1990, a small group of preferred shareholders sued for those reasons.

Every day seemed to bring a new challenge. If Steinberg's two principal competitors, Provigo and Métro-Richelieu, hadn't been struggling with problems of their own, they might have made life even tougher for Gaucher. As it was, Steinberg seemed to be holding its own in the Quebec food market in the months following the takeover. The supermarkets were still full of customers. Gaucher pressed ahead with his plans to franchise more of the stores, despite the opposition of the union. There was a growing belief in the industry that the Quebec food market couldn't support three major players. The betting was that one day Steinberg and Métro might merge.

Whatever happened to Steinberg, it would no longer resemble the company Mr. Sam had built. The irony was that the Steinberg sisters had sold to Gaucher rather than Oxdon, partly because they believed he would keep the company together and preserve their father's legacy. Within a matter of months the empire was in pieces and Steinberg was a shell of its former self.

# SOURCES

Evelyn Steinberg Alexander – Sam Steinberg's daughter

James Alexander – son of Evelyn Steinberg Alexander

Michael Aronovitch – longtime Steinberg family physician

Norman Auslander – former executive in Steinberg's Ontario division

Alain Bilodeau – Steinberg senior vice-president, corporate affairs

Jacques Bouchard – former Steinberg advertising executive

Don Campbell – former Steinberg board member; chairman of Maclean Hunter Ltd.

Jean Campeau – former chairman, Caisse de dépôt et placement du Québec

André Charron – former Steinberg director; chairman of brokerage firm Lévesque Beaubien Geoffrion Inc.

John Ciaccia – Quebec Liberal cabinet minister; former Steinberg real estate lawyer

William Cleman – former president of Steinberg's real estate group, now partner in Montreal investment banking firm

Marilyn Steinberg Cobrin – Sam Steinberg's daughter

Simon Cobrin – husband of Marilyn Steinberg Cobrin

Ross Cowan – Toronto-based financial analyst with Levesque Beaubien Geoffrion Inc.

Jean-Claude Delorme – board member, Royal Bank of Canada

Frank di Mauro – former member of Steinberg's communications department.

Mitzi Steinberg Dobrin – Sam Steinberg's daughter and former Steinberg executive and director

Ben Dobrinsky – longtime Steinberg artist; brother of former Steinberg chairman Melvyn Dobrin

James Doyle – retired Steinberg vice-president, general counsel and secretary

David Dunsmore – Steinberg employee during very early days

Graham Fletcher – manager, Steinberg Store Number Four, Westmount

Gaetan Frigon – former Steinberg marketing executive

David Gallagher – managing director of Toronto-based Canadian Association of Family Enterprise (CAFE)

Michel Gaucher – chairman of Steinberg Inc. and its parent company, Socanav Inc.

Sam Gerstel – former executive assistant to Sam Steinberg

Leo Goldfarb – former Steinberg real estate executive

Victor Goldbloom – former Quebec Liberal cabinet minister

Peter Golick – chairman of Grey Advertising Ltd., Montreal, who compiled a book of tributes to Sam Steinberg

Aaron Groper – former vice-president of personnel, Miracle Mart

Irwin Hockenstein – former Steinberg fruit and vegetables merchandiser

Steve Holt – Toronto-based financial analyst for Midland Capital Corp.

William Howieson – former Steinberg vice-president and comptroller

Bernard Isenberg – husband of Frances Isenberg

Frances Isenberg – president, Caplan Duval Gift Shoppes Inc., jointly owned by Steinberg

Stephen Jarislowsky – head of Montreal investment fund manager, Jarislowsky Fraser & Co. Ltd.

Martin Kaufman – Montreal-based financial analyst at Nesbitt Thomson Deacon Inc.

Michael Kershaw – former president, M Stores Inc.

Anita Knappe – head cashier, Steinberg Store Number Four, Westmount

Tom Kukovica – negotiator for United Food and Commercial Workers Union

Morris Ladenheim – former Steinberg executive

Marc Lalonde – former Steinberg director; partner in Montreal law firm, Stikeman Elliott

Diane Marcelin Laurin – former Steinberg vice-president, general counsel and secretary

Pierre Laurin – senior vice-president and Quebec manager, Merrill Lynch Canada Inc.

François Lauzon – president of Local 500, United Food and Commercial Workers union

Jack Levine – retired Steinberg president

Doug Long – former Steinberg director of communications

Irving Ludmer – former Steinberg president and chief executive

Malcolm MacIver – former Steinberg vice-president of labor relations

Morgan McCammon – former Steinberg lawyer

Paul Marchand – Montreal tax lawyer specializing in family businesses

Allan Mattison – former executive in Steinberg's Ontario division

Henry Mintzberg – McGill University business management professor, author of Steinberg study, "We Grew Like Topsy"

John Paré – former Steinberg vice-president of personnel

Billy Pedvis – son of Marilyn Steinberg Cobrin, and former director of real estate at Steinberg

Monique Plouffe – office manager, Steinberg Store Number Four, Westmount

Lily Steinberg Rafman – Sam Steinberg's sister

Louis Rochette – business partner of Michel Gaucher

Sam Roth – brother of Helen Roth Steinberg

Max Roytenberg – former Steinberg divisional manager

Maurice Segall – former Steinberg executive

Herb Shapiro – former equipment supplier to Steinberg

William Sherman – former Steinberg executive vice-president

Sam Shuster – former Steinberg company doctor

Herbert Siblin – senior partner in Montreal accounting firm representing some Steinbergs

Arnold Steinberg – son of Nathan, former executive vice-president, finance

Brahm Steinberg – son of Max Steinberg and former Miracle Mart executive

David Steinberg – son of Jack and former Steinberg restaurant group executive

Morris Steinberg – Sam's brother and former company executive

Murray Steinberg – Nathan's son and former Steinberg executive

Harry Suffrin – former director of Steinberg's market research department

Henri Tremblay – former group vice-president of human resources
Jean-Roch Vachon – appointed president, Steinberg Inc., in 1989
Charles "Chunky" Woodward – late chairman of Woodward's
department store chain
and others who preferred that their names not be mentioned.


## BOOKS

*For Good Measure*, Gerald Clark (McClelland and Stewart, 1986).
*Montreal: The New Cité*, Gerald Clark (McClelland and Stewart, 1982).
*Inside the Family Business*, Leon Danco, Center for Family Business (University Press Inc., 1980).
*Beyond Survival*, Leon Danco, Center for Family Business (University Press Inc., 1980).
*Controlling Interest*, Diane Francis (Macmillan of Canada, 1986).
*Quebec Inc.*, Matthew Fraser (Key Porter Books, 1987).
*The Woodwards*, Douglas E. Harker (Mitchell Press Ltd., 1976).
*We Grew Like Topsy: Strategy Formation at Steinberg's Ltd., 1917-1974*, Henry Mintzberg and James A. Waters (McGill University, 1979).
*The Bronfman Dynasty*, Peter C. Newman (McClelland and Stewart, 1978).
*Flame of Power*, Peter C. Newman (McClelland and Stewart, 1959).
*La Machine à milliards: L'histoire de la Caisse de dépôt et placement du Québec*, Mario Pelletier (Editions Québec/Amérique, 1989).

Other sources: News clippings from the *Gazette* (Montreal), *The Globe and Mail* and its *Report on Business* magazine, *The Financial Post*, *Le Devoir*, *La Presse*, *Canadian Grocer*, *Business Week Magazine*, *Harvard Business Review*, *Fortune Magazine*, *Maclean's* and Steinberg annual reports from 1955 to 1988.

# INDEX

Ciaccia, John, 60, 64, 104, 138, 139, 222, 223
Citibank Canada, 211
Claridge Investments, 216
Clark, Gerald, xii
Cleman, William, 3, 144, 150, 197, 198, 261, 270
Cleman Ludmer Steinberg Inc., 270
Cobrin, Marilyn (Steinberg), xiii, xv; attempt to gain control of Steinberg, 189-91; and family dispute, 198-207, 229-31, 238, 240; relationship with sisters, 266; role in managing family trusts, 181-88; sale of company 3, 5, 247, 258; sued by Mitzi, 4, 92, 95, 104, 117, 119, 144, 174, 176-78, 180
Cobrin, Simon, xiii, 144, 177, 181, 186, 204-06, 208
Cogan, Guy, 229
Connacher, Jimmy, 214
Consolidated Bathurst, 11, 12
Council on the Status of Women, 165
Currie, Richard, 270
Cyr, Raymond, 246, 258

Danco, Leon, 111, 114
DBRN Holdings Ltd., 174
Desmarais, Paul, 9, 11, 120, 194
DiMauro, Frank, 167, 168, 199
Dobrin, Lewis, 157, 185, 203
Dobrin, Mel, 69, 77; house bombed, 79; 103, 105-07, 108, as Steinberg chairman, 121, 125, 128, 140, 143-45, 153, 154, 157, 159, 170, 175, 181, 188, 197, 201-03, 207, 236; as Steinberg president, 109, 110, 112, 113, 118
Dobrin, Mitzi (Steinberg), xii-xv; childhood and education, 30, 49, 156-7, 158; confrontation with Irving Ludmer, 152-4, 170; efforts to sell company, 3, 5, 181-3; house bombed, 79; and Jack Levine, 125-7, 128, 133, 140, 143-5; and labor relations, 168-9; law suit against sisters, 4, 5, 204-08, 210, 217, 220, 229, 230-31, 236, 246, 248, 263; Lupton-Duvall store, 168; marriage to Mel Dobrin, 95, 96,

105, 106, 107, 109, 111, 117, 119, 121, 125; and Miracle Mart, 159-63; political views on Quebec, 166; relationship with father, 155-8, 162-3; relationship with sisters, 175-8, 173-6; resignation from Steinberg 170-71, 180-82, 266; role in family dispute, 184-91, 193, 197, 200-04; Royal Bank director, 163-4; Steinberg executive vice-president, 167
Dobrin, Terry, 157, 185, 203
Dobrin, Ronny, xv, 157, 174, 185, 203, 205
Dobrinsky, Ben, 105
Dominion Securities, 215
Dominion Stores, 57; Provigo's purchase of, 128, 130, 224; Steinberg's attempted purchase of, 65, 76
Domtar Inc., 270
Dorval Shopping Centre, 62
Doyle, James, 58, 66; on Sam Steinberg, 82-3, 89, 103-08, 109
Drapeau, Jean, 154
Duplessis, Maurice, 73

Eaton, George, 99
Eatons (family), 114
Eban, Abba, 154
Eberts, Gordon, 215
Economic Council of Canada, 165
Lionel Edie Co., 180
Elmridge Golf Club, 158

Fairview Ltd., 139
Family trusts of Steinberg, 4, 178, 179, 180, 203-04, 206-07
Financial Post, 211
First City Financial Corp., 245
Fletcher, Graham, 18-32, 34, 35
Fonds de Solidarité, 271
Ford family, 195
Ford Motor Co., 195
Four Stone Investments Ltd., 183, 184
Frigon, Gaetan, 132

Gallagher, David, 114, 115
Gaucher, Michel, xiv; business background 6-10; and Galen